D0385828

Seeing, Reaching, Touching

Seeing, Reaching, Touching

The Relations between Vision and Touch in Infancy

Arlette Streri

Translated by Tim Pownall
and Susan Kingerlee

The MIT Press
Cambridge, Massachusetts

First MIT Press edition, 1993

This book was printed and bound in Great Britain.

Library of Congress Cataloging-in-Publication Data

Streri, Arlette
(Voir, atteindre, toucher. English)
Seeing, reaching, touching: the relations between vision and touch in infancy / Arlette Streri : translated by Tim Pownall and Susan Kingerlee.
p. cm.
Includes bibliographical references and index.
ISBN 0–262–19343–4
1. Visual perception in infants. 2. Touch in infants. 3. Eye–hand coordination in infants. 4. Perceptual-motor learning. I. Title.
BF720.V57S7713 1993 93–11782
155.42′2214—dc20 CIP

For Charis and Aurélia

Contents

Foreword

What do infants perceive from the arrays of stimulation that meet their eyes and hands, and how does their perception change over the first few months of growth and experience? What relations do infants detect between the sight and touch of an object? How do infants coordinate their developing perceptions with their developing actions? For centuries, these questions were viewed as central to an understanding of mature human perception, action and knowledge. Unfortunately, they were also most viewed as beyond the reach of human science. More recently, these questions have been approached through a flood of experimental studies of human infancy, but their larger implications concerning mature cognition are less often considered. It is a distinctive achievement of Arlette Streri's book to bridge this long-standing gap between theory and research, bringing experimental studies of the early development of perception and action to bear on central questions about mature human knowledge.

Streri immerses the reader in the study of infants' developing perception of objects through vision and through active touch, infants' coordination of visual and tactile perception, and infants' coordination of perception and action. She presents a wealth of experiments, many of them her own, that use original and inventive methods to probe pre-verbal, pre-locomotor, and pre-reaching infants' perceptions. These studies are not presented in order to catalogue infants' positive accomplishments, but rather in order to probe the nature and limits of human knowledge through studies of its inception and of its early manifestations in perception and action.

Streri's work helps, as well, to bridge a gap between studies of early human development in French and English language traditions. Her thinking is informed by the work of Jean Piaget and by that of James Gibson and David Marr; her experiments combine the subtle behavioural analyses characteristic of much French research with experimental techniques that are more associated with the English language psychology. From these elements, *Seeing, Reaching, Touching* presents an original and worthy contribution to research and theory on early cognitive development. It merits a broad audience in all the cognitive sciences.

Elizabeth Spelke

Preface

The attempt to understand the nature of the relations between eye and hand during the course of development, and particularly during the first few months of life, is an almost obligatory path to follow for anyone who is interested in the cognitive capacities of very young infants and the way in which they organize their knowledge about themselves and about the world at large.

Vision, the spatial modality *par excellence*, constitutes a major source of information about the environment. As for the hand, it has two closely connected and absolutely crucial functions: a motor function for grasping, carrying, manipulating and changing/fashioning objects, and a tactilokinaesthetic perceptual function which is realized on the basis of sensory receptors in the surface of the skin and in the deep articulatory muscles. The precision and efficiency of the motor activities which are constantly executed by the hand are considerably refined when the visuospatial perceptual processing of objects is well coordinated with the programming and control of hand movements towards or actually on these objects. This coordination indicates that visual space and manual motor space must be integrated into a common spatial map. This is why the genesis of prehensile behaviour has been of such interest, and for so many years, to all those who are involved in the study of the sensorimotor and cognitive development of the neonate.

Combined with the investigation of this *perceptuomotor* coordination (coordination of visual perception and manual movements), it is also necessary to study the *interperceptual* coordination which connects the visual perceptions of an object with the tactilokinaesthetic ('*haptic*') perceptions of this object. In fact, because of the considerable anatomophysiological differences which exist between the visual and tactilokinaesthetic perceptual systems and, correlatively, between the visual sensations and tactile sensations which they engender, we cannot be certain *a priori* that the modes of functioning and of processing information are the same in both systems, nor *a fortiori* that these systems can communicate with each other straight away. The adult 'knows' that the visual impressions and tactual impressions extracted from, for instance, a cube specify the existence and the properties of one and the same object. Adults are also able to transfer the information received through one modality to another modality, thus achieving substantial economies in perception and learning. What about the infant? From what age are infants able to formulate coherent spatial knowledge on the basis of a single fused space?

These very old and still somewhat enigmatic questions have long remained only partially answered because observations have been chiefly concerned with infants of at least pre-school age who can understand the verbal communication of experimental tasks. The work of Arlette Streri, however, has been devoted exclusively to the study of very young infants, above all those under one year of age. In scrutinizing the most elementary forms of visuomanual cross-modal (or intermodal) coordination, this work has the great merit of grouping together and discussing the numerous studies which have emerged recently, but are so diverse that it was difficult to see any perspective in which they could prove mutually illuminating.

This is because the explosion of research devoted to the neonate over the last twenty or so years has called into question a number of notions which had long been regarded as certainties because the methodologies and techniques available to the field of infant psychology were unable to test such young infants efficiently. In this volume, Arlette Streri subjects several of these apparent certainties to critical examination. The first is the extremely plausible idea that because of the importance of the hand's reflex activity and the immaturity of the motor pathways which allow control of distal finger movements, the perceptual function of the hand during the first few months of life is so rudimentary that the baby can extract only a very small amount of the tactilokinaesthetic perceptual information which is engendered by manual functioning. In a series of original and highly ingenious experiments, Streri demonstrates that this is by no means the case, and that from the age of just 2 months babies extract the same relational invariants through touch as through vision, and can discriminate between objects varying in particular properties (their shape above all) just as well through manipulation only (without being able to see the object or their hands) as they can through sight only (without touching).

From a very early age, therefore, the eye and the hand are independently capable of apprehending and processing information about the spatial properties of the environment. But what about their coordination? This question is the central theme of Streri's discussion. In this domain, more even than in the preceding one, our knowledge has been turned on its head by the progress of research in the last few years. The hypothesis that the sensory spaces are radically separated at birth, and that they can be related only very gradually through the effect of simultaneous multimodal experience with the same objects, had become almost universally accepted and, towards the end of the 1960s, appeared unlikely ever to be challenged. This hypothesis had been advanced by Locke in answer to Molyneux's famous question, and then appeared to be confirmed in modern psychology by Piaget's observations (1936, trans. 1936, 1953) and the more recent and systematic findings of White, Castle and Held (1964). Thanks to the first research conducted by Bower and his associates (1970*a*), however, it is now known that the reality is quite different. Arlette Streri analyzes data drawn from the abundant contemporary literature on the subject in minute detail and, after comparing these findings with the observations she herself has obtained in a remarkable collection of experiments, arrives at the conclusion not only that eye–hand coordination does exist at birth, but that it persists throughout the first year of life despite the now well-known '*nonmonotonic*' development of some visuomanual behaviour. In fact, according to Arlette Streri, only the *expression* of this coordination changes from one month to the next because of the effect of newly emerging perceptuocognitive potentialities. Since the developmental rhythms of the visual and manual systems are very different (the former evolve much faster than the latter), the appearance of a new function in one or other of these systems will at first destabilize the fragile level of cross-modal organization which existed before. This organization is later reconstructed at a higher level of articulation but, meanwhile, it is possible for other forms of coordination to be manifested, indicating that the link between the systems has never really been interrupted.

One example which illustrates these changes particularly well is that of the 'silent period', between about 2 and 4 months of age, when the early prehensile behaviour of the neonate has disintegrated, while the new coordination which will emerge at the age of 5 months is not yet in place. During this period, eye and hand, having been united at birth, effectively appear to be functioning independently of each other, provided that the only indicator we consider is the prehensile gesture towards a visual target.

Nevertheless, this loss of perceptuomotor coordination between eye and hand at about 2 months of age is accompanied by the emergence of another form of behaviour which indicates that coordination is still operative. This time, however, the coordination is interperceptual – that is to say, it takes the form of a correspondence between visual perception and tactilokinaesthetic perception, and is observed in cross-modal perceptual transfers. Arlette Streri has in fact demonstrated that at 2 to 3 months of age – that is, before the motor activity of the hand is definitively under visual control – babies are capable of visually recognizing an object which they have previously explored manually without seeing it. This clearly reveals that visual and tactile spaces are in some way integrated.

But the existence of these cross-modal transfers at an early age also poses a number of problems. Arlette Streri suggests some elegant solutions to these, drawn from her analysis of the discontinuities of development. The trickiest of these problems is the nonreversibility of transfer. Transfers from touch to vision and from vision to touch are not, in fact, always obtained with equal frequency. Moreover, the direction of these imbalances varies from one age to another. For example, with 2-month-old babies, Arlette Streri shows experimentally that transfer is possible only from touch to vision, not from vision to touch. At 4 to 5 months of age, the opposite is observed. This apparent incoherence is explained when the changes which occur in *both* functions of the hand at these ages are considered. At 2 months of age, only the perceptual function is truly operative, the immaturity of the voluntary motor system being such that the hand has not yet acquired its function of carrying objects in order to use them or look at them. Hence the possibility of transfer from tactile perception to visual perception. By the age of 5 months, this carrying function has emerged. Its novelty and functional importance now absorb the perceptual function to such an extent that the hand becomes a motor instrument at the service of the eye, thus rendering the transfer of tactile perceptions to vision impossible, since they are too closely linked with the motor activity of carrying. Arlette Streri advances an explanation of the same kind – but based this time on the emergence of new perceptual capacities in eye and in hand – to account for the absence of vision-to-touch transfer in 2-month-olds, and for the appearance of this possibility at 4–5 months of age.

In other words, it is the intersection of observations of eye–hand perceptuomotor coordination with observations of vision–touch interperceptual coordination that permits hypotheses to be put forward to explain discontinuites of development which, at first sight, appear to be extremely contradictory.

It is thus evident that while eye–hand relations are present very early in life, their manifestations are unstable, since they are highly sensitive to the context in which the visual and manual systems are active. There is a perceptual context for grasping spatial facts and a functional context which is determined by the role and relative importance of the gross functions of eye and hand. If either one of these contexts changes under the effect of external circumstances, or of development, then this fragile path of communication is temporarily blocked.

A fragility of this kind would appear to be perfectly understandable in babies who are only a few weeks or months old. It is surprising, howcvcr, to obscrvc that it pcrsists wcll bcyond this stagc of infancy. In fact, imbalances in visuotactile cross-modal transfers are also observed in pre-school and school-age children, and in adults. What is more, the direction of these imbalances varies from one task to another – a fact which renders any general, unitary explanation of these apparent incoherences impossible. In order to explain them it will be necessary in each case to examine the nature of the constraints to which each of the systems involved is subjected, and the importance of the contextual and functional aspects specific to each situation.

All these recent findings throw new light upon the central problem underlying all the research: that of knowing how the perceptual data are processed. Is it a case of 'amodal' processing which extracts the abstract properties of objects, or of processes specific to each modality which coordinate with each other? The results Arlette Streri observes in neonates lead her, very logically, to reject the Gibsonian theory of amodal processing performed by undifferentiated perceptuomotor modalities in favour of a hypothesis of modalities which are differentiated very early but are also immediately capable of communicating with each other.

In conclusion, in taking stock of our knowledge of visuomanual coordination at the youngest age, this work introduces some indispensable elements into the discussion. With its great methodological thoroughness focusing essentially on recent experimental findings, it is clear and easy to read, which is no mean feat in this field. Finally, I would like to express my admiration for the patience and skill which Arlette Streri has had to deploy in order to test the hundreds of very young babies who took part in her research. By agreeing to look at and manipulate a few cleverly contrived pieces of wood, these babies of all kinds have enabled her to advance the field of psychological science.

Yvette Hatwell
Professor at Université de Pierre Mendès-France, Grenoble

Introduction

The objects in our environment have multiple properties, and only in exceptional cases is our knowledge of them gained through a single sense modality. Rather, each new impression is formed on a multisensory level. If we are to confer coherence on objects and events, we need to detect the relations between the properties of the objects and establish a balance between the different sensory data. If we are to adapt our behaviour in the light of external information, we have to respond in a manner which conforms to the perceived information. Coordinating the information gained by different sensory systems requires integrative behaviour at a central level.

Of the sensory equipment which human beings possess we intend to study only the relations between eye and hand, since their fields of action are so closely related. We shall be concerned with the way in which these two systems are coordinated during the first year of life. Any relationship, however, relies on elements which must be defined in terms of their properties and their function.

The systems compared

Let us remember that the haptic system and the visual system comprise both a sensory component and a motor component which are closely integrated in the functioning of their organs. However, the degree of importance accorded to these different components depends largely on the system under investigation.

The haptic system has a much greater receptive surface than the visual system, but its principal organs for receiving information can be reduced to just the hands and the oral cavity. It is essentially the functioning of the hands to which we shall turn our attention. While binocular convergence in the visual system permits perception of the unicity of objects despite the difference between the left and right retinal projections, there is no such mechanism for the hands. On the contrary, the independence of left and right hands gives the whole system a great degree of freedom which is specific to the human being. This, however, requires a certain amount of coordination between the various object-related activities, and raises the question of lateral preference in their manipulation. Our knowledge of early manual laterality is still very limited, and we shall attempt to clarify this problem (see Chapter 3).

Apart from the physiological differences between the various receptor cells, the sensory component of the two systems has the basic function of gathering the information provided by excitation of the receptors. An initial stimulation, intrinsic changes in environment or even a change in environment as a result of the subject's response are all circumstances which activate the sense cells. Recognizing these changes at receptor level requires an initial level of information processing which permits, among other things, discrimination between stimuli. Thus touching does not inform us solely of those properties of objects which are common to both touch and sight, such as their shape and texture. It also tells us about their weight, their temperature and, in a general way, about the surrounding temperature. Furthermore, the sense of touch has receptors for transmitting pain (Hatwell, 1981, 1986; Reisman, 1987).

It is in the motor component, however, that the essential difference between these two systems is found. The visual system depends on several motor mechanisms for orientating the receptors in order to improve the quality of reception of the information to be processed. Ocular fixation and eye movements characterize basic visual motor activity. Binocular convergence, lens accommodation and changes in pupil size provide further adjustment of the depth and luminance of the image.

The motor component of the manual system is more diversified. Stimulation of the hand, the sensory origin of which may be visual, auditory, olfactory or, indeed, tactile, prompts an orientating reflex which can end in the grasping of the object. In this behaviour, thumb and fingers are brought into various positions depending on the aim of the operation – power grip or precision grip, according to Connolly and Elliott's classification (1972). Simple contact of the palm's cutaneous surface with the object permits an initial stimulation of the tactile receptors. Manual exploration, when it occurs, consists either of moving the hand over the surface of the object, creating a series of depressions in the skin (tactile perception), or of an active movement involving the deeper muscular and articulatory layers (tactilokinaesthetic perception).

This dichotomy between motor and sensory components, as well as their interaction, is clearly indicated in the work of Lederman and Klatzky (1987, 1990), who regard the movements carried out by adults during the course of object manipulations as 'windows' through which it is possible to perceive and recognize objects haptically. The motor component of the hand improves the efficiency of the sensory component in obtaining information. These exploratory procedures (EPs) are specific to each property of the object. For example, the amount of pressure exerted on the object allows its degree of hardness to be detected; 'unsupported holding' enables an estimation of its weight; and 'enclosure' and 'contour following' serve to determine the object's general and exact shapes respectively.

However, the motor function specific to the manual system is exercised in the carrying, displacement and modification of objects – that is to say, in its effect on the environment – and this involves the use of the upper limbs (Hatwell, 1986, 1987). It is in this role that the proprioceptive function of the tactile system is fundamental in ensuring the positioning of the limbs in relation to the whole body during movement. It is essential that we are precise in our use of the terminology of proprioception. According to the Gibsons' theory (E.J. Gibson, 1969; J.J. Gibson, 1966, 1979), all the sense modalities have a proprioceptive and an exteroceptive function. Proprioception is not defined as an isolated sensory system. Information about oneself is obtained on the basis of all the senses. We prefer to give this term a less general meaning, reserving it for information obtained in behaviour which mobilizes muscles, joints, tendons, articulations, and the vestibular system – in other words, we use it to refer to sensitivity to movement and positions.

The properties specific to these modalities, and to the tactile modality in particular, mean that there is a profound difference between seeing and touching. However, there is close interaction between the two systems. On the one hand, information regarding space (direction) and the properties of objects (shape, texture, and so on) is common to both systems. On the other hand, visuotactile knowledge of an object is established in three ways in the adult: we can have an object in our hand without seeing it, although we would be able to recognize it visually; we can move to pick up an object within our visual field; we can visually explore an object which we have in our hand. Therefore, despite the specificities of the perceptual systems, our aim here is to demonstrate that relations are established, and to show how they are established. These relations are not opposed; they are complementary.

Vision–touch relations: a history . . .

If we concern ourselves with when the integration of the haptic and visual systems begins, and not with adult processes, the problem is complicated by the immaturity of the neonate's systems and the question of their development. What do we actually know about the baby's motor and perceptual capacities for touching and seeing? Curiously, the study of the ontogenesis of these systems has been carried out within the framework of a debate about whether vision or touch is dominant. Having believed for centuries in the dominance of the tactile modality on the basis of philosophical arguments, psychologists now assert that vision is in control of most of our activities. The history of this debate, whose path we shall now trace, will allow us to explain the extent of our current knowledge of the baby's perceptual and motor capacities in the two systems.

For a long time touch was considered the dominant sensory modality. On the one hand, it precedes vision phylogenetically; on the other, it is the first modality through which babies experience their environment. Contact modality *par excellence*, touch appeared to be the only concretely observable means of exchange with the exterior. In fact, it appeared inconceivable that the distal, directional perceptual systems, like vision, hearing, olfaction, should be able to inform the neonate about the external world. No tangible proof existed for the reception of information. In contrast, information which is gained haptically is always the result of movement of the hand over the surface of an object, and thus of the subject's direct contact with it. Furthermore, the fact that the haptic system makes possible three-dimensional contact with space led to the conclusion that it was through this modality that a truer – because more concrete – idea of reality was gained. The distal modalities, and vision in particular, seemed to take account of only two dimensions. Finally, the practical role of the hand and its capacity for activity directed towards its surroundings served to reinforce the idea of a high level of correspondence between reality and what is perceived by the tactile modality (Bernstein, 1967). Thus, for a long time, the first observations in this field were concerned with motor skills and babies' activities in relation to their environment, since this was the sole means of understanding infant development. These descriptions, however, have been largely responsible for the neglect of the sensory and perceptual aspects of the tactile modality. The motor functions of the arms and hands have been the subject of a much greater number of observations than tactile sensitivity.

The visual modality, on the other hand, was considered to play a minor role at the start of the baby's life. For centuries, and right up until the 1960s, paediatricians and psychologists believed that babies, like kittens, were blind at birth, and that they had a film over their eyes which would later dissipate. Change in the colour of the iris during the baby's first few months, as well as the vague, imprecise and hesitant fixations of the baby's gaze, served to confirm the notion that the neonate's vision was very immature, perceiving the world as a chaotic blur.

Of course, parents and professionals knew that babies can react to light with the pupil dilation reflex, and follow a moving stimulus with their eyes. However, they were not thought to be sensitive to shapes, depth, etc., and so the belief was held that the baby was functionally blind. Anatomical and empirical data have long supported this belief. The structure of the retina reveals cells, cones and rods, sensitive only to light but not to borders, shapes, movement, depth, or other complex perceptual qualities. The weakness of the retinal system also resides in its two-dimensional character, which reduces all retinal projections to a flat picture. Visual perception of the third dimension was supposed to be established either as a result of learning or with the help of information from other modalities, the tactile modality in particular (Berkeley, 1709). The notion that the three spatial dimensions are accessible to the hand but not operational for the eye appeared to confirm this dominance of touch over vision. Moreover, touch has the perceptual capacity to supplement the deficient visual system considerably. Vision was thus supposed to be dependent on touch.

Neuropsychological research on animals has somewhat overturned the belief that the baby's visual system is structurally deficient. Hubel and Wiesel (1959, 1963) demonstrated that the cortical cells of cats respond to bars, angles and borders and, moreover, that these cells exist at the animal's birth, even if they are not immediately functional. In the field of psychology, studies by Fantz (1961, 1963, 1965) have revealed that neonates are sensitive to the different shapes presented to them, and that they show a preference, given equal brightness, for complex and coloured patterns over uniformly grey stimuli. Recordings of ocular movement and the level of ocular fixation have confirmed the existence of a differentiated response in neonates exposed to homogeneous and heterogeneous visual stimuli (Kessen, 1967; Kessen, Salapatek and Haith, 1965; Salapatek and Kessen, 1966). In short, over the last thirty years, it is the facts more than the theories that have overturned the previously held convictions about babies' abilities. The image of a blind baby has been replaced by the idea that a baby has access to an organized world from the beginning and, consequently, is likely to understand a great deal (Mehler and Fox, 1985). In particular, it is certain that the baby's visual performances are by no means as poor as was previously supposed, despite the immaturity of the cells in the retinal system at birth (Banks and Bennett, 1988). Studies of the baby's visual modality have undergone considerable development in the last two decades. The structure and development of the visual system are now better known (Hickey and Peduzzi, 1987), as are its motor and proprioceptive aspects (Aslin, 1987). Psychophysical research into the baby's vision (Banks and Dannemiller, 1987) has thrown new light on what we already know about the baby's perceptual and discriminatory capacities (Atkinson and Braddick, 1982; Banks and Salapatek, 1983; Gibson and Spelke, 1983; Vurpillot, 1972). The sensory, perceptual and motor aspects of the baby's visual system are all currently raising numerous questions.

Nevertheless, the necessity of reconstructing the third spatial dimension from the retinal projection has long remained a thorny problem. We acknowledge the contribution of J.J. Gibson's theory (1950, 1966, 1979) in this domain. According to this theory, the perceptual visual data are sufficient to specify the characteristics of the environment, and need no external contribution or teaching. No information is lost in the retinal projection, and the third spatial dimension is preserved at the level of the receptor system. Two conditions must be fulfilled if it is to be perceived. The first supposes a change in the stimulus; the second implies active perception on the part of the observer. Motor activity in the eye is a determining factor in the production of these changes in the proximal stimulus. Furthermore, this activity makes it possible to differentiate between movements by the subject and those of the objects. The temporal component is reintroduced into visual perception, and learning is no longer necessary in order to see adequately. The three-dimensional spatial component of vision is provided, in Gibson's theory, by the notion that the world is constituted of heterogeneous surfaces, not homogeneous surfaces (we cannot see anything in fog). Differences in texture gradient, which are specific to the environment, give the observer an idea of the distance of objects. Retinal disparity and binocular parallax, peculiar to the visual system, contribute to the perception of distance. In this way, vision regains an autonomy of functioning which it should never have lost.

Experimental results have confirmed this theory, and there is an abundance of literature available today on the development of the perception of depth (see Yonas and Owsley, 1987, for a review of the questions surrounding this problem). Recent research suggests that the human neonate does have the capacity to perceive depth, without prior haptic learning, even if this ability is not yet fully developed. Granrud (1987, 1988) has demonstrated the neonate's capacity to perceive constancy of size. Fantz (1961) presented a disc and a sphere to 1-month-old babies who showed a marked preference for the sphere. This behaviour indicated that they were able to discriminate between the two stimuli. Campos, Langer and Krowitz (1970) placed 2-month-old babies on the shallow side and then the deep side of a visual cliff (Gibson and Walk, 1960). A decrease in heart rate indicated that the babies had distinguished between the two sides of the apparatus.

At present, the other sense modalities, especially touch, are arousing less interest. The baby's motor ability is described above all as being reflexive, disordered and anarchic, contributing to the notion that the tactile modality is far less essential to neonates in their interaction with the exterior than had previously been supposed. Attitudes to the relations between the two perceptual systems have also been modified. The tactilokinaesthetic system functions and develops in the service of sight. On this point, the literature about the baby is clear. The baby's manipulations are merely reflexes; they are poor, if not nonexistent (Lamb and Campos, 1982). When Bower, Broughton and Moore (1970*a*) first demonstrated the neonate's movement towards a visually presented object, it was the motor performance which was the initial subject of attention. Despite the 'noise' generated by the baby's arm movements, it is possible to identify some structured behaviour. It is not long, however, before this behaviour is obscured by visual activity which has been – justifiably – emphasized.

To sum up: our knowledge about the visual modality is sufficiently sophisticated to postulate the existence of a visual functioning which is adapted to the surrounding conditions from birth. Our knowledge about tactile motor skills rests on equally well-known observations. In contrast, we know very little about tactile sensitivity in general, and the hand in particular. In consequence, what hypotheses can we construct regarding the beginnings of the integration of haptic and visual systems?

Unity or differentiation of the systems at birth?

Only recently have researchers been able to start to formulate an answer to the question which was first raised by the philosophers of Antiquity. The theoretical debates raised by this question, and the experimental data to which they have given rise, have been the object of an exhaustive analysis by Hatwell (1981, 1986). Recent research on the infant, however, has brought to light detailed observations of the relations between the haptic and visual systems, which we shall be analyzing in this book. Starting from existing theories, we shall attempt solely to clarify which hypotheses concerning the relations between vision and touch in the baby are plausible (see Chapter 1).

It can be stated, however, that on the question of the unity or heterogeneity of the systems at birth, psychologists have responded from one of two perspectives. Either they have considered motor ability as the integrative link between the senses, or they have studied the relations between the information gained from two or more sense modalities.

The first perspective owes much to cybernetic models, particularly that of Bernstein (1967), and to contemporary neuropsychology (Held, 1968*a*; Paillard, 1971, 1974). This approach attributes a functional objective to all activity. The significance of the information retained by the organism is expressed in the integrated organization of afferences and efferences in behaviour.

The second perspective considers that there is a unique processing system which extracts 'amodal' meanings from the stimuli analyzed by sense receptors (J.J. Gibson, 1966, 1979). This 'amodal' information gives rise to an 'amodal' perception (E.J. Gibson, 1969) which is independent of the specificities of the sense modalities.

Current data on the infant lend support to both perspectives. The neonate's manual approach towards a visual target (Bower, Broughton and Moore, 1970*a*) and evidence of a transfer of information from the oral tactile modality to the visual modality in the 1-month-old baby (Meltzoff and Borton, 1979) plead in favour of a certain early unity of the systems. Bower (1974, 1979) infers from these facts that the baby is born with undifferentiated systems, and that development consists of the increasing autonomy of these systems.

Nevertheless, these results are insufficient to provide an understanding of the conditions necessary for the establishment of such a unity of systems. If motor ability is the integrative link between the senses, this would suppose that in order to grasp an object within their environment babies programme the distance and direction of their movement and take the visual information about the location of the object into account. In the same way, adjustment of the hand on approach to the object has to take the latter's intrinsic physical properties into account if grasping is to be successful. The fact that visually gained sensory information must be taken into account in the correct pre-positioning of the hand again reveals an integration of systems. However, the motor action has a dual significance. It translates the visual sensory information into movement, and reveals the presence of information which may or may not be confirmed later at the tactile sensory level. Correctly adapted movement in grasping an object thus implies a mutual adjustment, at central level, of the hand's visual system and motor system. There is currently an abundance of literature about the action of reaching for a visually perceived object. In order to evaluate such an early integration of the perceptual and the motor, we shall analyze the baby's behaviour in these situations in some detail (see Chapter 2).

As for amodal perception, this is possible under only two conditions. The first is that the two systems are functioning analogously. However, we know little about any perceptual information-gathering capacities of the hand which reveal a similar functioning to that of vision. The second condition is that equivalence of information is realized both from vision to touch and from touch to vision. The literature, however, tells us practically nothing about the existence of a transfer from vision to touch. In our research, therefore, we have attempted to determine first whether the perceptual component of the tactile modality is as efficient as that of the visual modality (see Chapter 3); and secondly whether there is a reciprocal transfer of information between the two modalities during the first six months after birth (see Chapter 4, I).

Just as it seems to be difficult to separate the perceptual function from the motor function, so this second specificity of the hand claims our attention on two counts. First of all, in the first six months motor skills are analyzed in terms of prehensile actions. As an integrative system of sensory information, the motor function of the hand has been the object of particular analysis. The function of transporting objects, however, does not appear at the same time during the course of development as the perceptual function of the haptic system. Thus these two functions are likely either to interfere or to coordinate. The establishment of prehension–vision coordination should certainly have an effect on the way the baby simultaneously and multimodally apprehends the different properties of objects. The baby has new possibilities: to contrast identical information arriving simultaneously from different modalities, but also to coordinate different information extracted from the same object. It is also through the baby's exploratory bimodal activity that we shall examine the coordination of the two systems (see Chapter 4, II).

Finally, we shall attempt to analyze what significance we should attribute to behaviours observed within the framework of these two approaches in order to gain a better understanding of the relationship between babies and their environment (see Chapter 5).

To sum up: if an 'amodal perception' and a 'nondifferentiation of systems' exist in the baby from birth, then we should be able to establish the existence of, on the one hand, a functional perceptual equivalence in the two modalities and, on the other, a reversibility of perceptual and motor behaviour. This is the hypothesis which we shall attempt to verify through an analysis of the modes of relation between vision and touch in the baby's first year.

Chapter 1

Theoretical perspectives and hypotheses

The study of the relation between eye and hand in babies was first performed on the basis of observations of their behaviour, which was taken as indicative of this relation. For example, the behaviour of reaching towards an object presented within the infant's visual field, which appears at about 4 months of age, was interpreted as the onset of coordination between the two systems. The inference was thus made that until that age the systems remained separate. Given the absence of any data on the infant's sensory and perceptual capacities, this interpretation seemed plausible. The appearance of prehensile gestures became a necessary condition for the realization of inter-sensory coordination. However, although a link had been established between these two fields, they continued to be studied separately. As a result, whether research is focused on sensorimotor relations or on the interaction between sense modalities, the way problems are envisaged and the explanations proposed are, necessarily, different. For us, however, the question which remains is whether, in these two approaches, haptic and visual systems are linked early and, if so, how.

A theoretical debate about reaching towards a visible target

Behavioural studies of the baby are currently conducted within the framework of a theoretical opposition between Piaget's developmental and cognitive perspective and the approach which centres on the ideas of J.J. Gibson (Butterworth, 1982, 1983). We shall start by analyzing the baby's behaviour from a theoretical point of view, but with the aim of going beyond this confrontation.

From separation to unity of systems

For many years Piaget's naturalistic observations have served as a landmark in the study of the development of the prehensile gesture. Several decades after Piaget, however, Bower has brought about a considerable modification to the very conditions of observation by demonstrating early manifestations of this behaviour. Current data on the development of prehension have led to the refinement of the Piagetian model (Mounoud, 1983, 1986).

Piaget's theory poses the problem of prehensile behaviour in terms of a coordination of schemes (Piaget, 1936, trans. 1936, 1953), but ignores the question of intermodal (or cross-modal) perceptions. For Piaget, sensory messages are very unstructured at birth. Through their functioning, neonatal reflexes receive information from the world and are transformed into specialized and independent action schemes. Thus the baby's activity has a primordial place in the organization of reality. These structures or action schemes are the means of exchange between each of the sense modalities and the environment.

Piaget describes with great care the evolution of coordination between vision and touch in the prehensile gesture. The pupil and eyelid reflexes which ensure adaptation to light and improved visual orientation give rise to visual schemes. Impulsive arm movements and the gripping reflex, when used repetitively, become prehension schemes. To begin with, the fields of touch and vision are totally autonomous. The eyes and the hand operate over distinct areas of space. Only the action schemes, which are coordinated in accordance with a process of reciprocal assimilation, can bring about the linking of the two domains in the realization of the act of grasping. Prehension–vision coordination begins at 4–5 months, but not until the visual scheme assimilates the tactile scheme. When the baby's hand enters its field of vision, it serves to 'feed' the visual scheme. Sight of the hands is a necessary stage in prehension–vision coordination, and gives rise to a very specific behaviour pattern: 'at a given moment, infants grasp the objects when they see them in the same visual field as their hands, and then look alternately at their hands and at the objects' (Piaget, 1936, p. 90, trans. 1936, 1953).

Then, until the age of 6 months, when infants look at everything they hold and pick up any object they can reach within their field of vision, there is a reciprocity of assimilation between the schemes. This is the period in which coordination between vision and prehension is established. The sensory domains then interact in a common space.

It is concerning the age at which reaching towards a visual target appears that Piaget's viewpoint has been contested. Since 1966, Bower has re-examined this problem and the approach to the baby's perceptual and cognitive development. He has demonstrated for the first time, in the newborn, the behaviour of reaching manually for a visually presented object (Bower, Broughton and Moore, 1970*a*). This initial research, although it was controversial at first, has given rise to a whole series of experiments on eye–hand relations, which we shall analyze below (see Chapter 2). Experimental confirmation of this behaviour calls Piagetian theory into question, and makes the hypothesis of a unity of spaces at birth plausible. In an explicit description of the neonate's initial state, Bower (1974) suggests that the infant is born with systems which are undifferentiated in the sense that young infants do not 'know' whether they are seeing, hearing or touching something. They simply respond to objects. They experience a world in which tactile space, visual space and auditory space are confused. From this point of view, the newborn's direction of gaze towards a sound (Alegria and Noirot, 1978; Butterworth and Castillo, 1976; Wertheimer, 1961) or manual reaching for a visual object are interpreted as revealing the existence of a primitive unity of the senses at birth. The newborn possesses abstract representations which retain only the very general dimensions of reality (Bower, 1979). Development, as a function of the organism's repeated encounters with the environment, is regarded as a differentiation and increasing autonomy of the sensory systems which leads to more specific representations of the properties of objects.

The hypothesis of an early relation between perceptual fields finds confirmation in neurological analysis of the brain. K.R. Gibson (1982) has demonstrated that in all vertebrates unity of the haptic and visual systems is based on clearly located neurophysiological foundations.

In the superior colliculi the centres responsible for the functioning of these systems are sited very close together. She has further demonstrated that early sensorimotor behaviour in the human neonate – for example, direction of gaze towards a sound or reaching towards a visual target – are also based on precise neurophysiological foundations. There is no cortical control of these behaviours, and in the human being they are similarly mediated by the subcortical region of the superior colliculi. These analyses find confirmation in the work of Stein and Meredith (1990). A large proportion of the cells in the deeper layers of the superior colliculi appear to be multisensorial – that is to say, capable of receiving information via the auditory, visual and somasthetic system. Ten per cent of these cells are common to both vision and touch, and 6 per cent to all three of the aforementioned modalities. Furthermore, each sensory topography interrelates not only with another sensory topography but also with the 'motor' topographies which are also present in the deeper layers of the superior colliculi.

These data may represent a solid argument for explaining the integrative behaviour between visual, tactile and auditory modalities. They do not, however, exclude the possibility of a cortically controlled reception system, capable of receiving and processing information obtained via each of the modalities separately.

Evidence of such early behaviour – and particularly that of manual reaching for a visual target – raises the question of what it actually means. Are sensorimotor relations a kind of reflex or do they, on the contrary, bear witness to the implementation of a higher level of integration of the systems involved, as Bower (1974) would appear to suggest? Observation of an organism's response to a stimulus requires that we determine the conditions for the realization, functioning and modification of this response into the more mature behaviour that occurs later.

This is what was achieved by Mounoud (1983, 1986; Mounoud, Vinter and Hauert, 1985), who characterized the different stages of evolution of the prehensile act in an exposition of his developmental model. Mounoud sets his model within the Piagetian framework, but departs from it on two fundamental points. Firstly, the structures are not constructed but pre-formed. The infant's object is to use them. Secondly, development is regarded as the elaboration of internal representations based on the appearance of codes for modifying the infant's interactions with his/her surroundings. The act of prehension during the first six months is described as a series of stages marked by profound reorganizations or 'revolutions', which may be summarized as follows (Mounoud, 1983):

1. The initial state is regulated by 'intersensorimotor coordinations' – that is to say, by a set of reflexes which are both differentiated and coordinated. The baby is capable of programming an action in response to excitation, but does not use the information provided by unsuccessful execution of the action: the movement is ballistic. The baby's means of exchange with the environment is based on sensory codes.
2. Through perceptual encoding, the initial action undergoes a profound restructuring; the programmes become local and dissociated.
3. Then, during the third stage (4–6 months), the disconnected representations of the previous stage become recoordinated. More unitary programming of the action is organized. The movement is again ballistic.

The apparent reorganizations of gestures are achieved between 6 and 18 months of age. The consideration of new properties of objects and the elaboration of other perceptual representations serve to characterize different stages in the development of prehensile behaviour. With the support of recent experimental facts, Mounoud integrates sensory information and motor components in his description of the act of prehension. However, this behaviour, defined as a programmed means of exchange between the organism and its surroundings, is largely dependent on the degree of sophistication of the baby's representations.

The 'perceptual' perspective

J.J. Gibson's theory (1950, 1966, 1979), which is very close to that of the Gestaltists (Costall, 1982), insists more specifically on the role of sensory input without, however, neglecting the role of action. This viewpoint makes it possible to interpret not only perceptual behaviour and interaction, but also the relations between perception and action.

The ecological approach of E.J. and J.J. Gibson and the notion of 'affordances' inverts the focus of interest in the relation between sensory and motor. According to J.J. Gibson, the proximal stimulus carries a huge amount of information about the external world, and the process of perception consists of discovering invariants in the stimulus. The perceptual act is 'direct', since it does not call upon any inference mechanism. It is 'immediate', because it does not demand a mental act of comparison between information stored in memory and the information presented, for example in the recognition of objects. Invariants allow the detection of 'sameness' across the different aspects of an object. Thus there is no necessity to resort to other nonperceptual psychological mechanisms, such as memory. This is itself a part of the process of perception. In the same way, from this perspective, to perceive is not, for example, to classify an object. One and the same object can take on different meanings depending on the conditions under which it is perceived. For example, a stone can be a projectile, a paperweight, a hammer, etc. (J.J. Gibson, 1979). It is this concept which best describes the notion of 'affordance'. 'Affordance' is the information which is potentially useful for an individual, the properties of things defined with reference to the presence and action of an observer. What is important is the description of the environment which makes it possible to define the information which is relevant for a given individual. This structured and significant information specifies the properties of objects and events. They form the observer's 'ecological niche', and an interdependent link is established between observer and environment. Environment does not exist independently of the organisms which act in it in order to survive. Conversely, observers use their perceptual systems to give objects the meanings for their activities. These perceptual systems play an essential role in receiving the information necessary for the subject's behaviour. For the purposes of adaptation, the senses detect valid information in the objects and events surrounding the individual, and this information, in its turn, controls the individual's actions. Behaviour is thus determined and modulated by information (J.J. Gibson, 1979; E.J. Gibson, 1982, 1984).

The fact that J.J. Gibson's work is primarily concerned with visual perception and the role with which he invests it in the detection of these 'affordances' is well known. Information plays the same role for manipulation as for vision. The shape and size of objects are perceived in relation to the hands – that is to say, in terms of their 'affordance' for manipulation. Objects are graspable, or they are not. Like eye movement, manipulation is behaviour which cannot be reduced to responses to environmental stimuli, or to behaviour guided by the brain. It is behaviour which is defined precisely in relation to information provided by the environment. As for the action of grasping objects, it is clearly presented in terms of the subordination of manipulation to vision. It is performed under visual control, and is inseparably linked to the visual perception of objects. This is the perspective from which the very young infant's behaviour of approaching and reaching an object is interpreted (von Hofsten, 1986; Rochat and Reed, 1987). The viewed object is also an object for grasping, so it possesses properties which direct the act of reaching and grasping. Nevertheless, J.J. Gibson (1979) considers that the manipulation of an object is a complex act for which it is difficult to formulate regularities.

By placing the emphasis on action, Piaget gives it too structural and epistemic a description. Action schemes are tools at the service of intelligence, which appears later. The factors which trigger the action and organization of movement are not analyzed as such. Moreover, the proprioceptive role of the hand does not exist in babies at the time when Piaget says of them: 'The hands they study evidently appear to them to be some kind of body in the same way as the objects they observe within their immediate surroundings' (1937, p. 201, trans. 1937, 1955).

Furthermore, Piaget does not tell us whether, at that time, babies differentiate between their hands and other observed objects. We do know that proprioception plays a major role, particularly in the traction response to stimulation of the hand as observed by Halverson (1937) and Twitchell (1965, 1970). By making the observer's behaviour depend on the properties of the stimulus, Gibson denies the organizational aspect of action and its effects on the environment.

In fact, the theories proposed by these two perspectives are quite complementary. According to Rochat and Reed (1987), for both Gibson and Piaget – though for different reasons – babies live in their environment in an adualistic way. These authors argue that the Gibsonian perspective views this interaction as a process of accommodation, whereas Piaget considers it to be one of assimilation. All the same, these theories do not tell us how the motor system of the hand is able to integrate the visually received sensory information at the time of approaching and reaching an object.

Other possible approaches . . .

Bernstein (1967) offers another point of view by taking account of both afferent systems and effections in his cybernetic model. On some points his conceptions agree with those of Piaget, since he attributes to action a dominant role in the exact knowledge of reality. Only the practical action of the subject makes correct access to reality possible.

Bernstein suggests that an organism is in a constant state of disequilibrium with regard to its environment. Consequently, subjects must be continually active: on the one hand evaluating their actions relative to the constantly changing conditions of their surroundings; on the other modulating their activities in order to satisfy their needs and realize their objectives. The evaluative function is realized by perceptual systems which actively explore the environment. The function of modulation is attributed to the action systems which construct, coordinate and adjust the individual's movements. The motor system thus undergoes constant adaptation to changing circumstances. This point of view does not disagree with the Gibsonian perspective. Nevertheless, it diverges from it fundamentally in that Bernstein's cybernetic model comprises a central command base controlling behaviour – that is to say, a memory. Bernstein draws a clear distinction between movement and action. The latter has a goal. For example, he describes voluntary movements in three stages as follows:

> Voluntary movements may be represented in the form of successive stages.
>
> 1. Perception, and the necessary evaluation of the *situation* and of its bearing on the individual caught up in it.
> 2. The individual determines in what way it is necessary to alter this situation; what, by means of his activity, the situation *must become* instead of *what it is*. The motor problem has already appeared at this stage. It is not difficult to guess that this motor problem must contain more information than is included in the bare perception of the situation, some of which is at least partially not present in the latter . . .
> 3. The individual must next determine *what* must be done and
> 4. How it must be done, and what are the available resources. (p. 148)

Here we find the assimilative pole of the action which is seen as the determining factor in Piaget's work. Let us remember that in this model of adult behaviour action is both a corrective system and a system for the translation of perceptions.

It is a corrective system, since the correspondence between perception and reality is essentially ensured by the practical actions performed by subjects in relation to their environment. The consequences of any errors inform subjects about their erroneous perceptions. It is a system for translation, since it is also these actions which give meaning to the signal when they are triggered with the aim of realizing a particular objective. All the motor components which are involved in a movement (joint, trunk, fingers, arms, etc.) and can operate independently of one another are organized in the service of a defined action which restricts their freedom. Furthermore, Bernstein demonstrates, in his physiology of activity, that the trajectory of a part of the body cannot be calculated without information reconstructed from the changes in muscular force which appear during the movement itself. In other words, any central command is ambiguous compared to the resulting patterns of movement, and has to be modified in consequence. The role of proprioceptive reafferences is, therefore, fundamental.

Like Gibson, Bernstein is very interested in locomotion and, to a lesser extent, in the movement of the hand. In contrast, on the basis of the Bernstein model (1967) and the earlier models of von Holst and Mittelstädt (1950), contemporary neurophysiological studies of the adult human or animal approach the relations between senses and motor activity in precisely the field of study which concerns us: the relationship between seeing and touching.

Three streams of thought dominate the literature, representing to some extent the theories of Gibson and Bernstein. The theory of motor systems is represented in France by Paillard (1971, 1974; Paillard and Beaubaton, 1978); the theory of action systems has been newly elaborated by Reed (1982), and the theory of dynamic systems has also emerged (Kugler, Kelso and Turvey, 1982).

The programming of motor systems

In an analytical and structural way, the theory of motor systems adopts Bernstein's analyses of the behaviour of grasping an object. This behaviour is essentially described as a sensorimotor loop. According to Paillard, two components of the act of prehension exist in the adult: one ballistic, the other corrective. The first is triggered visually; the second is controlled visually. The baby's behaviour is also thought to evolve in that order, as a result of the maturing nervous system and practice (Bower, 1974). Jeannerod and Biguer (1982) present a similar description to Paillard but include the corrective component in their analysis of the adult trajectory, describing it as a regular and continuous braking with feedback – that is to say, under visual control. The movement is thus uniform and visually controlled throughout the whole of its course.

In contrast, Jeannerod and Biguer (1982) make a clear distinction between the directional movement of the arm towards a target and the anticipatory adjustment of the hand in order to grasp the object. The movement is a response to locating the object in space; the organization of the fine manual system is a response to a property of the object. This description in terms of two sensorimotor systems is also used by von Hofsten and Rönnqvist (1988) and Jeannerod (1984, 1986), who find anatomical support for this division in Kuypers's research (1973). The directional movement of the arm is hardly affected by the absence of visual control (Jeannerod, 1984). Depending on the subject, it takes between 674 and 1,013 milliseconds (average 800 ms) in the case of a target situated 40 centimetres away. The course of the trajectory takes the form of an inverted U, and anticipatory adjustment of the hand takes place during the hand's journey towards the object. There is, therefore, a coordination between the two components of the act of prehension.

Numerous studies have been conducted on prehensile behaviour in the adult in the absence of visual reafferences – that is to say, without feedback, or in conditions of perceptual conflict – in order to analyze the adaptation of the eye–hand system.

In the no-feedback situation, Jeannerod and Prablanc (1978) have revealed major errors in aiming for a visual target when subjects cannot see their hands. They interpret this result on the basis of the duration of the movement's execution. In the normal feedback situation, the average duration of the movement is longer than with no feedback by 150 milliseconds. This time may be imputed to the final correction phase which is missing in the no-feedback situation. Sivak and MacKenzie (1990) examine more precisely the role of the peripheral and foveal retina in approaching and grasping an object.

Subjects wear either lenses which completely eliminate foveal vision or goggles which are adapted to eliminate peripheral vision. In the first case, both approaching the object and correctly grasping it are affected. In particular, the information obtained regarding the object's size and shape is inadequate. In the second case, it is only the movement of the arm for correctly locating the object which is flawed. In the case of perceptual conflict, a remarkable adaptation to prismatic distortions is performed by the adult even when the freedom of certain parts of the body, which are involved in the movement, is restricted.

The contributions made by Held (1968*a*, *b*) and Hein to our understanding of the role of voluntary motor activity in the eye–hand relation is well known. Let us briefly recall the roundabout experiment. A pair of kittens are placed in a roundabout. The 'active' kitten moves around quite freely. Its movements are transmitted to the 'passive' kitten, which is immobilized in a carriage. In visual placement tests the performance of passive kittens is far inferior to those of active kittens (Held and Hein, 1963). The importance of the animal being able to see its limbs for the establishment of visuomotor coordination, even when there is no restriction of the motor system, is brought to light by these authors. They have demonstrated that 4-week-old kittens deprived of the sight of their front limbs show an impaired extension reflex in placing their paws when they are put on to an uneven surface (Hein and Held, 1967). Similar results have been observed in monkeys for visually-guided reaching (Held and Bauer, 1967).

The act of pointing mobilizes not only the eyes and limbs but also the head. How are the movements of these three parts of the body coordinated in order to ensure the efficiency and precision of this action, given that each system has its own inertia? There are two contradictory hypotheses which account for this coordination. The first is based on the idea that the three parts of the body are controlled by a common motor command centre, and activated simultaneously. The time difference is small: mobilization of the eyes occurs 20 milliseconds earlier than that of the head and fingers (Biguer, Jeannerod and Prablanc, 1982; Biguer, Prablanc and Jeannerod, 1984). The second hypothesis suggests that the three systems are controlled by independent motor commands, and can be activated in any order (Gielen, Van den Heuvel and Van Gisbergen, 1984). Carnahan and Marteniuk (1991) put this idea to the test using the experimental task of pointing at a light. When subjects follow the target with pointed fingers and speed is given a higher priority than precision, the head moves before the eyes and hand. When the target is tracked only visually, the eyes move before the head and limb. These two results mean that the temporal organization of the eye/head system changes when arm movement is involved in pointing. Nevertheless, at the end of the trajectory the eyes always reach the target at least 200 milliseconds before the arm, irrespective of the order in which the three systems start to move. While looking may not always be necessary at the start, it is essential at the final phase, when it ensures the effectiveness of the action.

Similar situations to those used in the study of adults have been undertaken in the study of babies' behaviour, as we shall see. It will thus be possible to distinguish the motor programmes which are specific to the system of a young infant of a given age, and are therefore likely to be modified from those in the adult system which are already organized in the infant.

The notion of programming a motor movement assumes that we can determine the time when planning occurs. However, the role accorded to central and peripheral commands in the control of movement varies with the different theories proposed. For Adams (1971) it is the sensory reafferences produced during an action which play a primary role. They are compared to a reafference (perceptual trace) memory corresponding to the previously planned movement. Control of the movement is realized on the basis of a comparison of the present sensation and its perceptual trace. The peripheral systems are regarded as important, and the information obtained has a retroactive effect. This theory works well for describing movements which are slow or being learned. In contrast, Schmidt (1975) holds that movements are programmed prior to execution. Control is proactive, and exercised primarily in the case of rapid movements. Programmes are schemes which retain only the general features (invariants) of multiple movements. The role of central command is fundamental.

Reed's theory of action systems (1982)

Reed's theory, while it stems from that of Bernstein, is less analytical than its predecessors. At the level of behavioural organization, it completely denies the existence of any separation between central and peripheral command, sensory components and action motors. Functional movement is always controlled by the central and peripheral system. Input and output systems have both perceptual and motor functions.

The key aspect of Reed's perspective, however, lies in the attribution of meaning to actions. He proposes a synthesis of J.J. Gibson's theory (1966, 1979) with that of Bernstein (1967). Starting from Gibson's notion of action as the realization of an 'affordance' – that is to say, of information which is useful to the subject – Reed differentiates his theory from that of motor systems.

The study of movement is the study not of efferent commands or their effects, but of the way in which an organism uses valid information in order to modify its action. Following Gibson's example, Reed rejects the idea of a response being activated by a stimulus and, therefore, that of sensorimotor loops in so far as they take the form of an associative structure which can be interpreted according to the strict S–R scheme. Movements are not activated by a stimulus. Instead they are controlled, functional organizations capable of adapting to changing circumstances. Whereas according to the motor systems perspective movements are responses to stimuli or to central factors and, consequently, have only a single function, action systems possess a variety of functions owing to the fact that they adapt the organism's activities to significant properties of the environment.

Action systems are characterized by their functions, not by the muscles they activate. The two components of action are posture and movement. Actions are not discrete units with hierarchical levels; they are relations. A posture is an individual's orientation with regard to his/her environment, while movements permit changes in posture. Locomotion, for example, necessarily implies the coordination of different postures. Postures and movements imply nested afferent and efferent information paths.

Perception–action approach versus dynamic–systems approach

The baby's motor behaviour is currently expressed and explained within two theoretical approaches which appear to differ in the role they accord to the central nervous system (see von Hofsten, 1989). In the *perception–action approach* the success of an action depends on the mobilization of the appropriate tool for this action, and on the control of this tool to achieve the goal required. Taking account of the baby's perceptions and actions at one and the same time makes an optimized description of the stages of sensorimotor integration possible. The *dynamic–systems approach* also attempts to account for the changes involved in the baby's perceptuomotor behaviour. This second perspective is based on the general theory of the thermodynamics of complex systems, and on the general theory of systems (von Bertalanffy, 1973; see also Kugler, Kelso and Turvey, 1982). A complex multicausal and nonlinear system is characterized by a number of parameters which are self-organizing and produce stable patterns with a low degree of freedom. If the parameters operating in a system are no longer situated at the same level or are no longer synchronized, stability breaks down and a state of disequilibrium obtains until the system finds a new state of equilibrium in which to operate. Disequilibrium can have a number of causes, among them an increase in the system's energy – one example is the change from one form of locomotion to another. When the speed of locomotion increases, the initial state of walking loses its stability and is transformed into a new state: running. Physical growth is another factor of disequilibrium. When the size of an animal increases and reaches a critical value, the stability of movement patterns is lost, and the biodynamic system tries to establish a new stable state. In this approach, all the determining factors are equally involved. The brain loses its central function of commanding and controlling actions, and becomes just one element among the other possible elements. Its role is thus considerably reduced compared to the perception–action perspective.

The interesting thing about this approach is that it provides us with an explanation of the transitions between stages of development. The study of how weight is involved in the neonate's walking reflex (Thelen, 1985) is one example of how this perspective may be applied. When babies lose this stepping reflex at about 2 months, it is because their adipose, nonmuscular legs can no longer support their head and trunk. If they are helped to support their body – by being put in water for example – they rediscover their walking reflex.

According to von Hofsten (1989), the brain cannot be given an identical role to that of the other physical parameters of the body (weight, size, and so on). Physical constraints define the problems associated with realizable actions, while the brain resolves these problems. While the body's physical parameters define the most efficient moment to switch between running and walking, the brain exploits these physical constraints and can make it possible to walk quickly or run slowly.

The theory of dynamic systems is attractive, since it clearly defines the characteristics of a system and the importance of each one at a given moment and during the course of development. In defining the constraints of a system, it can explain the asynchronicities of development. However, while this theory can provide an interesting model for explaining motor changes as well as the development of expressive, communicative and social actions in the baby (Fogel and Thelen, 1987), it does not help us to understand the way in which sensory information is integrated at the perceptual level where the role of the brain must necessarily predominate.

What conclusions for the baby?

These approaches are characterized by a number of differences – above all, in the determination of the element in the subject–environment relationship which ensures control of action. According to Bernstein, central activity is involved in information capture, whereas for Gibson the value of the information extracted from the environment largely determines the adaptation of behaviour. The second difference lies in whether or not action is considered to be reflexive in nature. When behaviour is triggered by information it can take on this reflexive component; when it is controlled by information, or by a central command, it loses this automatic aspect.

We shall retain two of the essential ideas from these theories in our analysis of the start of integration of the tactile and visual systems. First, action is the realization of an item of sensory information, not a 'response' to this information. Therefore, it is not merely a link between the visual system and the tactilokinaesthetic system, it also represents the union of the two systems. Action possesses an integrational aspect. Secondly, it continuously adapts to changes in the environment. It cannot, therefore, be a reflex, a rigid and fixed reaction to a stimulus.

In the baby's prehensile gesture, it is the sophistication of the arm's visual programming as a function of changes in the stimulus and the pre-positioning of the hand to achieve a good grasp which serve as the behavioural indicators that reveal this integration. This behaviour has a dual psychological significance. While it reveals the visual sensory afferences, it also implies a programming plan which can be corrected in the way suggested by Bernstein. For example, anticipation of action reveals visual sensory information which the tactile sense then confirms or not when the object is grasped. When we observe a developing organism, however, this anticipation can also be regarded as expressing forms of organization of the knowledge which subjects possess about their environment, as Mounoud suggests (1983, 1986).

Several questions must be raised. Does the integration of haptic and visual systems exist in neonates, while their motor aptitude in general – and the finer motor skills of their finger movements in particular – is far less efficient than their visual afferences? If this is so, how are we to describe this integration? If not, then how is this integration established in the development of the act of prehension in the baby, given that perceptual and motor systems develop at asynchronous rates?

We do know that babies visually record certain spatial dimensions at an early age, and are capable of fine discriminations between the properties of objects. However, their still halting motor skills are unable to produce the finely adapted behaviour which would reveal all the recorded sensory afferences. Should we attribute the difficulty of adapting the hand to the low degree of maturation or to the absence of a motor programming plan in babies?

It is on the basis of an analysis of the behaviour of manually approaching and reaching a visual target, and of the properties of this target, that we shall attempt to answer these questions. Unlike Piaget, however, we support the hypothesis that there is an early relation between visual space and tactile space. While Piaget concludes that heterogeneous spaces exist for the neonate, this is because he bases his ideas essentially on the emergence of movements coordinating vision and prehension which, in his observations, do not appear until about 4 months of age. Furthermore, since Piaget's day new techniques for more refined observation of neonate behaviour have developed, and the resulting analyses no longer agree with Piagetian theory.

Nevertheless, unlike Bower, we hypothesize that systems in the baby are not undifferentiated. The visual system and the tactile system are to some extent functionally specific, and therefore enjoy a degree of independence. In fact, following Gibson's example, the literature points increasingly to the analogies, and less to the differences, between the visual system and the oral and tactilokinaesthetic systems (Bresson, 1972; Paillard, 1974; Paillard and Beaubaton, 1978). As we have seen, the tactile system ensures the operation of those functions which are specific to it.

On the other hand, another argument against undifferentiated systems is the difference in their effectiveness at birth. The visual modality, while it is not used *in utero*, appears to be prepared to function remarkably well in the newborn baby, and develops very rapidly. In contrast, while the overall motor ability of the organism is organized at a very early stage of life, it appears to be less performative and, above all, slower to develop. Bower *et al.* (1970*a*) demonstrate the existence of a 'visual capture' but describe the tactile system as weak, in that beyond actually grasping an object, babies do not bring it into their view. This asymmetrical behaviour argues against the nondifferentiation of systems. From birth there is a visual dominance which is linked to the difference in efficiency between motor and sensory.

The observation of this asymmetry is also explicable in terms of J.J. Gibson's 'affordance' theory (1979). According to this theory, the observer detects the useful information in the stimulus, and this information then controls the subject's action. This perspective makes it possible to interpret the action of approaching and reaching an object which is visually presented to the baby (von Hofsten, 1986; Reed, 1982; Rochat and Reed, 1987). The regarded object is also an object for grasping and therefore has properties which control reaching and grasping behaviour. Conversely, however, as far as we know, no one has ever observed that placing an object in the hands of newborns will cause them to carry it into their view or into their mouth. This is not because of some motor or muscular problem, since neonates lift their arms to reach an object and suck their thumbs even *in utero*. Does this mean that an object held in the hand does not contain sufficient information to control the motion of carrying it into view? In other words, does this imply that for neonates, a held object is not yet an object to be looked at? Or, on the contrary, does the held object contain all the interesting information in such a way that it is unnecessary for the baby to see it?

All the same, without totally rejecting the interpretation of the asymmetry of the sensorimotor relation in terms of sensory dominance, we should like to suggest an alternative explanation. The absence of an action equivalent to that of prehension – that is to say, the moving of a held object into the visual field – could result from the absence of the object-carrying function in the neonate. This function does not appear until several months later, and implies a programming of motor movement which is probably more complex than that demanded by prehension, for which the visual object situated in the space constitutes the goal towards which babies stretch their hands. The goal, therefore, is defined, whereas in carrying an object – that is to say, moving an object through space – the goal is determined by babies themselves. This action is therefore more difficult to plan.

Relations between the sensory modalities

Situating the problem

The human organism has to resolve the paradox of evolving in a stable and unified world while extracting information from the external world through sensory modalities whose structure and functioning appear to differ profoundly. What means does the human possess for unifying this mosaic of stimuli? According to Marks (1978*a*, *b*), philosophers since Democritus and Aristotle have regularly examined this question from a theoretical viewpoint. Each perceptual system, particularly at the level of sensory reception, possesses highly specialized structural characteristics which allow it to capture only one part of the information inherent in the environment. Furthermore, within this field the range of usable stimuli is limited by the capacity of the receptor.

For a very long time, it was primarily the particularities of the sense modalities which held the attention of philosophers and researchers (Revesz, 1933). Each sensory system has its own rules for receiving and transmitting information, and functions in a distinct space. To make the individual's environment unified and cohesive, the existence of mediators has often been postulated, by the associationist empiricists in particular (see Helmholtz, 1885). More recently, language (Ettlinger, 1967), images, mental schemes or the existence of codes for the transfer of sensory information from one channel to another (Bryant, 1974) have been hypothesized as plausible mechanisms for ensuring perceptual continuity in the adult, as shown by the behaviour of subjects in situations of perceptual conflict (Pick, 1970). These mediators, however, are not the necessary condition for this relation. What would be their nature and function at an age when the different sensory modalities are unable to realize all their functions, or in individuals with a different cognitive system from that of the human being? These mediators can be acquired only during the course of development.

The existence of suprasensory or 'intermodal' dimensions (Guillaume, 1937) postulated by the Gestaltists (Koffka, 1959; Köhler, 1964) and by Werner (1934) represents the opposite hypothesis. Perceptions coming from different sensory systems have elements in common, and one and the same perceptual quality can be obtained from several modalities at once. While this appears, perhaps, to be simpler for certain properties of the stimulus which are common to several systems, it is less so for the characteristics which are specific to any one modality. Even in this case, the Gestaltists still hold that a correspondence exists between the modalities, and is the result of a process of synaesthesia. The stimulation of one modality influences the functioning of another. Phonetically, for example, certain words will carry very particular connotations, or even – as revealed in Hornbostel's (1925) clever experiment – a certain smell will be associated with a particular colour or sound. Schiller's experiment on gudgeon (reported in Werner, 1934) is a remarkable illustration of the phenomenon of synaesthesia. Schiller trained gudgeon always to choose to receive their food in the best-lit chamber. After the training period, the experimenter gave the fish two chambers to choose from: one characterized by 'dark-smelling' indole, the other by 'light-smelling' acetone. The results showed that 75 per cent of the gudgeon preferred the acetone chamber, despite the fact that they preferred the smell of indole before the training session. One might object, however, that this is a question only of qualitative sensations, and that the modalities retain their specificity at the perceptual level. This, in any case, is what Werner has in mind when he distinguishes between a 'vital sensation' of colours, sounds, and so on and an 'objective perception' of the same colours and sounds. Synaesthesia occurs at the level of 'vital sensation'. The notion of quality of information, however, refers to the idea of sensation, and does not imply that the subject perceives it. Rather, the subject reacts to an 'ambiance'.

Nevertheless, the Gestaltist hypothesis of a unity of senses finds confirmation in certain types of animal behaviour. The imprinting phenomenon in ewes is well known to sheep farmers. The capacity for recognizing her own progeny depends on the ewe's olfactory modality. Removal of the ewe's olfactory bulb makes her unable to discriminate between her own lamb and a strange lamb (Bouissou, 1968). In contrast, she can auditorily recognize the bleating of her lambs if, at the time of their birth, she had auditory and olfactory contact which enables her to recognize her lamb solely through the auditory modality. It would appear that a set of sensory stimuli, commencing *in utero*, is essential for the successful reciprocal attachment between the lamb and its mother (Vince and Billing, 1986). In general, it seems that the rolc of prenatal stimuli in the animal is fundamental, and affects behaviour after birth (Gottlieb, 1983). This is also the viewpoint defended by Schneirla (1965), particularly with reference to intermodal perceptions. He stipulates that the tactile and proprioceptive stimuli to which the bird embryo is exposed influence its response, after hatching, to auditory and visual stimuli which it never perceived *in utero*.

In a similar perspective, experiments on the rat reveal that an intermodal process also exists in mammals. Teicher and Blass (1977) and Pedersen and Blass (1982) have demonstrated that if an odiferous substance with a particular taste (such as lemon juice) is injected into the amniotic fluid of the gestating rat, and the resultant baby rat is then made to choose between two smells, a familiar onc of lcmon juice and another which is new, it will choose the familiar smell. This behaviour lasts until adulthood, when the rat will choose, from two potential mates, the one which is impregnated with the familiar smell.

Spear and Molina (1987) have also demonstrated that the young rat, but not the adult, is capable of treating the smell and taste of alcohol as equivalent. Working within a Gibsonian perspective, these authors have also obtained transfers of learning between the olfactory and visual modalities of the young rat at the age of 16 days and, earlier still (4 days), between smelling and touching and between touching and taste.

The imprinting phenomenon bears witness to the memory of sensations. It is based on a simple learning process over which the animal exercises no control. Things are very different in the case of the intermodal transfer of object shapes. Such transfers suppose that the organism not only possesses receptor systems capable of fine analysis of this property of objects, but is also able to judge the equivalence or nonequivalence of objects presented in different sensory modalities. This kind of perceptual behaviour has been demonstrated in adult higher primates. After a long training process, these animals have shown themselves to be capable of matching or recognizing – by sight or touch, depending on the experiment – the shape of objects apprehended by one or the other system (Cowey and Weikrantz, 1975; Davenport and Rogers, 1970; Davenport, Rogers and Russel, 1973, 1975). These ingenious experiments have introduced new elements into the unity of perceptions. Certain mediatory principles – language in particular – no longer constitute a prerequisite for the existence of intermodal perceptions, as Ettlinger (1967) assumed. In contrast, they tell us nothing about the state of the relationship between intermodal perceptions in the newborn primate. In a general way, whatever the nature of the mediator which unites the perceptual systems in the adult, it can account only for fully developed systems or systems which are undergoing development. In no case can it predict the origins of this link.

Until very recently, the absence of data relating to the very young infant left the status of a number of hypotheses concerning the connection between perceptions undecided. As Hatwell points out (1981, 1986), the choice of hypothesis has important implications. The selection of either the hypothesis of a unity of sensory modalities at birth or the hypothesis of an initial separation leads to equally different conclusions being drawn about the way in which each modality functions at birth. Are they similar, despite the structural and functional differences they exhibit, or do they arrive at a certain homogeneity during the course of development?

Piaget never offered an explicit hypothesis of intermodal perceptions. It would be quite legitimate, however, to consider that within this perspective they can be implemented only once the coordination of action schemes is assured. The baby will then have the potential to contrast visual and haptic stimuli. According to this point of view, perception of a unified environment occurs late in the baby. In contrast, it is precisely in this field that J.J. Gibson's theory has reformulated the questions which have to be raised.

The Gibsonian view of perception

According to Gibson, visual perception is regarded as a pattern of stimuli specifying the properties of objects unequivocally. Perception is not the result of a set of sensations, specific impressions which are characterized by the system receiving them and which the subject then has to reassemble. His reasoning explains that the information specifying the properties of objects (distal stimulus) is retained in the proximal stimulus (the light energy reflected by the object) and in the transformations which this stimulus undergoes when it affects the subject's receptors and neural pathways. Nevertheless, for visual reception to retain all the characteristics of the distal stimulus the stimulus would have to change with time, and these changes would have to be the result of voluntary activity on the part of the subject. The stability of the perceived world depends on the extraction of perceptual invariants which correlate to these changes. Viewed from this perspective, the modalities function according to the same rules in their apprehension of space. Similar mechanisms to those employed in vision are possible in tactile perception (J.J. Gibson, 1962, 1966). It is active touching, not just simple contact with an object, which makes it possible to perceive the properties of objects. Passive touching can yield only a flow of stimuli which are difficult to identify. In this way, the classic distinction between contactual touch perception and distant visual perception no longer makes sense, since both systems function according to the same principles.

An ingenious experiment devised by White, Saunders, Scadden, Bach-y-Rita and Collins (1970), and repeated by Bach-y-Rita (1972), provides an illustration of this viewpoint. These researchers invented a system of remote tactile perception to compensate for the sensory deficiency of blind people. The TVSS (Tactile-Vision-Substitution-System) is a prosthesis which allows tactile perception of objects without hand contact and without the subject being able to manipulate them. The apparatus consists of a video system which projects the image of an object filmed with a camera on to a television screen. An electronic device transforms the light image into electric impulses which activate 400 tactile vibrators arranged in 20 by 20 rows on a plate positioned on the back of an armchair. Each of these vibrotactors functions fully or not at all, depending on the level of luminous excitation in the image. Point by point the system changes a light wave into an electric wave. The blind (or perhaps blindfolded) subject's naked back rests against the plate, and the cutaneous system is stimulated by vibrations which correspond to the light energy. The ingenuity of this prosthesis does not lie solely in the tactile system's potential for distal 'seeing'. The subjects are capable of recognizing the filmed object when they operate the camera themselves – that is to say, under conditions of active exploration. When it is the experimenter who is operating the camera (passive exploration conditions) the subjects have great difficulty in recognizing and naming the object.

This experiment is interesting for several reasons. First, the body area which is being stimulated is qualitatively and quantitatively poor in tactile receptors compared to those of the mouth and hands, which possess the largest number of cells necessary for a fine degree of tactile discrimination of objects. Nevertheless, recognition of objects is possible. This would imply that even a slight excitation would be sufficient to lead to perception. Secondly, substitution for the visual system by the tactile system appears to be achieved. It is not only the distal character of the visual modality which is put to the test, but also the two-dimensional projection of stimuli which is analogous to that of the retinal system. Furthermore, this device shows that the recognition of 'touched' objects is based on a stimulation pattern similar to that which could be used to describe retinal reception. It is not recognized by one particular system, since there is no manipulation of the object. Finally, it is through active, not passive, exploration of the object's contours by the subject who is manoeuvring the camera that perception is, nevertheless, possible.

Even though this experiment verifies many of the ideas proposed in J.J. Gibson's theory, some of the observations suggest that there is a limit to the tactile system's relatedness to the visual process. The 'distal' tactile perception is mediated through the subject's verbal account of what can be perceived. It is on the basis of the subject's comments that it has been possible to modify the system. On the other hand, it is on the basis of a two-dimensional representation of the object, not of the object itself, that tactile recognition occurs. Thus the hypothesis of symbolic mediators between the systems cannot be ruled out. Finally, like manipulation of the object, camera-aided exploration is still sequential. Shape identification is performed by moving the camera along the object's contours.

What conclusions can we draw from Gibson's theory concerning the relations between sense modalities in babies? The idea of an analogous functioning of the tactile and visual systems in the process of extracting perceptual invariants seems to us fundamental. If it is possible to demonstrate that these mechanisms do function in this way in infants, then the conditions for early amodal unity are present. However, Gibson's perspective, according to which the information about objects contained in the optic array is rich enough to allow the properties of objects to be specified uniquely, has met with a barrage of criticism from psychologists who subscribe to the information-processing theory. While they recognize the importance of the use of invariants in perception, they believe that Gibson has oversimplified the act of perception. We do more than find and extract physical invariants; we process this information and thus transform it. According to Marr (1982), for example, perception depends on a hierarchy of sketches. A series of processes transforms the optic array into a series of representations, each one exhibiting more complex properties of reality.

The notion of direct, immediate perception makes no sense in the context of the information-processing theory. Seen from this perspective, Fodor and Pylyshyn's (1981) demonstration is decisive. The properties of a surface are revealed in the properties of the light reflected from it and, conversely, the properties of the light contain information about the properties of the surface. This reversibility is compatible with Gibson's theory. In the epistemological relationship of specification, however, this reciprocity is no longer possible. The organism analyzes the properties of light in order to specify the structure of the surface, but cannot determine the structure of light on the basis of the surface. The perception of light is therefore, in a causal way, both necessary for the perception of the surface (without light, we cannot see the object) and sufficient (as in the case of the hologram). The organism, therefore, first of all determines the informative properties of the light, and then – or at the same time – associates these properties with those of the surface. Processes are postulated to account for the transition between the detection of light properties and the perception of surface properties. These processes assume that subjects are aware – although not necessarily consciously – of the correlation, and that they possess a mental representation of it. According to Fodor and Pylyshyn, the construction of a percept relies on the representation of the detected properties, and the representation of a correlation between the properties of light and those of a surface. While Gibson postulates that all the information is contained within the stimulus, in Fodor and Pylyshyn's theory the information about the objects which is contained in light is fragmentary, and only some of the object's properties (the sensory properties) are uniquely specified; the rest are mediated. The perceptual system makes inferences in order to reinterpret the sensory information transmitted to it by the transcoders (sensory receptors). In other words, the properties detected by the organism are less complex than the percepts to which they give rise.

At present, we do not have the means to postulate such inference mechanisms in the baby. However, while tactile and visual sensory systems do not present the same degree of efficiency for reasons relating to the receptors' capacity and the speed of their development in the baby, we can nevertheless postulate the existence of information-processing levels which would be seen to be a function of the capacity of the sensory systems. This hypothesis is not incompatible with the notion of an analogous functioning of the sensory modalities, though it would render the idea of intermodal equivalence more difficult.

Amodal information, amodal perception, intermodal transfer

In J.J. Gibson's theory, the relational character of the perceptual invariants means that they are not attached to any one specific sensory channel. The detection of invariants in the stimulus makes it possible to perceive the relatedness of modalities in several ways. Some properties are amodal because they can be specified by several perceptual systems. The shape and texture of an object are examples of this kind of property. An intermodal relatedness can be detected for properties shared by different events, such as rhythm in a piece of music and in the movements of a dancer. An intermodal relation is established when different information specifies one and the same object, as in the case of sound-emitting objects. It is by revealing the existence of intermodal relations that the reality of amodal information can be confirmed.

Let us take the example of sound-emitting objects. The observer has to establish a relation between two events, visual and auditory, for which the specified information differs according to the system but refers to the same object. It is the congruence of these two events in time and space which allows this relation to be made. More precisely, if an adult subject sees an object fall to the ground, the visual information of the falling object and the auditory information of its impact on the ground have no intrinsic link. However, if the sound reaches the subject's ear before or after the object's impact, or if the sound is perceived to be coming from some place other than where the object has fallen, the adult observer will be surprised by the temporal or spatial interval between the two events. In the case of thunder and lightning, this interval gives additional information (distance). This interpretation of the interval, however, is learned. The auditory and visual stimuli coming from a sound-emitting object, therefore, have an identical spatial origin. This commonality of place constitutes an intermodal spatial invariant in Gibson's formulation of the problem. When the sound-emitting object is moved, there is a synchronicity between the visual and auditory stimuli. The subject has to retain this synchronicity as an invariant memory across time, despite changes in the environment. This constitutes a temporal invariant.

In this perspective, it is not perception but perceived information which is amodal. E.J. Gibson (1969) makes it clear that an amodal property is not an intermodal relation in the usual sense of the term – that is to say, information received through one modality and recognized by another. An amodal property is information which can be picked up by several sensory systems, and is not specific to a single modality. In addressing the problem of the relations between sensory modalities, and not just of the nature of the information, E.J. Gibson (1969) talks of 'amodal perception'. She thus shifts the amodal characteristic from the stimulus to a capacity of the subject.

The notion of amodal perception was first used by Michotte (1950). He demonstrates that information which does not correspond to any of the senses is reassembled by the subject and determined by the whole stimulus (for example, the tunnel effect: a rectangle partially concealed by another will be perceived as whole by the adult). These experiences are called 'amodal' because the perception resulting from them does not come from excitation of the receptors. Amodal has a privative meaning. This term is also used by

E.J. Gibson (1969), but with a different meaning. In this perspective, information exists in the sensory stimulus, but the perception resulting from it is not linked to any one sensory modality. Amodal has an indeterminate, general meaning. An amodal perception is not a 'multimodal' perception in the sense defined by Marks (1978*a*) – that is to say, a way of linking the different perceptual systems, a faculty for integrating multimodal information. 'Amodal' perception means the capacity which different modalities have in common for extracting perceptual invariants. The information is unique because it is amodal, and can therefore be received by any system excited by the stimulus.

These two shifts of meaning in terms and definitions have allowed E.J. Gibson to apply J.J. Gibson's ideas to the infant and, more recently, to the newborn (E.J. Gibson, 1984). Since knowledge of the environment relies on innate mechanisms for finding invariants in the stimulus, and since perception is direct and does not depend on any inference, or on the re-creation of previous events – i.e. it does not depend on any mediator – intermodal relations between perceptions are possible very early in the human being. E.J. Gibson (1984) hypothesizes that amodal perception is present from birth. In effect, all the conditions necessary for such a unity of senses to be postulated in the neonate appear to be fulfilled. Nevertheless, E.J. Gibson admits that the baby's capacities are still immature, and that the effect of practice should not be discounted. From this perspective, the development of perceptions appears to be a capacity for finding invariants and perceiving new properties of objects which becomes increasingly refined as a function of practice. E.J. Gibson's perspective – which is very close to Bower's (1974) developmental perspective – does not postulate the existence at birth of internal representations of abstract properties of the world. However, these hypotheses remain to be verified in the baby. The existence of an intermodal transfer of information relating to objects from the oral tactile modality to the visual modality in babies aged 1 month (Gibson & Walker, 1984; Meltzoff and Borton, 1979) serves to confirm the theory of an early unity of the senses. From this, we can deduce that an amodal perception centre exists in the very young baby.

Nevertheless, the facts obtained in these experiments pose a problem. If an 'amodal' perception exists, we should also be able to find evidence of the same information being transferred from the visual modality to the oral tactile modality. So far, however, intermodal transfer in this direction has not been studied. What should we conclude from results of research into the reversible transfer of information between the two modalities if it obtained a positive result in one direction and a negative result in the other? Such a result would hardly be compatible with the notion of 'amodal' perception. This research would have found evidence only of an intermodal relation arising from one modality, but not of amodal perception.

When we analyze the situations of intermodal transfer encountered by babies, such a conjecture is plausible. Operationally, the situation of intermodal transfer between vision and touch has two phases (Gottfried, Rose and Bridger, 1977). A phase of haptic familiarization with one object is followed by a second phase in which two objects are visually presented, one familiar and the other new. The conclusion is that transfer of information from the tactile modality to the visual modality is realized if the subject looks at the familiar and new objects for different periods. The haptic object and the visual object carry redundant information at the level of the sensory system, but they also present specific properties. The weight of an object is perceived only through touch and proprioception, while colour is perceived only visually. Babies, therefore, discover properties visually which they have not previously perceived through touch. Conversely, through vision they no longer pick up haptic information. If there is a link between sensory modalities, babies should not be taking account of these specificities. On the other hand, if a transfer is obtained, it is possible to deduce that the babies have processed the information extracted from similar objects through vision and through touch as equivalent, but also that they have processed the properties extracted from different objects as nonequivalent. This assumes that they have compared them.

Under these experimental conditions, failure to transfer can be interpreted in several ways. The subject may or may not establish links between these situations and may think, for example, that the situation called 'recognition' is a new experience in relation to the situation called 'familiarization'. The results obtained reveal that babies establish this relation from the age of 1 month (Gibson and Walker, 1984; Meltzoff and Borton, 1979). Failure may result from the fact that at the recognition phase the baby does not 'know how to', 'can' not, or does not 'want' to choose from the objects the one which corresponds to the familiar object. Reasons other than lack of discrimination between objects are possible: the objects may be too differentiated, equally attractive, and so on. Failure may also be explained by inadequate memory of the information gained in the first phase, or it may mean that the information taken and processed in each modality is only partial, and is not the same for both modalities. The first two interpretations refer to a 'failure' linked to the constraints imposed by the situation; the latter two to a 'perceptuo-cognitive failure'. In the case of nontransfer, we need to be able to determine what comes from perceptual mechanisms and what can be imputed to the situation.

Thus, if nonreversibility of transfer is found, the hypothesis of a bias introduced by an experimental situation which is judged to be complicated for a baby is quite probable. In that case, we might object that in a more ecological situation, amodal perception could be demonstrated. However, it is these very transfer situations with which young infants are confronted in the course of their everyday life before prehension–vision coordination is clearly established – that is to say, before they can explore an object in a multimodal way. It is common enough for babies to look at an object they cannot pick up, and for an adult to place it in their hands or, conversely, for babies to hold an object in their hands and subsequently look at it – not because they bring it into view voluntarily, but because it is pointed out to them.

The perceptual mechanisms in intermodal transfer

The existence of an intermodal relation in animals encourages us to think that only relatively simple processes are involved. Thus, we might assume that these processes also operate in the human baby, whose brain and sensory modalities are remarkably more developed than those of an animal, though very immature compared to the adult state. Without being entirely convinced by the theory that ontogenesis replicates phylogenesis (Haeckel, 1891), we do think that the hypothesis of an early relationship allowing the perception of a unified environment is more economical than that of modal separation. The effort required to reconstruct this unity is considerable for an organism whose intellect is otherwise judged to be extremely immature.

What are the underlying mechanisms of intermodal transfer? When searching for one object amongst several in a bag without being able to see them, the adult will discriminate and find it – not on the basis of an exploration of all its properties of texture, shape, and so on, but through a simple clue which allows rapid identification. For this to be possible, the object must be familiar. The adult subject will immediately attribute a functional meaning to the unseen object: it's the car key, not the front-door key. For the newborn, the degree of familiarity with an object is poor. The relation between sensory modalities must therefore rely on a less complex mechanism than identification of an object. When an intermodal transfer of information between vision and touch is realized, we assume that it relies on the establishment of relations of equivalence between the properties of objects perceived via hand and eyes. When babies recognize an object visually, after tactile exploration of it, they do not necessarily recognize it as the same object as the one they have handled, but as having certain properties in common with it.

When intermodal transfer is achieved by a baby, it is not only a matter of the baby taking account of amodal information. Transfer also depends on the procedure used to reveal it, and on the activities which are necessarily implemented in the situation – for example, establishing a relation, choosing between objects, etc.

For such a theory to be supported and proved empirically, certain conditions would have to be taken into consideration.

1. First, the functioning of the tactile modality must be compared with that of the visual modality. It must be possible to obtain comparable data in both modalities – in particular, to demonstrate that besides simple reaction to stimuli, the tactile modality is as capable of processing information as the visual modality.
2. It must also be proved that there is a discrimination between stimuli within each of the sensory modalities. If there were not, the interpretation of the absence of an intermodal transfer would remain ambiguous. This absence might be explained by the inappropriateness of the situation to reveal such a transfer, or by a deficiency in one of the sensory systems involved in the information-gathering process. This problem has already been raised by Bryant (1974). Intramodal discrimination must be demonstrated before intermodal transfer can be established.
3. Finally, it is essential to demonstrate that if amodal perception

exists, transfer of information must be performed both from visual to tactile modality and from tactile to visual modality.

All these constraints point to the necessity of finding a new methodology which can fulfil these conditions. The methodologies which have been applied up until now are unable to solve all the problems we have raised.

Chapter 2

Manual approach to a visual target as evidence of perceptual coordination

Methodological aspects of observation

Observation of neonate behaviour and minutely detailed description of the development of this behaviour have long been documented. Among the best-known research, Gesell and Ilg (1943) and Piaget (1936, trans. 1936; 1937, trans. 1937, 1955) are excellent references. These carefully recorded logs have been the foundation for research on the neonate and young infant and, in particular, have provided a base for tests of motor development (Bayley, 1933; Brunet and Lézine, 1951).

Even when the baby's behaviour has been induced by skilful modification of certain environmental conditions, as in Piaget's work, the observation of behaviour in the conditions usually obtaining in the lives of babies has been insufficient to account for the entirety of their actual or potential abilities. It is often necessary to define the situation more narrowly in order to obtain from babies a systematic response which has either been obtained only by chance under their usual conditions, or has never been observed.

The behaviour of approaching and reaching an object does not depart from this rule. This behaviour, which does not appear to occur until the age of 4 to 5 months, has been brought to light in babies only a few days old by Bower *et al.* (1970*a*). This phenomenon, which was disputed for some considerable time, has been observed by other authors and analyzed precisely. Improvement in the technical methods used and – however slight – in the experimental procedures has been necessary to confirm the existence of this behaviour, and to describe it more definitively.

Initial observations were conducted with the baby in a supine dorsal position with the head held stable. This stabilization reduces uncoordinated arm movements, and manual reaching towards a visually perceived object can be obtained.

The first observations made by Bower *et al.* (1970*a*), recorded with the aid of a single camera, have been repeated in a more systematic manner. On the one hand, researchers have used two cameras (von Hofsten, 1982; Ruff and Halton, 1978; de Schonen and Bresson, 1984). This technical improvement allows all three spatial dimensions to be taken into account, with the result that the trajectory of the baby's arm and hand movement, and its final phase of reaching towards the object, can be analyzed more accurately. This allows a greater degree of precision than is possible with single-camera recording. On the other hand, reaching behaviour should not be confused with uncoordinated arm movements. Thus, von Hofsten (1982), Ruff and Halton (1978), DiFranco, Muir and Dodwell (1978), Dodwell, Muir and DiFranco (1976) and de Schonen and Bresson (1984) have compared the frequency of arm and hand movements over two periods: when the object is present, and when it is absent (control condition). This latter condition determines the subject's individual 'noise' level. When the object is present, reaching movements are analyzed as a function of the baby's attentional behaviour which accompanies these movements (ocular fixation of the object, nonfixation, closed eyes, undirected looking) (von Hofsten, 1982). Joint orientation of gaze and hand bears witness to the baby's ability to relate visual and proprioceptive information concerning certain spatial characteristics, such as the object's direction and distance.

Working from a clinical perspective, paediatricians have observed neonatal behaviour under one very specific condition (Amiel-Tison and Grenier, 1980, 1985; Grenier, 1980, 1981). This allows the baby's attention span to be maintained, and makes it possible to elicit from babies guided movements which do not appear under their usual conditions of attention. This highly delicate technique consists in the experimenter supporting the baby's neck and establishing a constant affective, social and spoken dialogue in order to induce a state of 'freed motor activity' – that is to say, to alter the baby's distribution of muscle tonicity. The result obtained is that uncontrolled movements are inhibited and organized, intentional behaviour emerges, usually several weeks after birth.

Under normal observation conditions, when the reaching situation entails a choice between two objects, the one which is touched provides a relevant clue to the perception of interobject spatial relations (von Hofsten and Spelke, 1985; Pineau and Streri, 1985; Yonas and Granrud, 1984). However, the absence of a reaching response towards an object is also considered to indicate that the baby visually takes account of a dimension of space, or of the object. For example, a distant object does not trigger the gesture (Bower, 1972; J. Field, 1976), neither does an oversized object (Bruner and Koslowski, 1972).

Finally, situations of conflict, as in the case of a virtual object, allow us to establish whether babies detect, in the terminal phase of the movement, correspondences between the properties of an object they can see and feel.

Depending on the research, it may be the motor component which is carefully analyzed independently of the nature of the stimulus; or, alternatively, it may be the nature of the perceptual stimulus which is studied for the purpose of provoking the action. This dichotomy is artificial, especially within the framework of Reed's ideas (1982). Mounoud (1983) and Mounoud, Vinter and Hauert (1985) have achieved an initial synthesis of these data in order to describe a development model based on grasping behaviour. Lockman and Ashmead (1983) have brought about a similar synthesis in which they emphasize the asynchronies in the development of this movement. These approaches, however, do not always take account of the baby's postural conditions, attention level, and so on, or of the most recent data. Thus, in an initial approach, it has been necessary to differentiate rigidly between sensory pole and motor pole, because the baby's still clumsy motor skills make the study of this behaviour rather complicated. Nevertheless, the way in which the motor system integrates the sensory afferences will continue to be redefined throughout this book.

The motor component of the reaching action

Postnatal manual reaching

In some studies, babies have been observed during the first two to three weeks from birth following a full-term pregnancy. De Schonen (1980), however, has demonstrated that the action of moving the hand towards an object can be observed from the fifth day after birth onwards, but not during the first four days. She describes (de Schonen and Bresson, 1984) the postural conditions for the appearance of this behaviour with much greater precision than Bower *et al.* (1970*a*). The baby is in a supine dorsal position. The target, a cube, is presented to the neonate in four positions angled at 30° and 60° to the left and right of the sagittal plane of the body, and at two constant distances: the distance to the wrist when the arm is extended, and 5 centimetres lower. A control situation without an object is conducted for each baby. Each observation lasts five minutes.

The arm is extended more frequently in the presence of a cube than in the control situation. This arm extension occurs with the arm which is homolateral to the target, while the contralateral arm remains immobile, with the hand closed. The number of times contact is made with the object is about a third of the number of extensions. In these circumstances the palm is always turned towards the target. However, in contrast to the results obtained by Bower for babies observed in the same position on the seventh day after birth, no manipulatory component following these contacts has been recorded. Bower (1974) points out that success rates (that is to say, of touching or grasping the object) are up to 40 per cent. Furthermore, there is no time lapse between neonates halting their arm movements at the end of their trajectory and closing their hands over the object. According to Bower, this reveals that anticipation is perfectly developed, and that grasping is not activated by touch. Neither of these two studies, however, notes whether the baby fixates on the object, or visual control occurs during the execution of the reaching movement. Such information, however, is essential if we are to conclude that vision–prehension coordination exists.

In other research, the neonate's posture and the presentation of the target are differently arranged. Von Hofsten (1982) placed babies ranging from 5 to 9 days old on a chair inclined at 50°. The babies were kept firmly seated, the chair supporting their heads and trunks. Thus they were able to move their arms freely. They were observed for eight one-minute periods. The mobile target was presented approximately 12 centimetres from the infants' eyes, and moved in a horizontal plane to attract their attention.

While the hand is open-palmed during the movement of extending the arm, as in Bower and de Schonen's observations, the frequency with which contact with the object is attained is less than in the previous experiments. Out of 232 arm extensions, von Hofsten records 22 contacts with the object, 12 of these occurring while the object is being looked at. When contact with the object is not achieved, the hand's angle of approach towards the object is narrower when the neonate is looking at the object than when it is not. Visual attention does, therefore, increase the accuracy of the action. The movement of approaching the object is described as a succession of pre-programmed, ballistic elements consisting of an acceleration phase and a deceleration phase. It can be seen that the hand, still open-palmed, slows down as it gets close to the object, which is now stationary. On average, the approach to the object takes approximately 1·04 seconds from the beginning of the movement. Between the ages of 18 and 21 weeks, this increases to 1·8 seconds (von Hofsten, 1979), thus confirming the ballistic nature of neonatal movement.

The difference in the success levels obtained – that is to say, successful contact with the object – does not seem to be due to the conditions in which the target is presented. Using a fixed target, with the baby seated, DiFranco *et al.* (1978), Ruff and Halton (1978), McDonnell (1979) and Rader and Stern (1982) have also recorded a lower frequency of contacts than those observed by de Schonen and by Bower.

According to de Schonen and Bresson (1984), posture probably plays a role in raising the level of success. The supine position with the head held stable and in slight traction leads to a decrease in uncoordinated arm movements comparable to that observed in situations of 'freed motor activity'. It is not posture alone, therefore, but also the level of attention which affect success levels. Fontaine (1984*a*) drew this same conclusion from his experiments on the reaching behaviour of babies aged 15 to 25 days under the condition of 'freed motor activity'. The attention level is comparable to that of level 4 of the states defined by Prechtl (1969) and Prechtl and O'Brien (1982). The babies' movements are described as saccadic, not ballistic. The reaction latency is shorter (quoted in de Schonen and Bresson, 1984). Moreover, the hand wanders over the object without grasping it.

Under the baby's normal conditions of experience (de Schonen and Bresson, 1984), when the target object is presented laterally the arm homolateral to the target is extended in 99 per cent of cases, while the contralateral arm remains bent, with the hand closed. When the object moves on one side of the baby, it is the right hand which is most often activated (von Hofsten, 1982). According to von Hofsten (1982), coordination between the baby's visual and motor activities appears to occur reversibly: as well from hand to eye as from eye to hand. He comments on several observations where the baby's hand accidentally touches the object. This causes the baby's gaze to be immediately directed towards the object. In this way, a reversible coordination between eye and hand can be obtained which is contrary to what occurs where the hand has to transport the object.

To sum up: the visuomotor space in which the newborn performs the movement of reaching for an object has a directional structure. The movement appears to be 'triggered' by visual information, since it is observed more often in the presence of this stimulus than in its absence. All the studies note that the indissociable phases of approach and contact succeed one another in a highly coordinated fashion. Depending on the author, these movements are described as pre-programmed, pre-adapted, ballistic or automatically controlled, and are thus distinguishable from the voluntary movements which will appear several months after birth. It is the absence of trajectory correction (failure does not have the same informational content as it has for the adult) and of correction of the manipulatory component that gives the neonate's movements their rigid character, sometimes making them seem like poorly controlled reflexes. The only information babies are likely to extract from their actions is essentially proprioceptive, although during the movement itself it does not, apparently, lead to the reafferences required for better regulation of the action. According to Mounoud (1983), the newborn possesses an 'evocation memory' but does not yet have a 'recognition memory'. Might it not be, however, that babies are unable to extract the proprioceptive information necessary to achieve their goal from the considerable level of noise generated by the activity of their muscles and still unpractised joints? Then, according to Lécuyer (1988), the unintelligible message could not be the object of a correction.

The 'extinction' phase

Towards the age of 4 weeks (Bower, 1974) or 7 weeks (von Hofsten, 1984) a decline is observed in the activity of moving the arm towards the object. The frequency of arm movements undergoes a significant decrease, and the baby's activity does not regain its initial level until around 10 to 12 weeks of age. This disorganization of action is particularly noticeable in the way the hand is held. During this period, when the arm is directed towards an object it is done with the fist closed, not with the palm open, as in the newborn (this is the 'swiping' action observed by White, Castle and Held, 1964). The proportion of closed-fist movements is at its greatest at 7 weeks of age, while the number of approaches with the palm open in anticipation decreases. Approach phase and contact phase become dissociated, and are thus only partially coordinated (von Hofsten, 1984, 1989).

Paradoxically, it is during this decline in tactilomotor activities that the visuomotor activities are predominant. The control of eye movements and the interaction between eye and head movements are crucial aspects of the young infant's capacity to access visual information. This control develops very rapidly during the first weeks after birth. The saccadic system, the tracking reflex and binocular convergence are already very efficient towards the age of 2 to 3 months (see Aslin, 1987). Information pick-up also becomes more refined around the second month (Vurpillot, 1972). Thus we witness not only the motor and sensory development of vision, but also an increase in attention. In an experiment observing the tracking of a moving visual target, Bullinger (1982) shows that the 7-to-10-week-old baby is practically transfixed by the moving object. Tracking is possible if the whole body participates in the movement. In a series of visual habituation tests using slides, Lécuyer (1987) records very long fixation of the stimulus in 3-month-old babies. However, he questions whether the entire fixation actually represents the time spent exploring the object, since atonic gazing at a stimulus is frequent at this age.

A number of interpretations have been postulated to explain this decline in the baby's activity in the presence of an object. It has been suggested that 'exuberant projections' (Frost, 1990) exist very early on in the course of development, then later disappear. For example, the axons in the retinal cells of a neonate hamster project into 'nonvisual' areas of the brain such as the thalamic nucleus, which is specific to somatosensory inputs, and the inferior colliculi, which are specific to the auditory process. These exuberant projections might mediate the multimodal perceptions or sensorimotor coordinations observed earlier. This, however, would be only a temporary phenomenon. According to McGuire and Turkewitz (1979), the increase in visual attention inhibits arm extension. Von Hofsten (1984) adds a physiological hypothesis to this argument. The agonist and antagonist muscles of the limb are activated at the same time, and this simultaneous activation blocks movement. These two explanations, taken together, may account for the decline in the baby's activity, but they do not explain the changes in the way the hand is held during or at the end of the trajectory. For Lockman and Ashmead (1983) there is no sychronization between the 'proximal' component of the movement – that is, the projection of the arm – and the 'distal' activity of the small muscles in hand and fingers. Their assertion of this behavioural asynchrony is based on an asynchrony in the development of the neurophysiological systems governing this behaviour. The pyramidal tract, which is responsible for fine finger movements, develops later than the extrapyramidal system, which is responsible for more global behaviour. In this theory, the motor system has recently come under the influence of the pyramidal tract, and the fine motor activity of the fingers is not yet integrated into the movement which was present at the very beginning. A more functional viewpoint is proposed by Mounoud (1976, 1983; Mounoud and Vinter, 1982) in his model of sensorimotor development. This entails a dissociation of the pattern of pre-programmed movement which exists in the neonate. This dissociation is for the purpose of restructuring – for the recomposition of the movement in which the hand, now opened again, will be better adapted for manipulation. Finally, lack of practice is thought to play a role in this decline. According to Bower (1974), the decrease in this activity is due to the absence of sufficient positive reinforcement – that is to say, successful reaching.

There is probably no single factor which is responsible for this disorganization of the system. It might be due to the combined effects of the organism's level of maturation and insufficient practice. It might also be the case that the development of systems does not occur harmoniously, and babies prefer to explore their new visual possibilities at the expense of movement which is still clumsy and difficult to perfect. We shall return to this question when we comment on the intermodal transfer of information between vision and touch. In fact, during a period when visual attention appears to be important, a touch-to-vision transfer of information can be observed but not, paradoxically, a vision-to-touch transfer (Streri, 1987*a*; Streri and Milhet, 1988).

Visuotactile recoordination

From the thirteenth week of age onwards, babies reach by slowly displacing their arms towards the object. This approach movement is less dependent on the baby's position. This displacement is visually controlled step by step (White, Castle and Held, 1964). Evidence of the discontinuous nature of this approach movement has been found by von Hofsten and Lindhagen (1979), who presented subjects with mobile objects.

The stages of approaching and contacting an object become recoordinated while still retaining their specificity. The hand approaching the object is visually guided, and the focus of gaze switches back and forth from the hand to the object to be grasped. The hand opens gradually in an anticipatory manner and, in this way, opening of the hand precedes contact with the object. When the hand comes into contact with the object, it tentatively feels the object several times before grasping it. Thus this action possesses several characteristics of the adult system (von Hofsten and Rönnqvist, 1988; Jeannerod, 1984, 1986; Jeannerod and Biguer, 1982).

The anticipatory opening of the hand reveals that a plan to grasp is integrated into the approach phase. This result is incompatible with the hypothesis of a dissociation between the two behavioural components, reaching and grasping. According to Bower, they are united in the newborn but dissociated at 5 months of age. The grasping phase then comes under tactilokinaesthetic control. Bower *et al.* (1970*a*) have demonstrated this phenomenon in a situation of perceptual conflict. Until the age of 4 to 5 months, babies faced with a virtual object will close their hands over the empty space where the object appears, while at 6 months they suspend this action until they receive tactile confirmation. Perhaps all that can be read into this dissociation is that it is an exceptional manifestation of behaviour in response to an unusual situation.

There are major structural and functional differences between the directional actions of the neonate and the more practised actions of the 5-month-old baby. In these five months the relation between vision and the tactile motor system undergoes a change. Movement is no longer a visually activated behaviour, but is guided by vision. Coordination – which, in the neonate, is based essentially on a visuo–motor correspondence – is transformed into a visuo–prehensile coordination. While the same order of phases is retained, the age at which certain transformations appear in the organization of the eye–hand system may vary according to the richness of the surrounding environment (White, 1970).

All these studies underline the importance of visually gained information for the triggering of action, and the role of vision in guiding action. According to Piaget (1936, trans. 1936, 1953), when the hand comes into the baby's visual field it has the status of an object perceived from a distance in the same way as a toy. How do infants react to the presence of two stimuli, one specifying a part of their own bodies and the other external to them? Does the hand have a particular status at the moment when prehension–vision coordination develops?

The role of hand vision: necessity or interference?

We have already mentioned the work of Held and Hein (1963) which examines the role of forelimb vision during the locomotion of a kitten. This is essential for the fine placement of its front paws in a task of positioning its limbs on an uneven support.

By completely suppressing baby monkeys' vision of their limbs and body during their first month of life, Held and Bauer (1967) demonstrated that hand-to-eye coordination is strongly affected as a result when the subjects' sight of their limbs is restored. The monkeys then concentrate more of their attention on their hands than on the object to be grasped. This interest in their moving hands persists even if the subjects recover the sight of their limbs during an intermediary phase before the test stage (Bauer and Held, 1975). The authors interpret this behaviour as revealing that during the course of development it is impossible for the subjects to close the 'loop' which links voluntary action by the subject with the perception of the consequences such action has on reafferent sensory inputs. In other words, sensorimotor coordination under the 'no-feedback' condition has deteriorated, just as in the adult human.

What, then, is the role of babies' sight of their hands? Piaget (1936, trans. 1936, 1953) places great emphasis on the importance of simultaneous sight of hand and object if the object is to be grasped, and on the pivotal role of this behaviour in the coordination of tactile and visual schemes. However, he accords only slight importance to the role of proprioceptive information in this action, and does not tell us whether infants distinguish between what belongs to them (their hand) and what does not (the object). The fact that they observe their hands at the same time as the object may have only a playful significance for babies, without constituting a necessary stage in the development of reaching behaviour.

Working within a perspective which is close to the Piagetian viewpoint, White, Castle and Held (1964) accord a privileged – though only indirect – role to vision of the hands in the process of prehension–vision coordination. These authors give the tonic neck reflex an important function in this coordination. Since this posture allows babies to see their hands, and possibly objects close to their hands, it appears to be the origin of the fusion of the two sensorimotor systems. Present from the age of 1 month, when the baby is in the supine dorsal position, the tonic neck reflex really takes on its essential function only from the age of around 2–3 months – a period when these authors, like von Hofsten, point to a decline in the baby's activity. Visual fixation of the hand when the baby is in this position becomes more frequent and less strained. Bushnell (1981) also subscribes to this theory.

Bower (1974) differs from these authors, and does not consider that vision of the hands is an essential stage in the establishment of the eye–hand system, since this system exists from birth. According to this author, the baby's action of bringing his/her hands into view is pre-formed behaviour which is already embedded in the motor programmes at birth, since it has been observed in newly born blind babies. If babies hesitate in grasping an object when their hands enter their field of vision, this is because they have to divide their attention between the two things, hand and object, and at that age attention is poor. Vision of the hand thus interrupts the act of reaching for and grasping the object.

Whether we regard the role of hand vision in prehension–vision (re)coordination as necessary or as an interference, the to-and-fro looking between object and hand is not produced systematically. This behaviour does not exist in neonatal ballistic action. It is never observed in conditions where a moving object is presented to a 4-month-old baby (von Hofsten and Lindhagen, 1979); the baby always fixates the moving object while reaching. The movement of the object, therefore, increases the visual attention focused on the object to the detriment of that focused on the hand. This fact confirms Bower's attentional hypothesis (1974). In contrast, Bruner (1970) emphasizes the role played by the baby's position when fixating an object. For example, infants who are half-seated always fixate during reaching on the object which does not appear to require vision of the hands. He suggests that the standing position is the one which provides the infant with the most effective proprioceptive and kinaesthetic information for guiding arm and hand. This hypothesis appears to find confirmation in the fact that in von Hofsten's experiments the babies are seated on an inclined chair, while in Piaget's or White, Castle and Held's observations they are lying on their backs. Moreover, it would appear that it is attainment of the ability to sit, rather than the age of the baby, which provokes the appearance of reaching for and grasping an object (Fontaine and Piéraut-Le Bonniec, 1988; Piéraut-Le Bonniec, Fontaine, Hombessa and Jacquet, 1988). Insufficient postural control during the first months of life thus seems to be an obstacle to the implementation of the motor programme, as observations of 'freed motor activity' suggest.

Attention and postural control are two determining factors in the performance of the motor act. It has been shown that both are involved in the appearance of neonatal movements in situations of 'freed motor activity'. While the appearance of the baby's hands in his/her field of vision does not seem to be a necessary stage in prehension–vision coordination, vision of the hands as they approach an object may play a role in the effectiveness of the programme's realization.

Reaching for an object at 4–5 months: ballistic or visually guided movement?

Bower (1974) points out that when 4-to-5-month-old babies' reaching for an object is inadequate, they do not attempt to correct their reaching but restart the action from the beginning. This ballistic movement resembles that of the neonate. It is not guided, but triggered by vision.

What happens when we suppress the ability to see the hand when the baby reaches for the object? A number of experiments demonstrate that the young baby of up to 5 months does not appear to be affected.

For example, Bower and Wishart (1972) presented 5-month-old babies with an object within reach of their hands, then immediately plunged the room into complete darkness. The number of successful approach movements and contacts was undiminished. Sometimes the action was not effectively achieved by certain babies until 90 seconds after the visual presentation of the object. According to the authors, neither the intention of the baby nor the location of the target was affected by the sudden change in the baby's visual conditions.

Lasky (1977) has systematically studied the role of the feedback provided by vision of the arm and hand during the action of approaching the object. Working with five groups of babies aged 2·5 months to 6·5 months, he used an opaque horizontal screen to mask the trajectory of the baby's arm and hand towards the target. The performance of the eldest babies was affected, particularly at 5·5 months. At this age, the frequency of approach movements and grasps of the object, as well as the position of the fingers and thumb before contact, differs from that of the control group, with which a transparent screen was used. In contrast, the opaque screen condition does not disturb the youngest babies. A similar result has been obtained by McDonnell (1975) using a different method. This author studied the trajectory of the arm in 4-to-10-month-old babies wearing prismatic glasses which shifted the visual target by 7 centimetres. Unlike the older babies, the young babies were disturbed very little by this situation, and scored a 90 per cent success rate. What changes with development is the strategy for approaching and contacting the target. The youngest babies (4–5 months) tend to alter their trajectory totally when their hand misses the target. In their case, the path of the trajectory is determined from the start by a ballistic movement, and is then visually guided when the hand is close to the target. In contrast, the fact that older babies make adjustments during the whole of the movement indicates that visual control is exercised throughout the trajectory. Von Hofsten and Lindhagen (1979) also describe this kind of movement. They presented 3-to-6-month-old babies with a mobile object to reach for. In babies of 4–5 months, they observed ataxic-type corrective movements during the approach to the object similar to those observed by McDonnell (1975).

In an experiment on adaptation to prismatic glasses, McDonnell and Abraham (1979) demonstrate that this is minimal when reaching is visually guided at around 7 months, then increases at 9 months. McDonnell (1975) suggests that visual guiding diminishes from 9 months as a more ballistic action, similar to that of an adult, replaces it. This decline in the visual guiding of reaching behaviour is interpreted as the result of a greater degree of control of motor skills in the baby's behaviour (Bushnell, 1985).

Proprioception, the neglected element

The research cited above confirms a fact which had long been in doubt: from the first few days after birth, babies have the ability to direct their arms and hands, and sometimes to touch an object perceived from a distance, despite their apparently uncontrolled motor skills. Furthermore, in the analysis of the movement's progression, the strategies observed later for approaching the object resemble the data which have been collected about the adult on a number of points (Jeannerod, 1981, 1984; Jeannerod and Biguer, 1982; Jeannerod and Prablanc, 1978; Paillard, 1974). Thus, from the age of 4 months, the baby's prehension–vision system has a degree of organization which is close to that of totally controlled movement. In contrast, the fact that at birth action is visually triggered but lacks any manipulatory component or correction in the event of failure to reach the object lends plausibility to the interpretation that what we are observing is a response triggered by a stimulus. It would be difficult to say that we are in the presence of a truly integrated form of behaviour in the sense understood by Reed (1982). The organization of the approach movement appears to be limited to a direction which is common to the space of visual attention and motor behaviour.

The establishment of a relation between visual system and motor system is described mainly as a result of the role of vision in gaining information about the stimulus, and guiding the path of the arm. The role of motor activity is reduced to the implementation of a visually controlled programme. There is actually no integration of the two systems, rather the subordination of one system to the other. Every time infants extend their arms and hands in order to reach the object, not only do they see a part of their own bodies, they also feel it. That is to say, they extract proprioceptive information from their movements. There is perfect correspondence between the visual information and the proprioceptive information about their own bodies. E.J. and J.J. Gibson would describe this correspondence as an invariant, an amodal relation which specifies the infants themselves. Only a few studies clearly emphasize the importance of proprioceptive information in the course of the reaching action and its role in the development of control of this behaviour. Before the age of 5 months this information appears to be essential, and it no doubt continues to be so after this age, even if it appears that visual control of the whole trajectory is the determining factor in the successful grasping of the target.

Nevertheless, these descriptions alone can only partially account for the reality of the behaviour. The analysis of the movement should be performed within the more general context of its habitual occurrence – namely, the environment and the perceptual conditions of its activation. In effect, if behaviour is a response adapted to information which the subject detects visually (Bresson, 1971), then the reaching action should be triggered by certain kinds of information and inhibited by others. In his own research, von Hofsten (1986) has been able to establish a relationship between the perceived information and the triggering of the action (see also the commentaries by Beek (1986) and Clark (1986)). We shall extend these descriptions to other research.

The sensory component of manual reaching

Beyond the 'noise' created by their uncoordinated movements, neonates extend their arm more often in the presence than in the absence of an object (de Schonen and Bresson, 1984; White, Castle and Held,

1964). Among all the visual cues the baby perceives, which are the ones that specifically trigger the behaviour of reaching towards a target? We shall analyze three categories of cue: properties intrinsic to the target responsible for triggering the movement; properties relating the object and the observer; and properties relating objects to one another.

The properties of the trigger target

Objects are characterized by intrinsic properties which can be perceived by both visual system and tactile system. If the hand takes account of properties which can be perceived visually, then it is possible to conclude that the two systems are integrated.

The object to be grasped is three-dimensional
Fantz (1961), Fantz and Nevis (1967), and Fantz, Fagan and Miranda (1975) have demonstrated that babies at least 2 months old prefer to look at three-dimensional objects (a sphere) rather than surfaces (a disc). Thus, in proximal stimuli, neonates differentiate between the retinal projection of an object and the projection of a flat surface of the same shape. Bower (1972) has attempted to determine whether neonates differentiate between an object and a picture of it, at the level not of the proximal but of the distal stimulus. An analysis of reaching behaviour is better suited to answering this question than target exploration time. Bower presented babies aged from 7 to 15 days with an orange sphere and a photograph of this sphere, both placed at a distance at which the babies could touch but not grasp them. If the babies express the intention to grasp the object, then it should be possible to observe their arm extensions. The results show that the photograph does not trigger an approach movement, while the object itself frequently does. The difference in behaviour towards the two targets is significant. Bower concludes from this that the behaviour of approaching and contacting the object is intentional at this age, not the result of a chance sweep of the arm. These results are partially repeated by Dodwell *et al.* (1976) and DiFranco *et al.* (1978). The fact that approach movements and contacts with the target have been observed by these authors confirms the reality of reaching activity. However, they have failed to find any difference in behaviour in babies faced with both the object and its image. Bower

(1978; cited by Hatwell, 1981) attributes this divergence in results to a difference in the posture of the babies and, above all, to the conditions under which the image is presented. In Dodwell's experiment, the image is presented on a support measuring 11 × 19 centimetres which, in itself, constitutes a graspable object. By using a framework of such large proportions that its edges were outside the baby's visual field, Bower claims to have observed differentiated behaviour in the presence of an object and that of its image.

On the basis of these observations alone, it is not clear whether the hand takes account of the inherent properties of three-dimensional objects. Piéraut-Le Bonniec (1985, 1986), however, has investigated whether a differentiated anticipation in the pre-positioning of the hand in approaching objects showing a difference in curvature might correspond to visual discriminations of flat, concave or convex targets. This important study used a sample of 80 babies aged 3–11 months, from whom a response had been obtained. The results show that the visual discrimination between convex and concave dimension obtained in an earlier experiment at the age of 3 months (Vurpillot and Piéraut-Le Bonniec; cited in Piéraut-Le Bonniec, 1986) does not necessarily lead to anticipatory behaviour corresponding to properties which can be perceived by the babies through tactile means. A differentiation in the approach of the hand between these three shapes is not realized until the age of 9 months.

The object to be grasped is tangible

Bower, Broughton and Moore (1970*a*) placed babies of 6 days to 6 months of age in an unfamiliar situation where they were faced with a 'stereoscopic shadow-caster'. An object is placed behind the translucent screen, and its image is projected on to the front of the screen by a dual system of polarizing lenses which makes it appear to have all the visual properties of a solid three-dimensional object while in fact it is completely intangible. The baby, wearing polarized glasses, is thus faced with a virtual object. The results show that at all ages babies faced with this conflicting situation are surprised, and cry when their hands come into contact with the virtual object but do not receive the corresponding haptic information. The frequency of attempts to grasp the object increases with age. What also changes with age is the babies' behaviour at the moment when their hands come into contact with the virtual object. Up to the age of 4 months they invariably attempt to grasp the object in a stereotypical manner. It appears, therefore, to be graspable because it is tangible. Babies of 5 and 6 months, however, do not close their hands over the object, and halt their action, with their hands open, when they do not receive the expected tactile information.

The size of the object

Bower (1972) takes either a fine response – opening the fingers and hand and, more precisely, the separation between fingers and thumb – or a more global response – the distance between the hands when babies contact the object with both hands – as indicating the baby's perception of size. Twelve babies 7 to 15 days old are presented with two cylinders, 0·5 and 2·5 centimetres in diameter, and two plastic balls, 3·5 and 7 centimetres in diameter. The results show that the finger–thumb gap and the distance between the hands increases with the object's size, the larger of each pair of shapes causing the interval to widen.

In a similar situation, Bruner and Koslowski (1972) have used a longitudinal method of study to observe the development of reaching behaviour in babies aged 8 to 21 weeks. A small ball (3·12 centimetres in diameter) and a large ball (25 centimetres in diameter) are presented in front of the babies and within their reach. Arm and hand movements are recorded during the 90 seconds following the first fixation of the object. The results show that before any contact with the objects, these movements are differentiated in young children according to the objects' size. Babies whose prehension–vision coordination is not yet established produce more movements involving an opening of the hands and manual activity directed towards the centre of the body (manipulation of clothing or of the other hand) in the presence of the small object than in that of the large one. The authors conclude that babies are sensitive to difference in the size of objects even before the different components of reaching behaviour are organized.

Lockman and Ashmead (1983) and Bushnell (1981) have serious reservations about the interpretation given to the results of these two studies. For Lockman and Ashmead, the behaviour of the babies in Bower's experiment might not have been adapted to the size of the object. They assert that the difference in strategy observed as a function of object size could be a product of the recording method. It should not be forgotten that in his experiment Bower uses only a single camera to record the babies' behaviour – a criticism which has often been levelled at him.

As for the experiment conducted by Bruner and Koslowski (1972), the authors interpret the babies' behaviour as a response not to the size of the objects but to their location. In effect, the large object is rather bigger than the centre of a baby's body, and in its presence babies extend their arms more sideways than forwards, as is the case with the small ball. We consider this argument to be unclear since it could, on the contrary, reinforce the idea that in extending their arms towards the side of the sphere rather than straight towards it babies do take account of the difference in size between the two balls. Another reservation which has been expressed about this experiment is that if there is greater hand activity in the presence of the smaller ball, this could be because babies are better able to make contact with an object positioned in front of them than at their side – for example, the hand is more likely to come into contact with and feel the baby's clothing and other hand.

Just as in the case of the properties studied above, the experiments which have been conducted are too vague to determine whether the difference in the size of objects is haptically taken into account by the baby. This type of observation demands a very high quality of recording material. There is no question that these differences in size are perceived visually by the baby. It is the way in which babies take account of this dimension at the level of the motor activity of the fingers before the hand reaches the object which remains unclear.

In contrast, Piéraut-Le Bonniec, Fontaine, Hombessa and Jacquet (1988) demonstrate that at 5 months the ability to anticipate the size of the object with the hands is closely linked to the baby's postural maturity. While the role of posture appears to be less important in grasping small objects (1·5 cm), it is a determining factor in the successful grasping of medium-sized (3·5 cm) and larger (5·5 cm) objects (see also Fontaine and Piéraut-Le Bonniec, 1988).

Von Hofsten and Rönnqvist's research (1988) is equally decisive concerning the hand's preparatory adjustment to the size of the object. These researchers placed two infrared diodes on the thumb and forefinger of each baby's dominant hand in order to gain a precise evaluation of when and how much the hand widens in the programming of the action. Reaching and grasping were recorded using an optoelectronic device. Three wooden objects, 1·5, 2·5 and 3·5 centimetres in diameter, were presented at chin height to infants aged 5–6 months, 9 months and 13 months.

The results reveal reaching behaviour with a high level of control from the age of 5 months. At none of the ages studied are the reaching for and grasping of an object separate actions, contrary to the findings of Bower *et al.* (1970*a*) in perceptual conflict situations. At the age of 5–6 months, the baby's hand plans the grasping of the target during its trajectory, not at the moment of contact, as Jeannerod (1984) has also demonstrated in adults. While preparation for grasping is integrated into reaching behaviour from the earliest age, this integration is not fully completed until the age of 13 months. The opening of the hand is adapted to the size of the target, but only in babies aged 9 months and over.

However, recent research by Newell, Scully, McDonald and Baillargeon (1989) adds another slant to the work of von Hofsten and Rönnqvist (1988). These authors subscribe to the theory of dynamic systems, and examine the difference in a baby's grip as a function of the properties of objects and of the respective roles of haptic and visual information in determining this difference. They present infants of 4 to 8 months with objects differing in size and shape (a 2·54 cm cube and three doll's cups of 1·25, 2·50 and 8·50 cm in diameter). The results reveal that from the age of 4 months babies show a different grip configuration as a function of the properties of objects, and particularly their size. Four-month-old babies are helped to differentiate their grips by both the visual system and the haptic system when hand comes into contact with object, and in this way they are helped to achieve an adequate grasp of the object. In contrast, the 8-month-old babies use only visual information to pre-position their hands before contact with the object as a function of its size and shape characteristics.

The orientation of objects

Precise recording of the pre-positioning of the hands and fingers in the face of objects exhibiting different properties or orientations reveals the way in which visual information is taken into account manually by the baby. In a cross-sectional study, Lockman, Ashmead and Bushnell (1984) have compared differences in reaching for a stick depending on whether it is presented horizontally or vertically to babies aged 5 months to 9 months. The orientation of the hand was precisely recorded at four points in the trajectory: at the start, in the middle, at the moment of contact, and during grasping of the stick. At 5 months of age, babies do not turn their hands in response to visual information, but do so after contact with the stick. Nine-month-old babies, in contrast, adjust their hands before contact with the stick.

Using a longitudinal procedure, von Hofsten and Fazel-Zandy (1984) have analyzed the capacity to use this information. They observed fifteen babies every four weeks from the age of 18 weeks to that of 34 weeks. As in the previous experiment, a stick was presented either horizontally or vertically. The results indicate that from 18 weeks the babies pre-position their hands in a way which is adapted to the orientation of the stick. Nevertheless, many further adjustments are made on contact with the object. This result is confirmed by Morrongiello and Rocca (1986), who filmed babies aged 5, 7 and 9 months reaching for a target which was either stationary or changed its orientation after the baby's movement began. The results demonstrate a change in the visuomotor system with regard to object orientation between the ages of 5 and 9 months. While 5-month-old babies pre-position their hands as a function of the orientation of the object when it is stationary, they become clumsy when the object changes its orientation while they are reaching for it, and adjust their hands badly on contact. Babies of 7 and 9 months, however, cope successfully, since they visually control their hand trajectory and make the necessary adjustments to attain successful contact with the newly orientated target. Thus the accuracy of hand adjustments improves with age. These results confirm the observations gained in tests of motor development in which the pincer grasping of an object between thumb and forefinger, considered to involve fine manual dexterity, is found at the age of 34 weeks.

From the very beginning, babies are probably capable of visually discriminating between the different properties of objects, as all the studies of visual perception in the young child indicate (Banks and Salapatek, 1983; Gibson and Spelke, 1983). For the first five months, however, fine motor action in the presence of the particular characteristics of objects is a poor representation of visual afferences. This does not mean that before the age of 5 months there is no manipulatory behaviour adapted to the properties of objects. What it does appear to reveal is that we are dealing not with manual motor difficulty but with a difficulty in the anticipatory programming of the shape of the hand.

Relations between observer and object: perception of the dimensions of space

When babies pre-position their hands with the aim of adapting their grasp to the object, they are providing clear proof of the fact that they take account of the relation between themselves and the object situated within their environment. However, the fact that they take certain properties of the object into account does not tell us whether they perceive the object within the three dimensions of space and locate it in relation to their own bodies.

Direction

We have reported the directional behaviour of the arm of a 5-day-old neonate towards a target located at 30° and 60° to the right and left of the subject (de Schonen and Bresson, 1984). The target may be situated at two distances for the same angle. When the target is successively presented at these two distances, the authors point to the frequent absence of any adjustment in the direction or amplitude of arm movement from one distance to the other. The babies extend their arms to the place the object occupied in the previous attempt. This absence of adjustment thus appears to reveal a memory of the previously presented distance. This fact is important, since it reinforces the idea of an association between a response and a determined object location, a change which temporarily disturbs the baby. In this case, no correction of the action takes place. However, the change in the target's location is taken into account in the following attempt.

The motor action of reaching for the object as evidence of perception of the third dimension

Bower (1972) complains that studies of visual perception – and particularly of perceptual discrimination – do not allow any clear answer to the question whether the subjects respond to differences between the objects or to differences between the retinal projections of these objects. Only evidence of appropriate observable behaviour in babies can begin to provide a satisfactory answer. The problem is particularly thorny when we consider the perception of the third dimension of space. According to Bower (1972), the action of reaching for an object is a relevant clue in the study of the perception of the distance of targets from subjects. He presents twelve babies aged 7 to 15 days with two spheres, 3 and 6 centimetres in diameter. The small sphere is presented at a distance at which the subject cannot touch it; the large sphere is presented at twice the distance of the small one. Thus the size of the retinal image is the same. The results indicate that the babies try to reach the small sphere significantly more often than the large one. The responses are therefore determined by the differences in distance between the objects, not by an analysis of retinal projections.

Gordon and Yonas (1976) and Yonas and Granrud (1985) employ Bower's (1972) argumentation with more precision in their studies of visual perception, and use reaching behaviour as a measure of the child's perception of depth. Two indicators can serve as a basis for studying the perception of distance:

1. The frequency of arm movements. This is influenced by the information obtained about the distance of the object in relation to the observer. For example, Cruikshank (1941) found that the frequency of attempts to reach an object is halved in babies aged 10 to 14 weeks who were presented with a rattle situated 75 centimetres away from them, compared to the same rattle 25 centimetres away.
2. The extension of arm movement in order to reach the object. This is a relevant indicator for studying the imperfect reaching of babies. To this end, J. Field (1976) gives the following operational definition of reaching for an object: the presence of a movement extending the arm more than 5 centimetres in the subject's median plane. Field compares the performance of two groups of infants, one aged 8 to 13 weeks and the other aged 18 to 22 weeks. In the older group this movement is observed in 87 per cent of attempts when the object is within reach of the hand, but in only 23 per cent when it is out of reach. The performance of the younger group is 50 per cent lower than that of the older group, and is a function of the distance of the object. Estimation of the distance between object and observer improves considerably with age, as indicated

by the improved adaptation of the movement with regard to the distance involved.

Gordon and Yonas's research (1976), which uses a virtual object to observe reaching behaviour, indicates that the binocular cues which specify depth can influence reaching. Children 5·5 months of age more often reach for and attempt to grasp a virtual object perceived as within reach than beyond reach.

Generally speaking, whether the condition of vision is monocular (Yonas, Cleaves and Pettersen, 1978) or binocular (see Yonas and Granrud, 1985, for a review of this question), whether the object presented is real (Cruikshank, 1941; Field, 1976) or virtual (Bechtoldt and Hutz, 1979; Gordon and Yonas, 1976), the infants always reach – or attempt to reach, depending on the age group being studied – the object closest to them.

Anticipation of the movement of the target

In anticipating the trajectory of a moving target, babies have to take into account not only the spatial references which they possess from the first few days after birth, but also an important temporal dimension. In a remarkable experiment, von Hofsten (1980) demonstrated the strategies employed by babies aged 18 to 36 weeks to reach an object moving at speeds of 3·4 to 15 or 30 centimetres per second. The results are based on a fine breakdown of the approach movement towards the object into ballistic units consisting of an acceleration phase and a deceleration phase. This analysis permits the calculation of the speed of movement, the acceleration or slowing down of the hand at different moments during the path of the arm and, therefore, a clearer understanding of the babies' strategy for catching the ball. The arm chosen – ipsilateral or contralateral – for reaching towards the object is also taken into account.

The results show that the infant implements the approach strategies predictively since the reaching actions are programmed from the start of the object's movement. Furthermore, these predictions are exact, since most reaching attempts are successful. Finally, this capacity does not develop with age over the period considered, since it is effective from the age of 18 weeks. The frequency of reaches with the ipsi- or contralateral arm depends on the speed of the object. At a slow object speed of 3·4 centimetres per second preference is shown for the ipsilateral arm, while at the faster speeds the contralateral arm is chosen in the majority of cases.

Von Hofsten (1983*b*) has attempted to find which strategy 36-week-old babies use to catch a target moving at speeds of 30, 45 and 60 centimetres per second. Whatever the speed, there are relatively few failures. Nevertheless, it is the slowest speed which most often allows the target to be caught or touched. The babies' strategy – evidently efficient – consists of directing their action towards the target in a movement which is simultaneous with that of the object. Reaching and tracking function together. This double system would seem to allow continuous control of the movement. Using this strategy, the baby's reaching attempts are made with reference to a system of coordinates based on the moving object, not on the stable background. The object can thus be reached at any moment in the target's trajectory, and does not require any prior calculation. Timing is remarkably precise (approximately a twentieth of a second).

While the act of reaching for a target is orientated correctly from the first few days after birth, it is not until the age of about 5 months that the visually gained sensory information is seen in the anticipatory action of the hand. Fine manual dexterity does not permit the hand to respond to the dimensions of objects – and to size in particular – with precision. This asynchronicity in motor development finds partial justification in analyses of the grasping reflex. Twitchell (1965) suggests that the stiffness of the hand, manifest at the moment of grasping, is still not fully controlled in the act of reaching. For example, at 5–6 months infants do not use the pincer grip for objects in a dominant way. They prefer to use the palmar grasp.

The manipulatory component in the grasping of an object

Even if the hand is prepared to receive visually obtained information, it is contact with the object which actually causes it to feel and manipulate it. If the hand does not meet with tactile stimulation – as in situations where a virtual object is presented – the babies' expectations are deceived. Their reactions should bear witness to their ability to integrate the information they receive through the two sensory modalities.

Bower *et al.* (1970*a*) have observed that in the presence of a virtual object babies from 6 days to 6 months of age are surprised and cry when, on contact with the object, the hand does not receive the corresponding haptic information. The existence of an emotional aspect in the baby's reaction has been strongly contested. In a situation similar to that used by Bower, Gordon and Yonas (1976) emphasize that at 5 months babies do not manifest any of the behaviour of surprise noted by Bower. They explain this by arguing that if the babies are not surprised when they try to grasp a virtual object, it is because at 5 months they often do not have their expectations reinforced when they reach for an object. J. Field (1977) observes only rare reactions of surprise in babies aged 7 months, and attributes the emotional reactions of the young babies in Bower's experiment to the distress caused by being made to wear glasses. Bushnell (1982) draws similar conclusions on the basis of the response of 8-month-old babies faced with situations of perceptual conflict.

It is very difficult to draw any conclusions on the basis of emotional or behavioural reactions, or the absence of these reactions, on the part of babies placed in unusual situations. The events they observe or participate in are perhaps perceived as magical and, therefore, likely to cause manifestations of surprise and astonishment. We do not yet know enough to be able to evaluate the baby's ecological environment at each moment of development.

The meaning of neonatal actions: reflexive or intentional?

We have analyzed in detail the perceptual and motor components which specify the act of reaching, and discussed the extent to which it integrates the baby's visual and tactile space. It would appear that prehension–vision (re)coordination at about 4–5 months of age reflects this integration. However, this does not exclude the possibility of a unity of motor and visual space before this age.

There is some degree of controversy about the nature and significance of neonatal actions. Numerous researchers are currently in agreement in recognizing the existence of a directional movement of the neonate's arm and hand towards a visually presented object (Bower, 1972; Bower *et al.*, 1970*a*; de Schonen and Bresson, 1984; von Hofsten, 1982). Given the low frequency of successful reaches, it is the actual meaning of these reaches that provokes the arguments.

The problem is to know whether neonatal 'pre-reaching' – to

borrow Trevarthen's term (1974) – comprises all or part of the components of the more mature reaching act, or whether it is a reflex in which, under certain conditions, optical input simply triggers the motor act. In the first hypothesis, the movement reflects the neonate's ability to perceive a world of organized objects. In the second, it equates to a response reflex which is excited by a visual stimulus (Bushnell, 1981; DiFranco *et al.*, 1978; Dodwell *et al.*, 1976; Ruff and Halton, 1978). In a way, this is what is expressed by the dichotomy between movement which is 'triggered' and movement which is 'controlled' by information.

What is the nature of the neonatal directional gesture? There are a number of arguments in favour of reflexive behaviour. In fact, contrary to Bower's observations, the object is only very rarely attained by the baby (von Hofsten, 1982), and when it is attained the manipulatory component does not come into play. The ballistic movement is stiff and the clumsy, nondirectional movements at the time of reaching do not lead to corrections. Similarly, it has not been clearly proved that neonates extend their arms more often in the presence of an object than of a picture (DiFranco *et al.*, 1978; Dodwell *et al.*, 1976). Neonatal reaching could well be merely an impulsive movement of the arm in response to visual stimulation. It seems difficult to exclude the hypothesis that there are reflex mechanisms at birth which are the basis of the voluntary prehensile behaviour observed later (Bushnell, 1981; Hay, 1985). As Spelke (1987) points out, there is no irrefutable proof which would allow us to state that the newborn and very young infant have a conception of an already organized and structured world, and much of the young infant's behaviour can be interpreted within the framework of both empiricist and associationist theories, Gibsonian or Piagetian.

Nevertheless, there are a number of arguments in favour of intentional action. The directional space is common to both modalities, since the movements are performed in the direction of the observed object. The degree of attention with which the infant looks at the object increases the frequency and precision of the movement (von Hofsten, 1984). Furthermore, the fact that the hand is presented with the palm open rather than closed suggests the intention at least of touching, if not actually grasping, the object. The absence of any behaviour is often ambiguous, and is difficult to interpret. However, the absence of a gestural response towards a picture or a stimulus which is too far away implies that the presence of such a response to an object possesses an intentionality from which its structure derives. The presence of a target is a necessary condition for the triggering of an action. It is not, however, a sufficient condition. The goal-orientated nature of the movement goes beyond the level of reflex. Even if we cannot call it voluntary motor activity, the act of reaching towards a visual target is directed behaviour.

The observation of other forms of behaviour brings to light the existence of an intentionality in the neonate – for example, the imitation of facial gestures and hand movements (Fontaine, 1982, 1984*a*, *b*) or the movement of the hand to the mouth for the activity of sucking (Butterworth, 1986*a*, *b*; Rochat, 1986). From the anticipatory opening of the mouth, Butterworth concludes that this behaviour is not accidental, and that there is an innate intentionality in the neonate. Why would such intentionality exist in this behaviour but not in neonatal reaching? We shall return to this problem in Chapter 5.

Von Hofsten's conclusions concerning his observations are clear: the beginnings of prehension–vision coordination do exist in the neonate. It appears that the conditions under which it is evoked (postural, baby's attention level) determine to a large extent the organization and success of the action, and very often explain the divergence between different researchers.

Finally, observations of reaching behaviour with 'freed motor activity' provide a decisive argument in favour of the existence of a space which is common to the visual and haptic systems from birth onwards. Even if there is a certain stiffness in the programming, performance and final manipulation phase of the neonate's movement, there is still a latent flexibility in the system.

It is clear from the development of this behaviour that the act of reaching undergoes major reorganization during the baby's first six months. Whether this organization is interpreted in terms of 'revolutions' (Mounoud, 1976, 1979, 1983) or 'key ages' (Vurpillot and Bullinger, 1983), the notion of stages and of discontinuous development keep reappearing in descriptions of its successive phases. This idea appears to stand out in the way the development of reaching behaviour is described. Overdependent on nervous and muscular maturity, the discontinuity of this behaviour in no way implies a discontinuity in the baby's perceptual and cognitive organization. While the development of technology during recent decades has enabled us to make good the gap in our knowledge of the neonate's sensoriality and perception, the new high-performance techniques which allow detailed observation of behaviour are still so recent that many questions remain unanswered because of a shortfall which is largely technical.

Reaching for and then grasping an object situated in front of them appears to cause problems for babies in their first six months of life. Once they have gained control of the action, further difficulties arise which appear to be linked neither to the object and its properties nor to the organization of the action, but to the spatial constraints surrounding the object.

Comprehension of the spatial relations between objects is revealed to be more complex than that of an object's dimensions and locality. However, prehensile behaviour cannot be reduced to simply taking account of elements perceived in space. It must also be organized in terms of the relation between these elements.

The space between objects

The boundary between two contiguous objects appears to affect babies' perception, and to modify the way they reach. In Piaget's *The Child's Construction of Reality* (1937, trans. 1937, 1955) he describes observing his son, Laurent. If Piaget presents him with a box of matches, for example, the baby tries to reach them, but as soon as the object is placed on a support, such as a book, the baby of up to 8–9 months does not grasp the object but draws the support to his mouth. Piaget interprets this behaviour as indicating the absence of understanding of the spatial relation 'on top of'. The grasping of an object on top of a support is achieved successfully at the fifth stage, around the age of 10 months.

The perception of two contiguous objects is more than a question of the spatial relation 'on top of'. Bower, for example (1974, 1977), proposes another interpretation of this situation. When the object is placed on a support, it loses its identity by virtue of the fact that it shares one of its boundaries with the support. The problem to be resolved relates not only to understanding the spatial relation but also to the ability to perceive as distinct units those objects which have two surfaces in contact with each other.

The grasping of an object on a support

These two interpretations are investigated in two experiments conducted by Bresson, Maury, Piéraut-Le Bonniec and de Schonen (1977) and Bresson and de Schonen (1976). The starting point for these authors is Piaget's observation that reaching behaviour is modified by variations in the dimensions of the support in relation to the object. When the support is medium-sized, the infant fails to grasp the object, but if the support is large, the infant does grasp the object. It is therefore necessary to discover under what conditions the modifications to the support surface contiguous to the object lead to a disorganization of the prehension–vision relationship.

Longitudinal and cross-sectional observations of babies aged from 17 to 40 weeks have been conducted in four situations with varying support dimensions (Bresson and de Schonen, 1976). An orange 2-centimetre cube was presented (1) on the fully open palm of the hand; (2) on a blue 5-centimetre cube; (3) on a white board (21 cm × 29 cm); and (4) on the tip of the fingers. The results show basically that from the earliest age, seizing the object occurs with just as little frequency in condition (4), with the object presented on fingertips, as in the other conditions, and that this frequency increases in the same way for all conditions as a function of age. Finally, at 25 weeks of age, seizing the object is performed in the majority of cases. The possibility of seizing and manipulating the object does not, therefore, depend solely on the nature and size of the support. In fact, an analysis of the various reaching actions indicates that behaviour differs depending on the situation. Between 17 and 21 weeks of age, ballistic reaching appears whatever the support. However, 'indirect reaching for the object with a differentiated role for the two hands', for example, does not exist for condition (4), and is dominant in the other three conditions. This behaviour consists of putting one hand on the support, then grasping the object with the other hand. The results also show that there is an age difference, which varies according to the support, between the appearance of indirect single-handed reaching (the same hand is placed on the support and then slid towards the object) and direct reaching for the object.

Detailed analysis of this behaviour leads the authors to reinterpret the very function of the support and, therefore, of the 'on top of' spatial relation. Without, however, permitting us to reject wholesale the hypothesis of the loss of identity of an object placed on a support, the difficulty of grasping the object in the 17-to-25-weeks age group seems to arise primarily from the presence of a double system of spatial references: the boundaries of the object and those of the support. At the very moment when the gesture is performed, the support boundaries are thought to interfere with the object boundaries (except when the support is of such large dimensions that it serves as a perceptual background). The support is perceived as 'surrounding' the object, not 'supporting' it. Thus there is no loss of identity of the object, as postulated by Bower (1974), since the ballistic actions are visually triggered by the object. This interpretation is contested by Lécuyer (1988), who believes that the baby may well perceive not a small object on top of a large one but the most interesting part of one and the same object (i.e. the small cube is the most interesting part of the big cube), and that the behaviour analyzed by Bresson and de Schonen does not invalidate Bower's hypothesis.

Lost and found, the unity of objects

Starting from the same Piagetian observation, von Hofsten and Spelke (1985) have posed the question of whether objects sharing a common boundary effectively lose their unity. However, they add an important factor to this question: the role of movement in the perceptual organization of objects into manipulable units, each possessing an internal coherence. They refer, in fact, to another of Piaget's observations according to which if the book is slanted and the box of matches gently slides, Laurent's behaviour changes and he tries again to grasp the box of matches. As Yonas, Granrud and Smith (1982) have demonstrated in babies of 7 and 5 months of age, kinetic information plays a determining role in the perception of surfaces, and influences infants' reaching behaviour.

Von Hofsten and Spelke (1985) have therefore conducted a series of experiments which combine the study of the influence of the spatial relations between objects, and that of movement, on the reaching behaviour of babies aged 20 to 23 weeks.

A small object is placed in front of a larger one of the same colour. Both objects are within reach of the baby's hand, and situated in front of a background of the same colour and texture. Depending on the conditions, the objects are either adjacent or separate, and may be stationary or moving, in unison or independently. If the infants perceive the two objects as distinct, the authors expect them to grasp the nearest one. If the infants regard them as constituting a single unit it is the largest object, which is also furthest away, which will be grasped, or possibly both objects together.

The results show that when the objects are presented so that they are stationary and separate the babies perceive them as constituting two distinct units, but perceive them as a single unit when they are contiguous. When two adjacent objects move together, they are perceived as one unit. If the small unit moves while the larger one remains stationary, it is the former which tends to be grasped. It might be considered that this is because the movement attracts the babies, not because they perceive two distinct units. This is not so: if the small object remains stationary while the large one moves – or, indeed, if the background moves and both objects remain stationary – the infants grasp whatever remains immobile. Thus movement, as Gibson's theory predicts, allows infants to structure their perceptual environment and organize surfaces into manipulable units with an internal coherence. This experiment also provides evidence that 5-week-old babies are sensitive to the Gestalt theory's law of common fate. Using a preferential choice technique, Spelke, von Hofsten and Kestenbaum (1989) obtained a similar result at the perceptual level in 3-month-olds. Bower (1965) had earlier demonstrated that from the age of 3 weeks babies are able to organize figural elements into coherent units when these move as a whole.

Although they are based on the same observation made by Piaget, the conclusions of the two experiments analyzed here (Bresson and de Schonen, 1976; von Hofsten and Spelke, 1985) differ. However, they are not contradictory. There is no doubt that when two objects share a common boundary, perception and manipulation of them are affected at an age when infants are perfectly capable of grasping an isolated object. In the first experiment the object can be distinguished from the support by its distinct physical properties. The baby has to resolve a perceptual conflict and programme an action strategy which permits this resolution. In the second experiment it is the movement

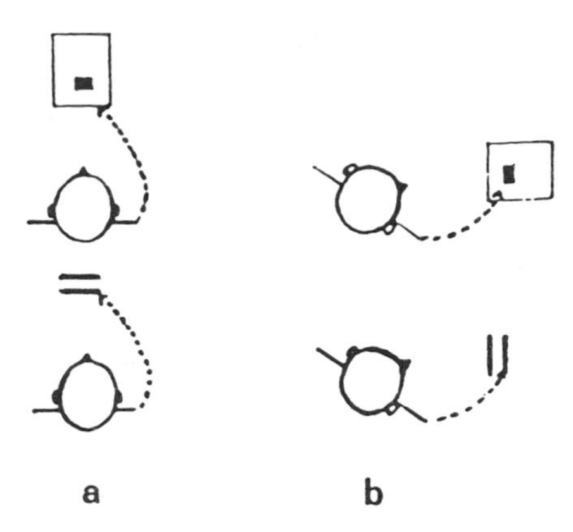

Figure 2.1 Trajectory of the hand (dotted line) when the object and its support are presented: (a) in the median sagittal plane (b) laterally. (*Source*: de Schonen and Bresson, 1984)

and separation between the objects which structure the whole picture and activate the grasping of the object.

How is the preferred object grasped when it is amongst others?

Even when the objects are perceptually individualized, the preferred object is not always grasped. De Schonen and Bresson (1984) have demonstrated that a 5-month-old baby will always grasp the nearer of two objects, whether they are identical or different, placed on the same horizontal plane, even when the preferred object (because of its bright colour) is further away. Presented on a vertical plane, each object is grasped with the same frequency. The nearer object thus seems to form an obstacle to the grasping of the further one. This obstacle effect disappears if the objects are presented to the side of the subject (90° to the sagittal plane). Under these conditions, the further object is grasped just as frequently as the nearer one. In the median direction the movement's trajectory would have to pass the nearer object, which therefore functions as an obstacle, while in the lateral direction the trajectory is wider and the further object can be grasped more easily (see Figure 2.1). For the authors, the position of the hand in the same visual field as one or other of the objects is taken into consideration in the plan to grasp the object.

A similar conclusion is drawn from the observation of visual and manual localization of an object situated between two other objects in 4-to-9-month-old babies (Pineau and Streri, 1985). Three identical objects are lined up on a support. During a familiarization period the baby learns to choose the object situated in the middle of the other two. It is detachable, and hides a flashing light which appears when it is lifted from the support. The other two objects are fixed. The actual experimental stage comprises three conditions in which the whole scenario is shifted: two rotations in the horizontal plane, one of 180° and the other of 90°, and a rotation which moves it 90° in the vertical plane. After each rotation of the apparatus (support and objects), the infant's direction of gaze and motor response are recorded. Amongst other things it has been demonstrated that the spatial relation 'between' remains invariant despite movement of the whole apparatus (Maury and Streri, 1981).

The results of Pineau and Streri's experiment (1985) reveal that the frequency with which the central object is grasped increases with age. It also changes at the same age, depending on the situation. While grasping of the preferred object is often successfully performed under the condition of 180° horizontal rotation, it is much less so under that of 90°, even by the older babies. The vertical rotation presents an intermediate difficulty. Nevertheless, manual localization of the objects is not necessarily accompanied by a corresponding visual localization. Hand movement is preferentially orientated towards the nearest object, while ocular fixation is preferentially directed towards the most interesting object.

These results serve to support the interpretations proposed by Bresson and de Schonen (1976) and de Schonen and Bresson (1984) of the obstacle role which appears to be played by the closest element in the choice of grasping one object out of several. The behaviour of grasping an object other than the central one should not be interpreted only as indicating absence of awareness of the spatial invariant 'between'.

The hypothesis which asserts that if the hand is positioned in the same visual field as an object then that object will be grasped preferentially is, to some extent, confirmed by the observations of visual guiding of the trajectory in the process of reaching for an isolated object. Simultaneous vision of hand and object increases the chances of success. In other words, what is important for babies is the success of their actions, even if the object grasped is not the preferred one.

What if a detour has to be made in order to grasp the object?

I do not intend to re-examine the abundant literature devoted to object permanence (see Bremner, 1980; Butterworth, 1982; P.L. Harris, 1983, 1987), but to attempt to understand why a baby fails to grasp an object from behind a transparent screen when to do so would involve a detour. Should we interpret these failures as indicating an incapacity on the infant's part to learn the in-front–behind spatial relation?

Jarrett (1981; cited by Butterworth, 1983) demonstrates that before the age of 13 months babies can find an object behind an opaque screen, but nevertheless fail to grasp it when it is visible behind a transparent screen. A toy is presented behind a transparent screen in which an opening is cut. If the toy is situated behind the opening, the baby grasps it without hesitation. If the toy is shifted so that is not behind the opening but to one side in such a way that the baby has to make a detour in order to grasp it, then the problem becomes insoluble to the baby, who tries to move the screen. The screen has become a barrier to the baby's action, preventing it from grasping the object. The baby cannot adequately conceive of the spatial relation *between* (emphasized by the article's author) screen and object which, correctly understood, would allow it to reach the object.

De Schonen and Bresson (1984) and de Schonen (1981) postulate quite another interpretation of the behaviour of 6-to-9-month-old babies confronted by a similar situation. De Schonen and McKenzie (experiment cited by de Schonen and Bresson, 1984) place the subject in front of an opaque screen in which an opening has been cut. An object is placed behind the screen, beyond the threshold of the opening but perfectly visible. The 6-month-old babies extend their hand towards the threshold but do not attempt to grasp the object. In contrast, if the object is placed astride the threshold, it is grasped immediately. Although by 7 months of age the problem has been resolved, the authors demonstrate that when the object is hidden behind an opaque or transparent screen without an opening, the difficulties linked to finding a path which circumvents the obstacle reappear, and remain unsolved until the age of 9–10 months (de Schonen, 1981). The baby leans over to look behind the screen, but does not manage to grasp the object. The authors interpret this behaviour as the result of an absence of any circumventing hand trajectory plan. Until the age of 9–10 months, 'the manual trajectory plan appears to be highly subordinate to the trajectory of aim'.

Diamond (1987) and Diamond and Gilbert (1989) obtain similar results, but interpret them slightly differently. Their experiment consists of placing 7–11-month-old babies into a number of situations which involve grasping a Lego object from a transparent, open-topped Plexiglas box. The object can be in various positions in relation to the box. When it is inside the box it can be against the front side, in the middle, or against the back. When it is outside the box it is positioned against the front. Finally, it is presented inside the box, which is tilted so that the open part is facing the infant. There is also a condition in which the Lego is presented in an opaque box.

The babies aged 7 months, and even those aged 8–10 months, fail to grasp the object when it is in direct contact with the far side of the front face of the transparent box, although they succeed perfectly when the Lego is in the middle of the box. On the other hand, 7-month-old infants correctly grasp the object in the other conditions when it is touching the back of the box or placed inside the opaque box. The authors interpret the failures as the result of an inability to perform two directional actions instead of only one: to circumvent the obstacle, then grasp the object.

In order to verify their interpretations more fully, a second experiment is conducted in which the obstacles which prevent grasping of the Lego are eliminated in different ways. For example, the height of the box is lowered, or the Lego is placed in a vertical position. In these conditions, the 7-month-old baby succeeds in grasping the object, but fails if the Lego is slightly separated from the front face of the box, and no longer in the middle. The argument of contiguity, therefore, is not sufficient to explain the failures. In all cases where it is possible to reach the object directly, the 7-month-old infants are successful. Otherwise it is the obstacle – that is to say, the screen – which is manipulated.

Diamond does not consider that an object encased in another has lost its identity for the 7-month-old infants. If they fail to grasp it, it is because they are not able to inhibit their reflex grasp and avoidance actions (Twitchell, 1965, 1970) when their hands come into contact with a neighbouring object. The infants succeed in reaching the object when no obstacle gets in the way of their direct path (Bresson and de Schonen call this the 'trajectory of aim') towards the fixed goal. Failures are caused by the necessity to circumvent another object, and therefore to change direction, in order to touch the target object (de Schonen and Bresson call this the 'circumventing hand trajectory plan').

Another interpretation of the results of all the studies on finding an object behind a transparent screen concerns the status which the baby confers upon the properties of the screen. Usually, a screen hides an object, which then becomes invisible. Searching for the hidden object requires manual exploration without necessitating visual control. If the object is visible behind the screen, it can be grasped directly, just as one can grasp an object plunged into a container of water. The baby's reactions might, therefore, testify to a lack of understanding about the nature of a rigid obstacle which, nevertheless, permits the sight of the object.

Conclusions

In seeking other interpretations for failures in the behaviour of reaching for an object situated among other objects or behind a screen, we can inject some coherence into the way we view the development of the prehension–vision relation. The absence of prehension in the very young baby of under 5 months has been interpreted as the absence of an underlying perceptual and cognitive organization. Nevertheless, we know that young babies' perceptions are better organized than their hesitant motor skills might lead us to expect.

Similarly, once control of the action is gained, failures to grasp one object among others has been interpreted as the inability to control a cognitive capacity. On this question, too, we are now seeing the rejection of an explanation in terms of incomprehension of the spatial relation between objects in favour of one in terms of a difficulty in planning the motor programming of an action.

This upheaval in the way the problems of the relationship between babies and their environment is approached is the result of precise observations of behaviour. We can no longer be content with a naturalistic view of the infant's motor development. At the same time, we are also finding another way of understanding the baby's motor ability. It is not only considered as a performance which reveals an underlying competence (in the Chomskyan sense). It is itself a competence.

Control of the organization of the reaching movement reveals not only the simple adjustment of an anatomo–physiological arm and hand complex to the perceptual conditions of the environment, but also an intention to ensure that the programme is successful. The young infant's anticipatory movements in the regulation of the hand on approach to the object are examples of the baby's 'cognitive' motor ability. The same applies when difficulties arise when the baby tries to grasp one object surrounded by others. Although these are visually perceived as objects, they are transmitted to the motor level as obstacles to be bypassed, an action for which the cognitive programme has not yet been developed. Motor organization thus appears to be more complex than the perceptual or cognitive organization which it is supposed to represent.

Taking into account the heterogeneity of the stages involved in reaching for a visual target, we might conclude that during their first year babies lead a disjointed existence, with their perceptual cognitive capacities being somehow discrete from their motor skills, and that perceived space and motor space are separated. The analysis of reaching behaviour shows that this is completely wrong. While reaching bears evidence of a simple directional visuo–motor coordination at birth, during the course of development the relevant dimensions are integrated for more effective performance and the realization of its goal.

Manual laterality and the behaviour of approaching an object

The organization of the eye–hand system appears still more complex if we compare the independence of the left and right sides in the upper limbs with the convergence of the eyes necessary to ensure the fusion of images. A whole range of motor responses to a single visual target are possible. In the adult, the manual preference in behaviour is certain. The right hand, which is the more skilled for 90 per cent* of the population, is assured a privileged role in the individual's perceptuomotor behaviour. This lateral specialization requires the coordination of both hands in bimanual tasks. This collaboration is possible only if the hands have different functions in the fulfilment of the task. How does the baby manage this important motor potential when reaching for an object?

Neuropsychologists and psychologists have devoted a large body of work to manual laterality in the baby (Young, Segalowitz, Corter and Trehub, 1983). The problem appears to be important, since for centuries philosophers, anatomists, biologists and neuropsychologists have been constantly preoccupied with it (see L.J. Harris, 1983).

Family origin determines the child's manual dexterity. In all probability, children whose parents are left-handed will be as well. From this observation the existence of a genetic link has been deduced. This, however, does not resolve all the problems posed by the functional asymmetry of the hands.

The fundamental questions which have been posed concern the existence and origins of this laterality. From a phylogenetic perspective, these origins are ancient. Corballis (1989) dates the origins of manual laterality to probably 2 to 3 million years ago, which would imply that *Homo habilis* was endowed with manual laterality; and definitely to 1.5 million years ago, the time when *Homo erectus* was able to stand erect. From an ontogenetic perspective, Previc (1991) asserts that the origins of lateralization in the human are to be found in the asymmetrical prenatal development of the ear and labyrinth. The hypothesis of an advantaged auditory laterality in the right ear (therefore specialization of the left hemisphere, favouring the perception and production of language) is confirmed by the asymmetrical development of the cranium, while the vestibular or labyrinthine dominance of the left side (therefore specialization of the right hemisphere for the performance of spatial tasks) is due to the

* Different percentages of right-handed people in a population have been defined by various authors. The most precise study on this subject is by Annett (1970), which postulates 65 per cent right-handed, 31 per cent ambidextrous, 4 per cent left-handed.

position of the foetus in the last three months of gestation. When and how is this specialization expressed during the course of development? When does right-hand preference become observable in the infant in a stable and concrete way? Does some stage exist when the infant prefers the left hand? Is this manual asymmetry controlled at the cortical level, or is it the result of encouragement by parents in their interactions with the child? Is manual laterality closely linked to other asymmetrical behaviour? The manual approach to a visual target represents one of the elements which describe the organization of the system in the baby.

Which hand is chosen?

For a long time it was believed that neonates and babies were principally left-handed. This belief rested mainly on the observations of Gesell and Ames (1947), who noticed a slight preference for the left hand in reaching behaviour between 16 and 20 weeks of age, followed by a period of preference for the right hand. This first impression found confirmation in a study by Seth (1973). Babies aged 20–52 weeks prefer to grasp objects in their left hand, except for a critical period between 28 and 32 weeks of age when the right hand is activated more frequently. In younger babies aged 1 to 4 months, DiFranco, Muir and Dodwell (1978), McDonnell (1979) and McDonnell, Anderson and Abraham (1983) find similar results in reaching for an object. However, this preference for the left hand is slight, and has a low level of statistical significance in all these studies except McDonnell's.

Young, Segalowitz, Misek, Ercan Alp and Boulet (1983) attempted to examine the reality of these data in an exhaustive analysis of seventeen studies of reaching behaviour in which the limb used is clearly stated. These studies cover the age range from birth to 4 months. This analysis reveals that only four of the studies – those mentioned above – indicate a preference for the left hand, while in the other thirteen the right hand is preferred. Moreover, in discussing McDonnell's data, Liederman (1983) does not find this preference for the left hand between 3 and 10 weeks of age. Bloch and Ennouri (in a personal communication) compare the frequency of neonatal hand movements in the 'freed motor activity' condition and in the presence of an object with their frequency in a control condition (without an object). The frequency with which the right hand is moved towards an object situated to the right of the baby is significantly higher than in the control condition. A similar result is not obtained for the left hand.

This initial impression that babies are left-handers is not, therefore, unanimously supported by researchers. However, the results suggesting the dominance of the right hand have also not received significant confirmation. Preference for the right hand between 0 and 4 months of age would appear to be a tendency rather than a clearly established fact, especially in the case of the youngest babies. A closer analysis of the data by Young *et al.* (1983) has demonstrated that the right hand is preferred for activity directed towards a nearby target on which the baby's gaze is focused. In contrast, the left hand is frequently in motion when there is no clearly directed activity.

Results at 6 months of age do not seem any more decisive. Michel, Ovrut and Harkins's study (1986) clearly indicates a right-hand preference in the reaching activity of babies from the age of 6 months; while McCormick and Maurer's (1988) does not indicate a similar result. In contrast, developmental research by Cornwell, Harris and Fitzgerald (1991) with girls aged 9–13 and 20 months shows clear evidence of a preferential use of the right hand in activities involving manual skills from the age of 9 months onwards. This preference would appear to depend on the activity required. Drawing with a crayon is the activity which shows most evidence of laterality and is thus a good predictor, while putting a sponge into a cup is a poor predictor.

What are the origins of laterality?

Early manual asymmetry is often interpreted as revealing that a functional asymmetry of the cerebral hemispheres is present from birth. The left hemisphere is assumed to be responsible for processing temporal, sequential events; the right hemisphere for processing configurations in a more global way. While the right side is preferred for reaching behaviour and the manipulation of objects, these activities, as well as the processing of speech and musical sounds, are thought to be controlled by the left hemisphere. The model proposed by Young, Bowman, Methot, Finlayson, Quintal and

Boissonneau (1983) brings greater precision to this general configuration, attributing to the left hemisphere a primordial and highly complex role in reaching behaviour. The left hemisphere would thus appear to be responsible not only for the activation of appropriate behaviour but also for the inhibition of inappropriate or interfering behaviour.

To test the reality of their model, they present the right ear of 2-day-old neonates with a series of musical sounds and syllables while placing their hands on a bar situated at shoulder height. They observe the direction of the head when the sounds are heard, and the exploratory movements of the hands both during and after the auditory stimulation. These two forms of behaviour should be concurrent in the case of left hemisphere processing. The results show that the head is turned to the right in response to the auditory stimulation. In contrast, the right hand remains immobile during presentation of the stimulus; movements appear only two to four seconds later. The authors interpret this result as indicating that the left hemisphere gives priority to the activation of listening to the sound at the expense of manual activity, which is inhibited until after the sound has been heard.

Nevertheless, environmental influence is not neglected by their model, and the authors attribute an important role to adult interaction with the baby in the process of differentiating the hemispheric functions. These authors find a positive correlation between the degree of parental verbalization and vocalization and the degree of lateralization in the directional activity of the arms in 1-month-old babies. The more social interactions the infant experiences, the more the process of hemispheric specialization develops. A study of asymmetrical mouth contortions on audition of a sound confirms the role of educative practice in the asymmetrical behaviour of the neonate. Alegria and Noirot (1978) and Noirot (1983) demonstrated that bottle-fed babies show preferential distortion of the mouth towards the left, irrespective of the sound source, while breastfed babies show positive contortions directed towards the sound whether it is presented from the left or the right. These results reinforce the theory developed by Turkewitz (1980) and Turkewitz and Birch (1971), which asserts that asymmetrical sensory input from the environment determines postural and behavioural differences in babies (see also Harris and Fitzgerald, 1983).

Trehub, Corter and Schosenberg (1983) have sought evidence of these early lateral asymmetries in neonatal reflexes other than reaching behaviour in premature and full-term babies. The subjects undergo a set of ten tests, such as spontaneous head-turning, strength of grip when holding an object, pedalling movements, and so on. Although a preference for the right side is manifested as much in premature as in full-term babies, the authors point out a lack of stability in the responses during the tests, and find a significant right-side preference in only two out of the ten: namely spontaneous head-turning and the rooting reflex. The authors conclude from their observations that lateral asymmetry is not a general property of reflex behaviour. In reflex responses there would appear to be some lack of lateral asymmetry, which seems to be of more importance in voluntary responses. These conclusions confirm those of Young *et al.* (1983), who have particularly emphasized right-handed dominance in directed activity, and left-handed dominance in nondirected activity. A reflex response is not, strictly speaking, behaviour with an underlying goal.

Among the reflexes which contribute to the clinical description of the neonate, spontaneous head-turning to the right has often been noted (Michel, 1981; Turkewitz, Gordon and Birch, 1965). This behaviour is one of the components of the tonic neck reflex (ATNR, or Asymmetric Tonic Neck Reflex). In this reflex, the position of the arms and hands alters in such a way that the limb on the same side as the face is extended, while the opposite limb is flexed. This reflex, rarely observed at birth, becomes frequent at 6 to 8 weeks of age. It is asymmetrical, and the majority of infants in the supine position will turn their heads towards the right (Coryell and Michel, 1978; Gesell and Halverson, 1942). A number of authors consider this reflex to be the origin of eye–hand coordination (Bushnell, 1981; White, Castle and Held, 1964). Visual perception of the hand during ATNR is predictive of a preference for this hand in reaching behaviour at 12 weeks (Coryell and Michel, 1978).

Michel, Harkins and Meserve (1990) have demonstrated that preferential head orientation in the very young newborn, only a few hours old, depends on the baby's gender and attention level. This orientation towards left or right occurs during the alert state in girls and the sleep state in boys. Moreover, girls are more often in a state of alertness than boys, and for longer periods. This behavioural difference between the sexes occurring at such an early stage might throw light upon other behavioural differences or other forms of hemispheric specialization.

According to Michel (1983), preferential head orientation, such as ATNR, of babies in the supine position is the origin of lateralization to the right in infants. The visual, proprioceptive and tactilokinaesthetic information involved in these asymmetrical activities of head, arms and hands facilitates the creation of cortically lateralized sensorimotor programmes.

This point of view is, therefore, opposed to that of Young *et al.* (1983), who regard hemispheric specialization as the origin of asymmetrical behaviour, not the other way round. It is probably the correlative evolution of both factors during the course of development which determines the manual preference of child and adult.

Bimanual coordination and hemispheric specialization

The problem of early laterality and the meaning of this laterality is particularly acute when both hands compete in accomplishment of the same task. Does this result in interference or a complementarity of roles? As de Schonen (1977) and Peters (1983) point out, when the arm and hand reach the object, the other arm performs complementary coordinated movements. This is the case in ATNR, where one arm flexes while the other is extended. In the simple alternation of arm movements in ATNR, Peters (1983) sees the basis of adult coordinated bimanual activities. From the beginning there is no interference, only complementarity. This coordination can show itself in two situations. Either both hands cooperate in achieving the same aim or, if one is unable to perform the task, the other provides a replacement.

In the first situation, de Schonen (1977) has clearly demonstrated this functional division of the hands in babies aged 17 to 40 weeks. When the infant reaches an object with both hands, the right hand makes contact with the object while the left remains on the support next to the object. This pattern of complementary movements varies according to the nature of the object and the way in which it is presented (Bresson, Maury, Piéraut-Le Bonniec and de Schonen, 1977). Ramsay (1983) has also observed this pattern in infants aged

11 months. The right hand is preferred in the activity of handling objects, while the left hand holds and supports them.

This collaboration between the hands is established particularly towards the end of the infant's first year. Peters (1983) shows that at 12 months of age there is a preference for the right hand in reaching for and handling objects, while no such preference exists at 6 months of age. His interpretation of this is original in that he regards grasping the object not as an end but as a means to an end. The infant intends to move the object. At the age of 6 months, the object is grasped and carried so that oral exploration may take place. This activity does not necessitate any manual preference. At 12 months of age the infant's exploratory activity is transformed into playing, which involves a distribution of roles between the hands.

Two recent studies confirm that it is at the end of the first year that collaboration between the hands is established (Cornwell *et al.*, 1991; Michel *et al.*, 1986). Both these studies, however, bring to light a change in manual preference in coordinated activity during the second six months of life. This change appears between the ages of 9 and 13 months in the research conducted by Cornwell *et al.* (1991), which confirms the results already obtained by Ramsay, Campos and Fenson (1979).

In all the studies reported here, it is clearly demonstrated that it is the hand which is ipsilateral to the presented object that is activated in reaching behaviour. What happens when an object is presented to the right, and the right hand cannot grasp it because it is immobilized or occupied? In such a situation babies have to cross the median line of their body with their left hand in order to reach the object. Bruner (1969, 1970) describes the difficulty experienced by infants in crossing the 'midline barrier'. This difficulty constitutes a stage in the development of the coordination and complementarity of the hands. However, the problems Bruner presents to the baby are extremely complex.

Provine and Westerman (1979) replicated Bruner's research with babies aged 9 to 20 weeks. One of the baby's arms is immobilized and the behaviour of the free arm is observed in three conditions of object presentation: to the left, in the middle, and to the right of the baby. The results show that the frequency of reaching depends on the distance between the free arm and the object, the 'midline' barrier representing an intermediary condition. Babies of 9 to 11 weeks of age are unable to reach the object when it is presented to the side opposite to the free arm, and 100 per cent success in this task is not achieved until the age of 18–20 weeks.

Two important points must be emphasized in these studies of manual laterality. First of all, it appears that mobilization of the right hand is preferred in directed activities quite early in the infant's life, but it is during the second half of the first year that an evident functional difference between the hands is established. The majority of research into the act of reaching for a visual object in babies under 6 months old notes that the right arm is most often extended. This observation provides an additional argument in the refutation of the idea that this action is essentially reflex in nature, particularly at birth. The arm would appear to be extended towards a goal. Furthermore, it has not yet been clearly demonstrated that a behaviour such as the tonic neck reflex plays a role in establishing prehension–vision coordination. However, research in this domain is still at a descriptive level.

Chapter 3

The motor ability and sensoriality of the haptic system

The beginning of tactile sensitivity and motor ability

The neonate's visual mechanisms are now sufficiently well known for us to accept the notion that this sensory modality functions with a degree of precision from birth. In contrast, we are a long way from knowing as much about the tactile modality. All we know is that foetal and neonatal reactions to haptic stimulation indicate the receptive system's level of sensitivity. The aesthesiometric method refined by Michotte (1905) has made it possible to observe that in the adult the fineness of haptic discrimination varies depending on the part of the body which is stimulated, and that 'regional signs' exist within the hand. Each mobile segment of the hand possesses its own 'regional sign' – that is to say, its sensitivity threshold. This difference in sensorial receptivity appears to guide our prehensile actions even when we are in a state of inattention.

Adopting a method similar to Michotte's, Hooker (1938) and Humphrey (1970) offer a precise description of the tactile sensitivity of the foetus. In their experiments conducted on organisms which survived for a short period after their expulsion, they stroked the surface of the skin using graded hair aesthesiometers. Withdrawal of the head in response to mild stimulation is obtained in foetuses aged 7·5 weeks (Humphrey, 1964). One week later this initial reflex is followed by that of opening the mouth and swallowing. Anatomically, the only part of the central nervous system which is differentiated at this stage of development is the part of the trigeminal nerve which is responsible for the transmission of pain and general tactile sensations. The functioning of tactile sensitivity is based on Meissner's corpuscles and those Pacinian corpuscles which are already encapsulated. Their anatomical development begins in the peribuccal region at 7 weeks of intrauterine life. At 11 weeks they are present in the palm of the hand. These corpuscles do not develop synchronously. Pacinian corpuscles, for example, appear in the fingers at 11 weeks, while Meissner's become individuated between 24 and 30 weeks (Lecanuet, Granier-Deferre and Busnel, 1989).

Thus the parts of the body which respond to tactile stimulation are the peribuccal area (8·5 weeks), the genital area (10·5 weeks), the palm of the hand (between 10·5 and 11 weeks) and the sole of the foot (12 weeks). These small surfaces possess the greatest number and variety of receptors in the adult (Humphrey, 1964). All the specialized cutaneous receptors are present at birth, although they have not yet fully matured. Meissner's corpuscles, for example, which are sensitive to pressure and are particularly numerous in the palm of the hand, the sole of the foot and the genital organs, are not yet encapsulated, and are still not so in 1-year-old babies (Humphrey, 1964). In the visual system, in contrast, the peripheral retina is structurally fully mature in the newborn, and the entire retina attains its adult form during the first few months after birth (Abramov, Gordon, Hendrickson, Hainline, Dobson and Labossière, 1982). Thus the visual system possesses the physiological capacities which allow it to function much earlier, and with greater efficiency, than the haptic system.

Descriptions of motor behaviour in the foetus are also fairly precise. Thus Ajuriaguerra (1978) – who takes the research of Minkowski (1938) and Hooker (1952) as a starting point – reports the emergence of the first behavioural manifestations. These appear between the fifth and eighth weeks of foetal life. Complete opening of the mouth is observed at around 9·5 weeks. The first palmar response to stimulation is noted at 10·5 weeks and consists of incomplete closing of the fingers, with the exception of the thumb. The hand's reaction to tactile contact thus occurs very early. Prehension, which is weak at 18 weeks, is strong enough to support the weight of the foetus briefly at 27 weeks.

At birth, tactile sensitivity becomes more important. Rose, Schmidt and Bridger (1976) have compared the threshold of tactile sensitivity in premature infants with that of full-term infants by touching their abdomens with three different thicknesses of Semmes-Weinstein filaments during sleep. Using heart rate and leg movements as observable indicators, Rose *et al.* (1976) find that only full-term babies show an increase in heartbeat in response to this stimulus. These babies' leg movements are also more vigorous. A cardiac response can be obtained in premature babies using a stronger tactile stimulus, thus reinforcing the idea of a higher threshold in these infants (Field, Dempsey, Hatch, Ting and Clifton, 1979; Rose, Schmidt, Riese and Bridger, 1980). In contrast, these authors observe no decrease in cardiac response in premature babies as a function of the repetition of the stimulus. This indicates an absence of haptic habituation, which the authors interpret as revealing the immaturity of the central nervous system. We know that the phenomenon of habituation is general, and that a large number of organisms are susceptible to it (Bornstein, 1985; Pêcheux and Lécuyer, 1988; Tighe and Leaton, 1976). Slater, Morison and Rose (1984*a*) have shown that visual habituation exists in neonates. However, the baby's level of attention greatly influences the likelihood of obtaining either a cardiac response to a tactile stimulus (Rose, Schmidt and Bridger, 1978; Yang and Douthitt, 1974) or habituation to air being blown on the eyelids (Martinius and Papousek, 1970).

We know little about the processing abilities of the manual tactile receptors, and we are particularly ignorant of their distribution and development in the baby, in terms of both number and specialization. Such knowledge would allow us to formulate a precise hypothesis about the information the baby can grasp beyond simply reacting to a stimulus. Research into tactile sensitivity shows that young babies are capable of receiving information and reacting to it, despite the poor specificity of their tactile receptors. Nevertheless, observations have concentrated on the ability to react to haptic stimuli rather than the discriminatory capacities of the receptors. However, this area of research is important for the study of relations between touch and vision. Even though the tactile receptors are clearly less efficient than the visual receptors during the first few months after birth, the conditions for an early perceptual unity require a certain degree of similarity in the functioning of these two sensory modalities. It is therefore important to discover whether the baby is capable, beyond simple reflex reactions to a stimulus, of the haptic processing of information and of a differentiated response to varying environmental stimuli, such as has been demonstrated in the visual domain.

The reflex and motor component of the hand

The reflex reaction of the hand is described by paediatricians as one of the organism's basic behavioural acts. It therefore forms part of the clinical description of the set of reflexes used for examining the neonate and the infant (Ajuriaguerra, 1978; André-Thomas and Saint-Anne-Dargassies, 1952; Prechtl and Beintema, 1964).

The palmar grasp response is obtained when the neonate's hand is stimulated by lightly pressing on its palm with, for example, an index finger. The response is considered positive if the infant's fingers flex around the examiner's finger. Such a response is obtained, in particular, when the baby is awake and alert; it is negative when the baby is asleep or deeply absorbed in a sucking activity (Prechtl, 1970, in Connolly, 1970). In contrast, it is not produced under the condition of 'freed motor ability'. This response is the 'tonic finger flexion reaction', also called the grasp reflex or reaction.

There is a continuity between foetal and infant reflex. Twitchell's systematic observations (1965, 1970) complement the now classic early observations of Halverson (1937). Twitchell has described not one but three hand responses to stimulation: the traction response, the grasp response and the avoiding response. The first two are reflexes involving finger flexion and closing the hand; the third, in contrast, is a reflex which involves spreading the fingers and opening the hand. These reactions coexist during the first few months, but sometimes one of them dominates at a particular age. Below is a summary of Twitchell's (1970) description of the conditions under which these reflexes are produced, and the age at which they appear.

1. Proprioceptive dominance. The traction response, which is essentially proprioceptive in nature, is observed from birth to 8 weeks of age. Pulling the arm elicits closing of the fingers and flexion of all the joints in the limb. Finger flexion appears as a synergistic component of the flexion of the limb. The reaction can be intens-

ified by further stretching of the flexor muscles. This traction response is not a static reaction, since it can be facilitated or depressed by the tonic neck reflex, or even inhibited by concomitant stimulation of the back of the hand. This response can be elicited by stimulation of the surface of the palm at between 2 and 4 weeks of age.

2. The grasp response, which is obtained until the age of 2 weeks by a pressing stimulus on the palm, can be elicited more locally between 4 and 8 weeks of age. At this age, stimulation of thumb and index finger produces adduction and flexion of these digits. This local reaction is immediately followed by flexion of all the joints in the hand. According to Twitchell, this constitutes the first stage of development of the grasp reflex. During the next few weeks, the receptive field widens to include the radial aspect of the palm and the proximal part of the phalanges.

   Between the ages of 8 and 20 weeks, the grasp reflex splits into two stages. An adequate stimulation elicits a sudden quick flexion of fingers and thumb (the catching phase). This flexion is maintained by traction of the fingers (the holding phase). As the grasp reflex develops, the synergistic traction response disappears. The tonic neck reflex is no longer so effective in altering flexion of the arm. However, stimulation of the back of the hand still elicits opening of the fingers.

   From the sixteenth to the fortieth weeks of age, the grasp reflex develops considerably. Twitchell describes several stages. First of all, the fingers flex independently in response to stimulation. Only the finger which is subject to tactile stimulation flexes. This fractionation of the grasp reflex is obtained first in the index finger and then later in the other fingers. In a second stage, hand orientation reactions are elicited (between 16 and 36 weeks of age). A light contact stimulus to the radial part of the hand will produce a supination of the hand towards the stimulus. Later, stimulation of the ulnar part of the hand causes a corresponding pronation of the hand towards the stimulus. In a third stage (between 20 and 44 weeks of age) a new form of behaviour appears, and this constitutes the final phase of the grasp reaction. The hand adjusts to the contours of the object, and makes slight groping movements to recover it when it is withdrawn.

3. Avoiding reflexes. In the newborn, a light stimulation of the back

of the hand will elicit only a slight avoiding reflex consisting of dorsiflexion and abduction of the fingers. Between 3 and 8 weeks of age, even a slight contact stimulus is sufficient to cause the hand to be withdrawn. This mode of responding to a stimulus is produced more locally between 12 and 20 weeks of age. The instinctive reaction is fully developed between 24 and 40 weeks of age. It is more easily elicited from an irritable infant, and can become generalized to affect the entire posture of the very young baby.

4. For Twitchell, grasp and avoiding responses are more than mere reflexes. They play a fundamental role in prehension–vision coordination. From the organism's general reflex behaviour, which is evoked by the traction response, there is a development towards specialization of each joint and greater control of the hand's motor ability. Twitchell attributes a highly important and specific function to each reflex. They are the basis not only for grasping objects, but also for rejecting them.

   While the trajectory of the hand is visually guided from the age of 4 months, anticipatory opening of the hand quickly occurs at the start of the approach movement in reaction to visually gained information about the properties of the object. The hand's subservience to vision in reaching behaviour will disappear as hand adjustment improves and the dexterity of the fine finger muscles develops. In the final phase of reaching for the object, the manipulatory component is controlled by the tactile system, and freed from visual constraints.

It is a pity that Twitchell still speaks of reflex in connection with grasping behaviour. For example, when the grasp response splits into two stages, the holding phase can no longer be regarded as a reflex reaction or a prolonged grasp. A reflex is a fleeting reaction; and holding on to an object is not. Bruner (1970) makes a similar criticism of Twitchell's work. Reflexes exist, and must be taken into account in the study of grasping behaviour. Beyond this reflexive component, however, we need to discover whether babies are capable of perceiving the properties of the objects they grasp. We shall attempt to demonstrate that the sensory component of the tactile modality, and of the hand specifically, is by no means this rudimentary.

The sensory component of the tactile system

During the last thirty years, the development of vision in the baby has been accorded so much importance that the study of tactile sensoriality, and of the hand in particular, has been somewhat neglected. Descriptions which are made purely in terms of reflex mechanisms mean that the real abilities of the hand during its interactions with the environment are considerably underestimated. Such descriptions cast doubt on the possibility of active touching which, according to J.J. Gibson (1962), is essential to the perception of the properties of objects. Let us remember that in the foetal stage the tactile modality is the first modality through which external information is received and communicated to the brain. This is one rcason for supposing that the gathering of such information is possible very early, despite the poor degree of fine motor ability in the hand. Curiously – and no doubt for technical and methodological reasons – it would appear that nothing is yet known about the sensory potential of the baby's hand. In infants, it is the oral mode of the tactile modality which has attracted the greatest interest. Therefore, we shall briefly switch our attention to this particular pole of the tactile modality: the baby's buccal cavity.

Oral information pick-up

Like all the activities that characterize neonatal motor movements, sucking has long been regarded as invariable and rigid – that is to say, as a reflex behaviour which plays an important role in babies' relationships with their environment.

Bullinger and Rochat (1985) describe sucking behaviour 'as a rhythmic activity whose temporal components have a relatively rigid structure' (p. 56). A graph of this behaviour in situations of non-nutritive sucking is obtained with the aid of a device which transforms the infant's pressure on a dummy into an electric signal. The regular sucking pattern obtained is sometimes interrupted by an irregular trace of lower amplitude which corresponds to the mechanical misshaping of the dummy caused by all the components of the buccal cavity. This temporary signal is attributed to active movements of the mouth, which the authors compare to manual exploratory palpations, and which reveal an expressive activity on the part of the baby. This activity, largely unassociated with nutrition, is capable of modification and corresponds more to an exploratory activity.

Crook (1977) and Lipsitt (1979) have even observed a variation of responses in babies during gustative sucking depending on the level of sucrose concentration in water. The neonate prefers the sweetest liquid, and expresses this by increasing the duration of sucking periods and shortening the pauses between sucks. Therefore, the gustative function of the mouth is present from birth.

Sugar solutions appear not only to have a lasting calming effect on the baby, but also to be a factor in activating hand–mouth coordination. Rochat, Blass and Hoffmeyer (1988) and Blass, Fillion, Rochat, Hoffmeyer and Metzger (1989) have obtained a response of carrying the hand to the mouth in 1-to-2-day-old neonates given a sugar solution. This behaviour ceases when the sweet stimulus is withdrawn, and is not obtained with plain water. This hand–mouth coordination is described not as the expression of a motor pattern triggered by the sugary taste, but as the activation of suckling–feeding mechanisms which give rise to the integration of motor activity in head, mouth and hand.

Rochat (1983) has studied the development of the expressive function of the oral cavity. He presents neonates and 4-month-old babies with a series of dummies varying in shape and substance (rigid or elastic). He observes that the duration of the regular sucking pattern decreases as a function of age while, correlatively, that of the exploration pattern increases. Furthermore, he notes that there is an interaction between the age of the infant and the type of dummy. Neonates respond differently depending on the substance, while the exploration performed by older babies differs with the shape of the object.

Research by Pêcheux, Lepecq and Salzarulo (1988) has demonstrated the capacity for oral discrimination in babies aged from 35 to 85 days. After a 90-second familiarization period with a flexible dummy into which either a cube or a tetrahedron with small spheres attached to it is incorporated, the baby reacts with an increase in irregular exploration patterns to buccal presentation of the unfamiliar dummy.

Buka and Lipsitt (1991) have studied the relationship between sucking and grasping which had already been noted by Halverson

(1937). They activate the traction response, as described by Twitchell (1965), in 72-hour-old neonates during two periods of sucking activity: sucking without absorption of liquid and sucking with absorption of sugared water. A metal rod is placed in the baby's right hand in such a way that a traction response is obtained. Four conditions are produced: sucking without fluid intake with and without grasping; sucking of sugar solution with and without grasping. The results reveal that presentation of the sugar solution alters sucking behaviour and heartbeat. The presence or absence of grasping has no effect on sucking. In contrast, the sucking mode does have an effect on grasping. The neonate holds the rod more firmly when sucking than when not sucking, and still more firmly when the sugar solution is presented.

While there is a relation between sucking and grasping, it is interesting to note that this is not reversible. Moreover, there are differences in functioning between oral mode and manual mode in the tactile modality. The function of the mouth is essentially to ingest food, and it is used for exploration only incidentally and for a limited period in the life of the human being. As Peters (1983) has demonstrated, from the age of 12 months onwards buccal exploration no longer holds the same interest for the baby, whereas the hand has an exploratory function which, whilst it appears to be limited at birth, develops rapidly and, no doubt, to the detriment of oral exploration.

Working within a Gibsonian perspective on this problem, Rochat (1987) has studied the ability of the neonate and 2-to-3-month-old baby to detect the information relevant for triggering behaviour of oral and manual exploration of objects ('affordances'). He compares the differing amounts of pressure exerted on objects made of materials which are either rigid or pliable. The objects presented to both hand and mouth are absolutely identical. The frequency of the pressures exerted on the hard or soft object, either orally or manually, is registered on a polygraph. Pressure is defined as a positive response to the stimulus. A positive response has an amplitude which is greater than a third of the maximum amplitude obtained for each infant.

The results show a clear difference between oral and manual exploration of the hard object and the soft object. The important result, however, is that at all the ages researched, the hand exerts pressure more on the hard object than on the soft object, whereas in the case of oral pressure the opposite tendency is more frequently observed. What changes with age is the frequency of positive responses in the different modes of exploration. In the neonate, oral exploration represents a much more important activity than manual exploration, while it has the same degree of importance in the 2-to-3-month-old baby. Sucking is, therefore, the most essential activity for the neonate.

A qualitative analysis of the pressure exerted reveals specific types of exploratory behaviour. Two forms of pressure pattern are defined: clutches and squeeze–releases. The former correspond to squeezing followed by a slow release of the object; the latter correspond to squeezing followed by a quick release of the object. The proportions of these pressure patterns also differ depending on the type of object explored, the mode of exploration and the age of the baby. At all ages, and for both types of object, the proportion of quick squeeze–releases is higher in oral exploration, while clutches occur most frequently in manual exploration. At birth, the squeeze–release-type pressure is exerted more frequently on soft objects than on hard objects during oral exploration, whereas in the case of manual exploration the opposite is observed. The evolution of this kind of behaviour as a function of age is quite remarkable. From the age of 3 months these tendencies are reversed: the baby exerts more squeeze–release pressures on hard objects than on soft objects.

We have presented these results in such detail because to our knowledge they are the only ones which compare the performances obtained in both modes of exploration at such early ages. As the results indicate, these modes of exploration exhibit very real specificities from birth. However, this experiment does not tell us whether babies are capable of extracting and processing information about substances, and thus of discriminating between the properties of the objects explored. In fact, the presence of different pressure patterns may be due to the solid or pliable nature of the object, and the oral or manual systems of reception. It reveals a mechanical adaptation of the sensory receptors as a function of the properties of the object. It is therefore this ability to adapt to the constraints imposed by the object on the mobilized system of information pick-up which has been studied, not the detection of relevant information for object-directed activity.

Manual information pick-up: intramodal tactile transfer

There are very few studies which demonstrate the apprehension of information about the properties of an object while it is being handled. Nevertheless, an ingenious experiment by Insel (1987) shows that the tactilokinaesthetic activities of the hand in response to a palmar contact stimulus cannot be regarded merely as a reflex reaction. A palm imprint is taken in quick-setting paste which is used as the contact stimulus for the palmar grasp response of neonates (from birth to 5 days old). Then a positive of the obtained imprints is taken in plaster and used to describe the response patterns. This subtle analysis reveals, in particular, the thumb's participation in the grasp of all the infants, and a wide diversity of responses with, none the less, a certain intrasubject stability over the course of successive trials. These results run counter to the classic descriptions of the grasp reflex, and reveal that the system is flexible from birth.

Therefore, babies do gain information about objects from holding them. However, we do not know what information is obtained, or what fine discriminations they are capable of making between the properties of objects. The stability of responses from one trial to the next suggests that a habituation which would indicate a system memory does not occur during the presentations. It is this aspect of the problem, however, which has claimed our attention.

If an analogous functioning exists in all the sensory modalities, and notably in the extraction of perceptual invariants, then it is necessary to test the perceptual and discriminatory capacities of touching in order to compare them to those of vision in babies of the same age. However, no procedures existed for testing the tactile knowledge of object properties in the very young baby, although their visual knowledge has been clearly demonstrated.

Cowey and Weikrantz (1975) have invented a situation in which it is possible to obtain touch-to-vision transfer of object shapes in animals by training them in intramodal tactile discrimination. The original aspect of their method lies in finding a direct link between the stimulus, the object of transfer and the reinforcing agent. In the evening, the animal is placed in darkness. Scattered haphazardly around its cage are twenty articles of one shape and twenty articles of another. These articles are made either in edible form with powdered food, or in inedible form with a mixture of powdered food and sand. All the articles of one shape are edible, while those of the other shape are not. For some subjects the shapes are reversed. In the morning the experimenters make a note of what has not been eaten, and the presentation is repeated on five consecutive nights without the animals being able to see the shapes in question. The only test takes place on the morning of the fifth day: it consists of visually presenting the animal with one article of each shape, and noting which one it chooses first. The entire procedure is then repeated with another pair of shapes, using the same chronology as before. Out of sixty pairings, the authors note that at the test stage the edible objects are chosen in two out of three cases. They conclude from this that a touch-to-vision transfer of the shape of objects is present in higher primates.

An almost identical procedure has been used to attempt to test the haptic memory of babies over 6 months of age (Gottfried and Rose, 1980; Soroka, Corter and Abramovitch, 1979). These studies show that at 10 and 12 months of age respectively, infants are able to discriminate the shape of objects haptically without visual control. The subjects are plunged into darkness and filmed with an infrared camera. The principle of the technique lies in familiarizing the infant with a number of objects in an initial phase, then mixing the familiar objects with new ones in a test phase and noting the differences in exploration times.

Our research on babies under 6 months old differs from that of Cowey and Weikrantz (1975) by separating the discriminatory learning phase from the intermodal phase, and uses a procedure applicable to both modalities which was not possible in the research undertaken by Soroka *et al.* (1979) or Gottfried and Rose (1980). The habituation procedure followed by the reaction to new shapes appeared to be the most suitable approach. We tested both the monomanual and the bimanual possibilities of object exploration.

Monomanual exploration

Manipulation, habituation and discrimination. As far as we know, the habituation procedure, used extensively in connection with vision, has never been employed in the tactile modality without visual control. Willatts (1983), however, has noted that tactile manipulation time decreases in a sequence of object explorations in both modalities at once. A precondition for the study of transfer is that the babies do not visually control their tactile exploration.

We have therefore adapted the situation of visual habituation. The baby is seated in a baby chair facing a white screen. A hole pierced in the panel makes it possible to film the baby's face and hands. One side of a large white cloth bib is tied round the baby's neck; the other is attached to the screen, preventing the baby from seeing his/her hands and the object, but allowing complete freedom of exploration (Streri and Pêcheux, 1986*a*) (see Figure 3.1).

The familiarization period consists of repeatedly placing the same object in the baby's hand. The trial is deemed to begin as soon as the baby grips the object, and to end when he/she drops it. It is thus an infant-controlled procedure (Horowitz, Paden, Bhana and Self, 1972). Presentation of the object ceases when object holding-times have decreased by 50 per cent in relation to those of the first two trials, which are taken as the reference times (an adaptation of the habituation criterion as defined by Cohen, (1973)), in which case haptic habituation is observed. The test phase for discrimination consists of presenting the baby with a new object once or twice. A significant difference between the mean times of holding the new object in test trials compared with the mean times of the last two trials in the habituation phase indicates a haptic discrimination between the two objects on the baby's part. For the study of visual discriminatory ability, we have adopted the infant-controlled procedure which has been standard practice ever since Horowitz *et al.* (1972) demonstrated its advantages. A visual trial begins when the baby looks at the stimulus and ends when he/she turns away for a period of at least one second.

There is some advantage in using the same procedures for both visual and haptic presentation. It becomes possible to compare the way in which information about the same objects is extracted and processed, notably in the case of parameters such as exploration time, number of trials until fulfilment of the criteria, habituation profiles, and so on (Streri and Pêcheux, 1986*a*). The drawback of this procedure is that it requires a control group who undergo two additional trials in the habituation phase instead of trials with the new object. This is necessary in order to confirm that the increase in exploration time is indeed due to the awareness of a new object and not to a chance increase in the times of the habituation phase.

a

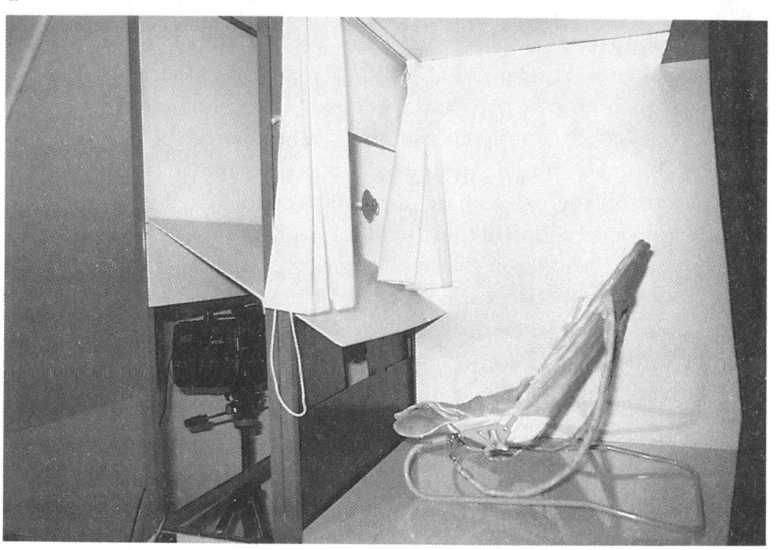

b

Figure 3.1 Apparatus used in the intermodal transfer trials. (a) Tactile manipulation of objects without visual control (b) Visual presentation of objects.
(*Source*: Streri and Pêcheux, 1986*a*)

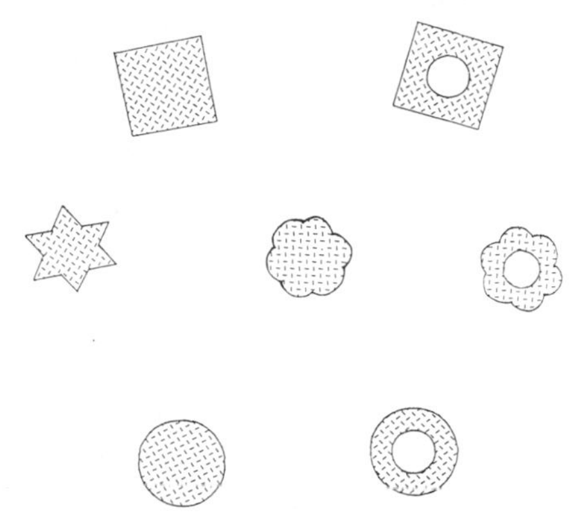

Figure 3.2 Shapes of the objects used in experiments on intermodal transfer.
(*Sources*: Streri, 1987*a*; Streri and Milhet, 1988; Streri and Pêcheux, 1986*b*)

Therefore, the test trials of the experimental group have been compared with the post-habituation trials of the control group (see Bertenthal, Haith and Campos, 1983).

The objects used were 45 millimetres in size, and could easily be held in the baby's hand. The characteristics of the study objects varied – either rectilinear or curvilinear; some with a hole in, others unpierced (see Figure 3.2). As we observed in Chapter 2, manual lateralization emerges very early, and we therefore concentrated our tests on the right, most adept hand. These studies have been conducted with two age groups: at 2 months (Streri, 1987*a*), the age at which a decline in the activity of reaching for a visual object is observed, and at 5 months, at the time of vision–prehension recoordination (Lécuyer and Streri, 1986; Streri and Pêcheux, 1986*a*, *b*).

The results show that 5-month-old babies, like 2-month-olds, do exhibit tactile habituation to the objects presented to them. They hold them for progressively shorter times during successive presentations. Moreover, they react to novelty, holding on to an unfamiliar object for longer. Similar results have been obtained for vision at the same ages and using the same objects.

Table 3.1 Haptic exploration of objects

	2 months	4–5 months	5 months
Mean of first 2 trials	22.3 s	19.2 s	18.5 s
Number of trials	6.4	6.6	7.4
Total exploration time	91.1 s	90.8 s	112.1 s

Comparison of haptic habituation criteria, depending on age and in three experiments. s = seconds.
Sources: Lécuyer and Streri, 1986; Streri, 1987*a*; Streri and Pêcheux, 1986*a*.

These results are important for three reasons. On a technical level, they demonstrate for the first time that the tactile modality lends itself just as well as the visual modality to the habituation technique followed by a test for reaction to novelty. Secondly, the decrease in object holding-times provides evidence of manual tactile recognition, and therefore of a system memory. Thus babies extract information when they explore – or, indeed, even grasp – an object. Finally, at the ages researched, the tactile modality possesses the same capacities for recording information and discriminating between different shapes as the visual modality.

We have compared the data obtained for three parameters of haptic habituation, at 2 and 5 months of age, in three experiments using monomanual trials (Lécuyer and Streri, 1986; Streri and Pêcheux, 1986*a*; Streri, 1987*a*). There is no significant difference between the three experiments – in the mean times of the first two trials, in the number of trials before fulfilment of the habituation criterion, or in the total exploration times (see Table 3.1). We should point out that the habituation criterion adopted in Streri and Pêcheux's research (1986*a*) is not quite the same as that employed in Lécuyer and Streri's (1986). This difference does not affect the overall results at all. Thus no evolution of the characteristics of tactile habituation has been observed as a function of age. It is possible, however, that the parameters observed are not relevant indicators of such a development, and that a qualitative analysis is necessary.

The exploration patterns are difficult to analyze qualitatively, since the video recordings do not always allow a detailed picture of the hand during fine exploration of the object. The periods during which the baby grips the object tightly are important during the habituation trials. However, as no polygraphic recordings of the grasps of the object have been taken (Rochat, 1985, 1987), it is difficult to determine whether these grasps are simply reflex-type grasp reactions, or whether the baby is sometimes exerting active, controlled and differentiated pressure on the object. It is important, however, to point out the existence of exploratory behaviour during the habituation sequence at both ages and in all three experiments.

We have observed fine prehensile activity in 5-month-old babies. This behaviour consists of: running fingers and thumb over objects; attempts – sometimes successful – to pass the object from one hand to the other; carrying the object to the mouth or attempting to look at it, even through an opaque screen; frequent opening and closing of the hand; and reactions of suddenly avoiding or rejecting the object. Avoiding reactions are numerous at the start of habituation, but these short trials have not been taken into consideration since they last for less than one second. At the end of the habituation phase they turn into reactions which can legitimately be termed rejection of the object. These are less sudden, and occur after several seconds of holding the object.

We have observed the same response patterns at 2–3 months of age, with a few exceptions. These patterns are less frequent. The attempts to pass an object from one hand to the other are rare, as is carrying the object to the mouth or into view. Avoiding reactions are also infrequent, and it often happens that babies simply put the object down, whether on to themselves or on to the floor. Although these analyses do not run counter to Twitchell's descriptions (1970), they indicate that intentional manipulation without visual control does exist in the baby, and that holding an object cannot be regarded as a mere reflex.

Manipulation and laterality. The reflex of grasping an object appears to occur most often on the right. Young *et al.* (1983) point out that in the majority of the research analyzed the grasp reflex is at its strongest, and lasts for longer, when it is the right hand which receives the stimulus. Trehub *et al.* (1983) researched the intensity of the grasp reflex in premature babies and in full-term babies, and found a clear difference in the strength of the right-hand reflex in premature babies of 32 weeks from conception, although they point out that the responses during trials were not consistent. In contrast, Strauss (1982) failed to find a (left or right) manual preference in the duration of holding an object in 1-to-5-day-old neonates or in 1-to-4-month-old babies.

In a haptic habituation sequence without visual control, 2-month-old babies handle the object with the right hand for an average of 91 seconds (Streri, 1987*a*). This period does not appear to develop as a function of age, since it is about the same at 5 months (Streri and Pêcheux, 1986*a*). Hawn and Harris (1983) have made a systematic study of the duration of object holding in the left hand and in the right hand at the same ages. The average duration of two object-holding trials in the right hand is significantly longer than with the left hand. This result confirms those obtained by Caplan and Kinsbourne (1976) and Petrie and Peters (1980). In contrast, Hawn and Harris (1983) observe an increase in this duration as a function of age, a result which we have been unable to replicate. In their research, 2-month-old babies hold the object in their hands for 54 seconds. This period increases to 110 seconds at 5 months of age. The difference between the durations obtained in our experiments (22·3 s and 19·2 s respectively for the first two trials (see Table 3.1)) and those of Hawn and Harris (1983) is probably due to the difference in the procedures and material employed. In our experiments, the object was held without visual control. The screen no doubt hindered the 5-month-old babies, if not the 2-month-olds. Nevertheless, the right hand is clearly favoured for holding objects from the age of 2 months onwards. This right-hand preference is confirmed in older babies. The developmental research undertaken by Michel *et al.* (1986) demonstrates that 6-month-old babies tend to use the right hand for handling objects. The preference shown in this activity appears to be more marked in girls than in boys.

Bimanual exploration

Exploration, habituation and discrimination. A number of studies have made it possible to observe the bimanual exploratory behaviour of 4-month-old babies deprived of visual control (Milhet, 1989; Streri and Spelke, 1988, 1989). With the exception of a few variations (base trials for the calculation of criteria), the habituation situation employs the procedure adopted by Streri (1987*a*) and Streri and Pêcheux (1986*a*). A habituation trial begins when the baby grasps the object with both hands and ends when he/she releases it with one or both

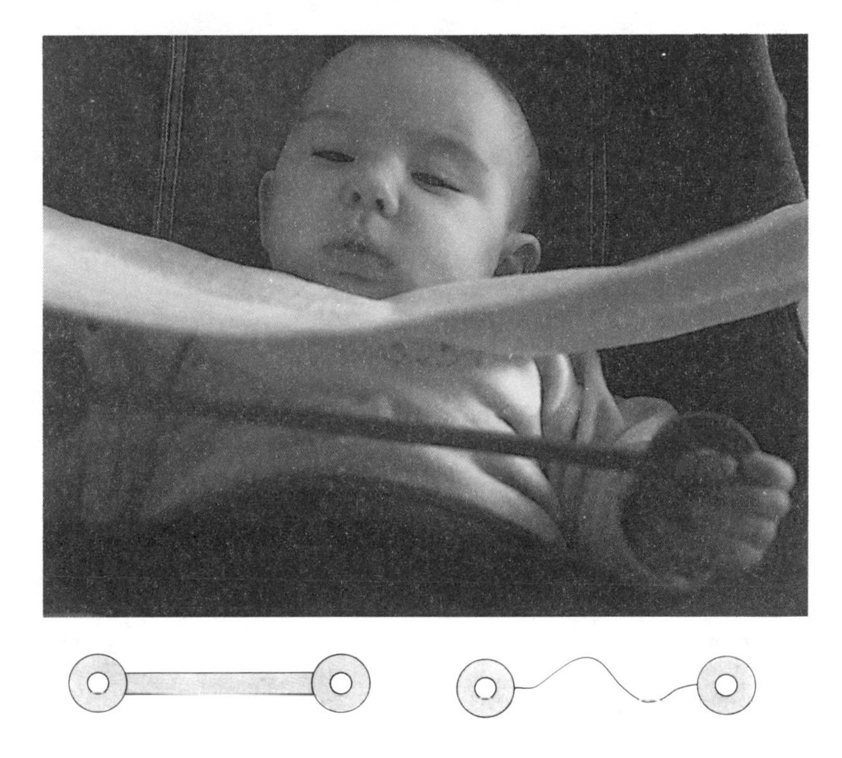

Figure 3.3 Situation and material used in bimanual exploration. *(Source*: Streri and Spelke, 1988).

hands. In the test phase, the familiar object and a new object are presented alternately over six trials. In order to test intramodal haptic discrimination, the difference between the times of the three test trials with the familiar object and the three test trials with the new object is compared. If the familiar object is held for a shorter time than the new object, the babies are assumed to have discriminated between them.

In Streri and Spelke's research (1988), the babies were given a ring display to manipulate. This consisted of two identical rings connected by either a flexible link (an elastic band) or a rigid link (a bar). The rings were placed in each of the baby's hands in such a way that the baby could not feel the connecting link (see Figure 3.3). After

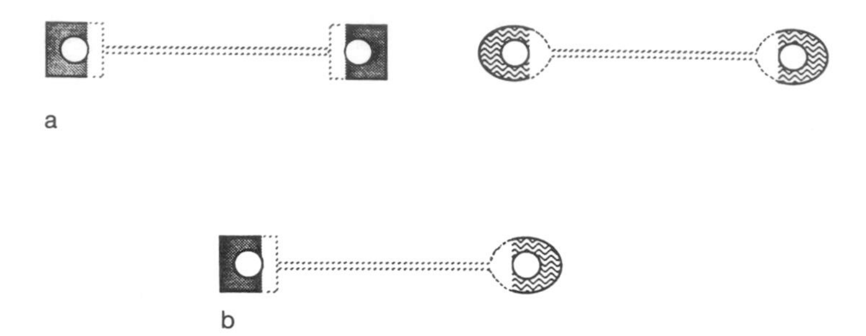

Figure 3.4 Material used in Streri and Spelke's experiment (1989). (a) Symmetrical assembly (b) Asymmetrical assembly.

habituation to one display, the babies explore the new object for longer than the familiar one during the test phase. In a second experiment (Streri and Spelke, 1989), the objects held in the hands are linked by a rigid band. However, they are either identical (symmetrical assembly: two squares with a hole in them or two foam-rubber rings) or different in shape, texture, weight and material (asymmetrical assembly) (see Figure 3.4). The results indicate discrimination between assemblies which have the same type of connecting link.

Finally, we have used a similar procedure to confirm Milhet's observations (1989) that babies aged 4 months can distinguish one assembly, on which the objects to be handled are of an identical weight, from another with objects of different weights.

The duration of bimanual exploration of objects is generally very long at 4 months of age, lasting between 2 and 2·5 minutes depending on the experiment. Exploration of an object using both hands appears to require more time than one-handed manipulation. For example, in Streri and Spelke's experiment (1988), the objects presented to both the babies' hands are the same shape at each end, but the connection is either flexible or rigid. Exploration of the whole display thus requires not only manipulation of its contours but also activity which involves both arms and both hands acting together. The role of motor ability and proprioception in this experiment is important. Analysis of the video recordings indicates that there is a difference in the patterns of exploratory movement associated with the different types of links, but no difference in the patterns associated with symmetrical and asymmetrical objects with the same link types (Streri and Spelke, 1989).

Bimanual exploration and laterality. Hawn and Harris (1983) placed identical objects into both hands of 2- and 5-month-old babies to test their hold durations. In general, overall times were greater than those in the monomanual condition for babies of both 5 months and 2 months. In contrast, the behaviour of releasing the object from the left hand more quickly than from the right hand is significant only in the 5-month-olds.

In our experiments on the bimanual exploration of objects (Streri and Spelke, 1988), we also noted which hand was the first to release the ring for both types of display connection, flexible and rigid. The results show that 4-month-old babies drop the object from the right hand in 37 per cent of the observations, from the left hand in 44 per cent, and from both hands at the same time in 11 per cent. The difference between left-hand and right-hand releases is not significant. Left-hand releases occur slightly more frequently when the connection is flexible, but the results are similar when the connection is rigid.

It appears, on the other hand, that the weight of the objects reveals a difference between the competent and less competent hand. In a tactile habituation sequence without visual control, Milhet and I (Streri and Milhet, 1992) presented 4-month-old babies with objects of the same shape, and with weights which were either the same or different. In this experiment, the heavier object was presented to the left hand of some subjects and to the right hand of others. With objects of the same weight, we observed that the object was released more frequently by the left hand (70 per cent). With the differently weighted objects, this percentage increased when the heavier object was given to the left hand (84 per cent). Thus it appears that the right hand is the more efficient for holding a heavy object. Moreover, the profiles of the habituation curves are different, and match those defined by Bornstein (1985). When the weights are the same, a regular, falling, exponential curve is observed. When the heavy object is in the right hand, the duration of the trials is short at the beginning of habituation, then gradually rises, only to fall again until the criterion for habituation is reached. This is an 'increasing–decreasing' type of curve. The profile of the curve is 'fluctuating', or 'sawtoothed', when the heavy object for exploration is in the left hand.

However, manual laterality is not evident solely in the haptic exploration of the weight of objects. One of the differences between the hands which is most often mentioned is that the right hand appears to specialize in fine, sequential exploration of objects, since it is controlled by the left hemisphere. It seems that this hemisphere is involved in the processing of information which stems from events that develop sequentially. The left hand, in contrast, would appear to excel in overall spatial activities, such as gross motor movements.

Mebert (1983) has tested this hypothesis by observing babies aged 4, 6, 8 and 10 months exploring different toys. She defines eleven categories of exploration: power grasp, precision grasp, fine motor activity of the fingers and hand, gross motor activity involving the whole arm, bringing the object to the mouth, removing it from the mouth, approach to the object, contact with the object but without holding or handling it, transferring the object from one hand to the other, releasing the object and, finally, just resting the hand on the table.

While power grasps decrease as a function of age, precision grasps and transferring the object from one hand to the other increase. The author observes only one effect of laterality: in all the age groups, the right hand is more often activated for fine exploration of objects than the left hand. In the other activities, both hands are involved with the same frequency in gross movements, even if the right hand appears to be more active than the left.

Mono- or bimanual tactile exploration is not limited to the simple holding of the object but involves a range of activity, from precision grasps and fine exploration with the fingers to more global behaviour involving the whole of the upper limbs. If the perceptual and discriminatory possibilities of the hand are thus confirmed by our experiments, how, then, does the hand succeed in coordinating this ability, which is present from a very early age (from at least 2 months), with the function of carrying the object, which will be its dominant function when prehension–vision coordination occurs? Do the two functions interfere with each other?

Manipulation and carrying of objects: two incompatible activities?

Hatwell's theory (1987) provides a good summary of this incompatibility of behaviour. Perception and motor activity are closely linked in the tactile modality. When the movement made by arm and hand has a particular goal, the perceptual functioning is absolutely necessary for realization of this goal. In the competition between the two functions of the hand – for perception and for carrying – it is very often the second function which predominates among children of pre-school and school age (Hatwell, 1981, 1987). We have attempted to demonstrate that this is also true in babies of 5–6 months when prehension–vision coordination is actively practised (Streri and Pineau, 1988).

This study was composed of two experiments which were undertaken without visual control and entirely in the tactile mode. The first consisted of testing the baby's tactile ability to discriminate between a sphere and a cube. The situation and procedure employed were much the same as in the previous experiments on monomanual exploration of objects (Streri, 1987*a*; Streri and Pêcheux, 1986*a*). The experiment comprised a habituation phase and a discrimination test phase. The aim of the second experiment was to test how actions performed by babies affect their manual perceptual capacities. This also was conducted without visual control.

The object is a musical box. The babies are presented with this box, which has had its sound mechanism disabled so that the music does not attract their attention. The infants are expected to wind the handle of the box in a circular movement in eight trials of 10 seconds each (the average time obtained in the habituation phase of the first experiment). The end of the handle consists of either a sphere or a cube, which are identical to those used in the first experiment (see Figure 3.5). The experimenter helps the babies by placing the end of the handle (the cube or sphere) in their hands, and turning it. In doing this, the experimenter holds the babies' hands very lightly allowing them complete freedom of manipulation (see Figure 3.5 again). The test phase is identical in both experiments: haptic presentation of a cube and a sphere alternately for six trials.

The results of the first experiment show that tactile intramodal

Figure 3.5 Material used for tactile exploration without visual control. (*Source*: Streri and Pineau, 1988)

discrimination occurs. The sphere and the cube are clearly differentiated. In the test phase of the second situation, in contrast, the babies do not recognize the object which was on the end of the handle in the learning phase. This is the first time haptic intramodal discrimination has not been obtained in babies of this age. This experiment clearly demonstrates that movement activity interferes with the perceptual capacities of the hand. The baby cannot pay attention to both the activity of turning the mechanism and the properties of the held object.

This result appears to be incompatible with those obtained by Streri and Spelke (1989). Let us recall that in this situation the objects placed in the hands and connected by a rigid bar are either identical (symmetrical assembly) or completely different (asymmetrical assembly). At the time of exploration, the movements required by this type of connection are difficult and require the cooperative activity of both arms, which is hardly natural at this age. It might be thought that when practising exploratory movements on the whole assembly the babies would not be sensitive to the properties of the objects they have in their hands. However, the results clearly demonstrate that despite the constraints imposed by the assembly, the babies are capable of discriminating between an assembly whose ends are the same and another whose ends are different. Therefore, the hand's perceptual ability to pick up information is not hindered by all types of movement. In Streri and Pineau's experiment (1988), the turning of the handle imposes a definite circular movement in a particular direction on the baby's arm. This constraint is very strong, and hinders the apprehension of sufficient information concerning the properties of the held object. In order to turn the handle, it is no doubt necessary for the baby to grip the end of it very tightly. This would prevent any exploration and, therefore, differentiation between sphere and cube. This constraint is much weaker in Streri and Spelke's experiment (1989). While the rigid connecting bar reduces the variety of possible exploratory movements, it does not definitively impose any particular movement (see Streri, 1988*b*).

While within the visual system the motor aspect works towards the improved reception of sensory input, in the manual system motor functioning can, under certain circumstances, inhibit the perceptual function.

Vision/touch analogies but tactile specificity

What emerges from all these experiments is that, probably from birth onwards, the apprehension of information by the tactile system is equally assured in both its oral and its manual form. These two modes of pick-up collect the same information and function in a similar manner. However, the status of the buccal cavity will alter as a function of age. While it is now accepted that the oral exploration of objects takes place at birth, the mouth becomes a goal to which the hand carries objects.

Our experiments have demonstrated that from the age of 2 months manual tactile functioning is similar to that of vision. Babies are able to pick up information, and to discriminate between the shapes of the objects they manipulate. This result is important in that a similarity of functioning between the modalities makes intermodal relations between vision and touch possible at a very early age.

The tactile system, however, possesses specificities which are not shared by the visual system. Babies have to learn to control their grasp and avoid reflexes in order to promote the fine manual exploration of objects. Nevertheless, the reflex component does not appear to hinder information pick-up. The baby can extract certain information about the object simply by grasping it. This information is less precise than that provided by fine exploration, but it is information none the less. The participation of active arm movements in an attempt to explore the object does not in any way prevent the fine manipulation of objects. In contrast, a defined movement which is imposed by the situation, such as turning the handle on a musical box, hinders exploration and the apprehension of information concerning the properties of objects. Thus we can observe the existence of an interference between the baby's practical and perceptual actions on an object. Everything happens as if haptic perception is subordinate to the subject's practical action. There are thus complex interdependencies between these two functions of the hand, exploration and practical action, which must be taken into account in the young infant's behavioural development. Furthermore, the existence of two hands which are symmetrical from a physical point of view but capable of acting independently adds to the complexity of information gathering by the system. This division of labour – which, at a very early age, is accompanied by specialization and by the dominance of one of the hands – is what makes the haptic system unique, and increases its specificity. In the visual system, the opposite is the case. The dominance of one eye over the other increases retinal disparity and contributes to the perception of depth in the necessary fusion of the two images. Poorly regulated binocular convergence, such as often exists in the first few months after birth, makes perception blurred. Left and right visual systems are pathologically independent.

It has thus been demonstrated that similar mechanisms exist in the visual and haptic processing of sensory information. The conditions for establishing a perceptual unity of information received via the two sensory modalities seem to be fulfilled. It would not appear justifiable, however, to conclude from this that the systems are undifferentiated at birth. Our experiments have shown that the tactile system may operate independently of the visual system. However, similar functioning of the modalities does not necessarily mean that the quality of perceptual performance is the same. The mainly biological constraints at the beginning of the baby's life render this second conjecture implausible.

Chapter 4

The perceptual relations between vision and touch

Intermodal relations

The methodological approach

Studies which analyze the nature of the relations between the sensory modalities adapt a number of experimental procedures which have proved their worth in the study of the perceptual mechanisms of vision and audition (see Gottlieb and Krasnegor, 1985). Nevertheless, the specificity of their methodology lies in the fact that a single paradigm can account for the subject's ability to process information extracted via different modalities. Thus we pass from the study of unimodal perception to that of bimodal and even multimodal perception.

Rose and Ruff (1987) describe two outlines of the conditions for relating the information gained through different sensory modalities.

1. The objects or events are perceived simultaneously by the two modalities. It is necessary for us to study the existence and nature of any link between them. The subject must establish a correspondence between the information about the objects which is simultaneously apprehended via two sensory systems.
2. The data are gathered by the two modalities successively. When the second modality is stimulated, the subject recognizes the

information which was gathered about the objects or events in the first modality.

It is on the basis of these outlines that we shall look at the different situations employed in studies of the relation between touch and vision. The choice of procedure depends on several factors: the age of the subjects, the sensory systems being studied, the type of information to which the receptors are sensitive, the possibility of information being accessed by more than one system at once and, in some research, the theoretical viewpoint adopted.

Simultaneous bimodal apprehension of information

Under this heading we shall restrict our investigation to a specific type of intermodal exploration: simultaneous bimodal exploration. What interests us is the process through which information is gained by the two modalities, and the resulting intermodal relationship. The second half of this chapter will be devoted to the situation of simultaneous visual and manual – therefore bimodal – exploration of the same object; here manual exploration strategies are the particular subject of analysis (see below: Multimodal Relations).

When two modalities are stimulated at once, a number of possible cases arise.

1. The stimulation of one modality affects the functioning of the other. Here, it is a matter not of coordination of the sensory modalities but of 'elementary cross-modal interaction' (Hatwell, 1981, 1986). For example, the brightness of a room can affect the way we listen to music. Synaesthesia is a good illustration of this interaction.
2. The types of information are different in nature, but in order for the situation to be plausible they must be synchronized and produced in one place, as in the presentation of sound-emitting objects. Here – as opposed to situation (1) – coordination between sensory modalities is required if we are to understand the situation.
3. The perceptual systems have access to the same object-specifying properties. Thus it is the ability to match objects in one or more of the dimensions perceived by both modalities which is being tested.

4. The perceptual systems have access to different information, but its coordination leads to perceptuo–cognitive conflict. It is the subject's ability to react to this conflict which is tested, and provides proof of intermodal integration.

All these situations present individuals with the necessity of simultaneously relating the information which different sensory channels make available to them. They may therefore appear to be simple, since no temporal component is introduced. The difficulty for the experimenter is in finding relevant indicators which provide evidence that a relation is being established between the modalities. There is a wide variety of these indicators, depending on the experimental situations constructed. Only situations (3) and (4) test the matching of touch and vision.

Vision and touch have simultaneous access to the same properties: the information is concordant

Where vision and touch have access to identical properties of space between places and objects, these properties are said to be amodal – that is, they are not specific to any one modality. Thus if the observing subjects deem the shape of the object they are handling to be identical to that of the object they see, they are matching the information regarding this dimension of the object, and its unity of shape is assured. This situation may seem simple, since it does not involve the storage of information and its later recognition. We might suppose that it can be realized by animals whose cognitive capacities for intermodal transfer are as yet poorly understood. There are some difficulties which have yet to be overcome.

Studies of animals. Studies of animals differ from studies which investigate the human baby. The problem is not lack of language, which is common to both, but the tasks involved. In babies, the behaviour elicited by the tasks forms part of their natural repertoire of responses. In studying animals, on the other hand, it is necessary to teach the subject a form of response which can be decoded by the human experimenter. Without this prior training we do not know any means of interrogating the animal about its own capacities. In addition, the experiments usually have to be conducted over a very long period of time – this can sometimes extend over several months.

In the study of intermodal relationships in the great apes, transfer of training situations have long been used, but with very little success (see Hatwell, 1981).

The situation of intermodal matching has proved more fruitful. Davenport and Rogers (1970) and Davenport *et al.* (1973, 1975) attempted to discover whether the great apes treat the objects they simultaneously see and manipulate as equivalent. The experiment was conducted in two stages: a long training phase during which the experimenters taught the subjects how to respond to the situation, followed by a test phase in which the response was generalized to objects which were different from those used in the preceding phase.

The experimental situation and apparatus are relatively simple. They differ depending on whether the control object for comparison is perceived visually or tactually. In the first situation (intermodal matching from vision to touch) the subject can see one object through a transparent window while at the same time manipulating two objects, one in each hand, of which one is identical to the visual object and the other is not. These objects are fixed at either side of the window; the animal cannot see them, but can handle them with complete freedom. The animal has to compare what it perceives visually about the control object with what it perceives about the different objects for haptic comparison. The equivalence response consists of pulling on the haptic object which is identical to the visual one. Good responses receive positive reinforcement. In the second situation (intermodal matching from touch to vision) the subject feels a control object held in front of it, but cannot see it. To the subject's left and right, the experimenter presents two objects for comparison behind a transparent window. One is identical to the felt object; the other is different. They are visible to the subject, but cannot be touched. The response consists of pressing the window showing the comparison object which is identical to the felt control object. Again, good responses receive positive reinforcement.

The training period for establishing the response which can be interpreted as satisfying the instruction 'Show me the two identical objects' takes place over several weeks. The experimenters require a performance from the subjects which is equal to or greater than 90 per cent correct responses, and only those subjects achieving this result take part in the test phase. This consists of a single trial using different objects to those employed in the learning stage. If the frequency of correct matching responses is significantly different to that which would be obtained by a randomly responding subject, the indication is that coordination between the modalities does occur. Using this procedure – which, though time-consuming, employs simple apparatus and is not dependent on language – the authors have demonstrated that the higher primates are capable of performing intermodal matching on the basis of both visual and tactile stimuli. In our work with 2-month-old babies we have used a similar system in order to eliminate the difficulties inherent in procedures in which items of information are presented successively – namely, the memorization and recognition of information. However, the constraints and modes of response are not comparable, and it is therefore justifiable to ask whether it is the same problem that is being dealt with.

Studies of the human baby. In order to demonstrate that a mechanism which is common to touch and vision is present in 2-month-old babies, we (Streri and Milhet, 1988) employed an intermodal matching situation which we judged would be simpler for babies of this age than the one used earlier (Streri, 1987*a*).

One of the difficulties with studying babies is that all their responses may not be available at the time of the experiment, and it is necessary to elicit them within the spatio–temporal dimensions which can be tolerated by the infant.

We used the apparatus employed by Streri (1987*a*) (see Figure 3.1, p.102 above) to elicit intermodal matching between touch and vision. The experimenter draws the babies' attention to two things at once: one object presented within their visual field, another placed in one of their hands (generally the right). The felt object is either the same shape or a different shape to the one presented visually. Each simultaneous presentation trial lasts for 50 seconds and several trials are conducted with each baby. All the babies are confronted with both situations: the one in which the two objects are identical and the one in which they are different. Thus the length of the trials is fixed and not controlled by the infant, unlike the experiments in haptic habituation conducted with the same age group (Streri, 1987*a*). A control group is formed in which the subjects are stimulated through only one modality. Each baby is successively presented with a visual object and a tactile object. The duration of each presentation trial is also 50 seconds. The reactions of the babies in both groups are recorded. Among the behavioural indicators observed, looking away or dropping the object are the modes of response which best reveal matching behaviour. In the experimental group, a difference of reaction when the objects presented are of the same shape and when they are different provides evidence that infants can (1) simultaneously extract information about two objects, one they can see and the other they hold in their hands; (2) compare at least one of their properties, that of shape; and (3) discriminate between the two conditions of object presentation: same-shape objects and different-shape objects.

In the experimental group, the results indicate that the babies turn away or drop the object more often when the objects are identical in shape than when they are different. The frequency of this behaviour in each situation is compared with that of the control group. The performances differ significantly only with the presentation of different objects. These two results provide clear evidence of the 2-month-old baby's ability to perform intermodal matching, and to react to redundant information. There is therefore a definite link between the sensory modalities concerned. However, what happens when the information is discordant – that is to say, when the babies see an object of a particular shape but haptically perceive the same object as having a different shape?

The perceptual systems access the same properties simultaneously: the information is discordant

Situations in which visual and tactile information is contradictory were first created for research on the adult in order to observe how visual perception of an object seen through a distorting lens leads to erroneous haptic perception of it (Rock and Victor, 1964). Without seeing their hands, the subjects handle an object whose size is different from the one they see. They then have to point out or choose from several other objects the one which they think they have just held. The results show a strong visual predominance, and the researchers refer to this as the effect of a visual 'capture' of tactile perception. Attempts to obtain a haptic 'capture' despite visual distortion proved unsuccessful (see Hatwell, 1981, 1986). Visual dominance appears to manifest itself in situations of perceptual conflict.

In babies, the emotional reactions of surprise and crying in conditions of perceptual conflict are indicative of coordination between the sensory modalities. Using an ingenious device involving reflective mirrors, Bushnell (1982) has subjected babies aged 8, 9·5 and 11 months to two conditions of perceptual conflict: one resembles presentation of a virtual object; in the other a seen object and a manipulated object occupy the same space but differ in size, shape and texture (a fur-covered cylinder and a smooth plastic object with protrusions). The babies are unable to see their hands during exploration. As well as noting their emotional reactions, the author recorded the total durations of visual and tactile exploration and compared them with those of a control group who undergo the experiment with the same apparatus but for whom the information is concordant. She concludes from the absence of behavioural differences between the two groups of 8 months of age, and from the lack of any emotional reaction at this age, that babies do not detect the differences between visual and haptic information, and that they are unable to integrate visual space with tactile space. From 9·5 months of age, in contrast, both the babies' emotional and exploratory behaviour indicate the existence of such integration. Bushnell notes, however, that 17 of the 33 8-month-old babies refused to take part in the experiment, while only one out of 17 11-month-olds refused. Might this perhaps indicate a negative reaction to the conflict situation? Although the experiment does not include the situation of visual or haptic intramodal discrimination, it hardly seems probable that the 8-month-old babies would not have differentiated between the two objects in one or other of the modalities, given that the objects contrasted to such an extent in all their attributes. It is possible that in these babies what we are witnessing is a 'visual capture' of the kind which has often been observed in adults.

The situations we have just described rely on the same principle. The individual apprehends the information coming through different sensory channels at the same time. Adaptive behaviour on the subject's part reveals good integration of the information. As we have seen, these intermodal matching situations are very heterogeneous, varying with the problem to be studied and the population to be examined. Nevertheless, except in the perceptual conflict experiments, they do reveal the existence of simple mechanisms for relating information. When items of information are apprehended successively by the subject, the perceptual and cognitive capacities required for good integration of the information appear to be more complex.

Successive bimodal apprehension of information (intermodal transfer)

The transfer of information specifying the properties of an object from one modality to another demands at least three processes: (1) the information must be extracted by the subject in the first modality; (2) it must be memorized; (3) it must be compared to the information presented in the second modality. This comparison may or may not lead to recognition of the object familiarized with in the first modality. It is in the context of situations of intermodal transfer that researchers have most often raised the question of the possible existence of a mediator or learned code for translating the information sourced through one sensory channel in order for it to be received by a second sensory channel (Bryant, 1974). The early existence of intermodal relations has weakened the relevance of this hypothesis to babies.

The major paradigms employed in investigating intermodal transfer are the paired comparison method (with a variant, the preferential choice technique) and the habituation procedure.

After the ingenious experiment conducted in three stages by Bryant, Jones, Claxton and Perkins (1972), the transfer situations used have classically comprised two stages. The work of Bryant *et al.* (1972) consisted of two experiments. The aim of the first, discrimination between objects, was to demonstrate that babies between 6 and 12 months of age prefer to grasp and manipulate those objects which make a noise when shaken than those which do not. In the second experiment, intermodal transfer, the babies were visually presented with two differently shaped objects which were beyond their reach. In a second phase, one of the objects was presented to the babies behind a screen, where they could manipulate it but not see it. This object made a noise when shaken. Finally, in the third stage, the manipulated, sound-emitting object was presented as in phase 1 at the same time as the other, non-sound-emitting object, and the babies' choice was recorded. The results obtained revealed a partial transfer (for one of the two object pairings) from touch to vision. Nevertheless, the experimental procedure was flawed by important methodological imperfections. The absence of a situation permitting intramodal haptic discrimination means that the lack of a transfer of information concerning one of the two pairs of objects cannot be interpreted. The arrangement of the experiment in three phases – visual–haptic–visual – complicates the interpretation of the results. Phase 1 could have affected the manipulation occurring in phase 2 in such a way that the results of phase 3 (test of transfer phase) remain ambiguous.

The two-stage paradigms produce clearer results. The first stage consists of familiarizing the baby with an object in one modality. It is during this period that information is gathered and memorized. The second stage involves another modality. The infant is simultaneously presented with two objects, the familiar one and a new one, and it is recognition of the familiar object or nonrecognition of the other one which is tested.

In situations of intermodal transfer, researchers rely on two natural forms of behaviour in babies. First, they become habituated to or familiar with an object which they then regard with less interest as soon as they recognize it; secondly, they react to the presentation of a new object by paying greater attention to it. We shall not discuss the theoretical foundations of this behaviour here (see Lécuyer, 1987). If, however, after getting used to an object in one modality, babies then spend more time exploring a new object rather than the familiar one in another modality, we conclude that they have generalized their habituation to the familiar object, and have therefore recognized it.

The technique known as the 'paired comparison' method

Gottfried, Rose and Bridger (1977) used this procedure for the first time in order to discover whether touch–vision transfer of the shape of objects is possible in 1-year-old infants. The experimenter places an object into the hand of the baby, who is prevented from seeing it. After a fixed 30-second period of haptic familiarization, the baby is visually presented with the familiar object alongside a new object for a period of 20 seconds. The fixation times for each object are measured, and the object the baby chooses first is noted. The percentage fixation time for the new object is calculated as follows: $A/A + B \times 100$, where A is the new object and B the familiar object.

If the percentage fixation time differs significantly from 50 per cent, the authors conclude that a touch–vision relationship has been observed. Within this paradigm, it hardly matters whether a preference, evaluated by the length of visual fixation time, is shown for the familiar or the new object. What is essential is that a difference in the exploration times of the two objects is observed.

This procedure has been repeated in order to study visual recognition of the shape of manipulated objects in babies aged from 6 months to a year (Gottfried, Rose and Bridger, 1978; Rose, Gottfried and Bridger, 1981*b*; Ruff and Kohler, 1978). This technique can be used to study the transfer of the texture and substance of objects from the oral to the visual modality (Gibson and Walker, 1984; Meltzoff and Borton, 1979). Depending on the experiment, the familiarization times vary from 30 seconds to 90 seconds, and are adapted to the age of the infants. Rose *et al.* (1981*b*) have demonstrated that if the familiarization time is too short, this can affect intermodal transfer.

The reverse transfer – that is, in the vision–touch direction – can be studied using a similar, though not identical, method. In this case, for the tactile recognition phase, the babies are plunged into darkness and an infrared camera is used to record their haptic exploration times of unseen objects presented alongside the objects with which they have already been familiarized in a visual phase (Rose, Gottfried and Bridger, 1981*a*). This procedure has been employed only with 1-year-old babies.

The paired comparisons method does not appear to account adequately for all the phenomena involved in information transfer. First of all, the fixed time allowed to all the babies in the familiarization stage does not take individual differences in haptic exploration into account, and risks being inadequate for some of the babies to gather all the information. For these subjects it is possible that intermodal transfer will not occur. Moreover, the influence of tactile exploration on visual recognition has been the object of many studies, though the reverse process has been studied only rarely. If we are to support the hypothesis of a unity of perceptions, and thus of an amodal code, evidence of an intermodal relation in both directions must be provided.

In the test phase, the drawback of simultaneous presentation of two objects has frequently been pointed out: the risk that the baby – and particularly the very young baby – will look at only one object. This risk can, however, be reduced by reversing the positions of the objects halfway through the visual testing stage. Nevertheless, the authors do not indicate whether this change in the situation might sometimes disturb the baby's visual exploration. Finally, this procedure tests visual discrimination but not haptic discrimination. The majority of studies of intermodal transfer are accompanied by tests of intramodal visual discrimination of the same objects, but rarely by tests of intramodal haptic discrimination. An exception is Rose *et al.*'s study (1981*b*) in which the familiarization phase and the test phase were conducted in the dark. The absence of intermodal transfer may sometimes be interpreted as an absence of differentiation between the object properties in one or other of the tested modalities. An intramodal tactile discrimination without visual control should be obtained in the same way as intramodal visual discrimination is realized (see Chapter 3).

The habituation technique

In order to avoid the drawbacks inherent in the paired comparison technique, it is necessary to use another procedure in which the baby's visual and tactile exploration of objects is not interrupted. This procedure should allow the same technique to be used in the study of intermodal transfer of information both from touch to vision and from vision to touch. The habituation method, using a procedure which is controlled by the infant (Horowitz *et al.*, 1972), appears to be suitable for and to unite all the conditions required for such a study.

Providing evidence of intermodal transfer necessitates the simultaneous fulfilment of three criteria for which the experimental study is conducted successively as follows: after a period of habituation, the infant has to (1) explore the familiar object presented in a different modality for less time than the new object presented in this modality; (2) recognize the familiar object presented in the first modality after presentation of this object in the second modality; and (3) discriminate intramodally between the objects.

Such a procedure has been used with 5-month-olds (Streri and Pêcheux, 1986*b*) and with 2-month-olds (1987*a*). However, this procedure proved unwieldy and costly. On the one hand it necessitated the formation of a control group for comparing the results of the test stage – here, condition (1) – and on the other, the task of remembering information is a hard one for 2-month-old babies. We have therefore adopted a simpler procedure which combines the habituation technique and the paired comparison method which, like Spelke (1985), we have called the preferential choice technique.

The preferential choice technique

This can be distinguished from the paired comparison method in that at the test phase, the new and familiar objects are presented successively, not simultaneously. This method was first adopted by Kellman and Spelke (1983) for studying the baby's visual perceptual abilities. Adapted for studying intermodal transfer, it takes place in two stages: a habituation phase in the same form as the one employed by Streri and Pêcheux (1986*a*, *b*) and Streri (1987*a*) and a test phase. In the test phase, the familiar stimulus and the new stimulus are presented alternately over six trials. If the exploration time for the new object is significantly different from that for the familiar object, we conclude that the familiarization phase has influenced the test phase, and that transfer has occurred. Nevertheless, one methodological precaution is necessary. A control group receives the six alternate presentations of the two objects, but without prior familiarization. The formation of a control group permits us to make sure there is no visual or tactile preference for one of the shapes. Moreover, comparison of the performances of the two groups in the test trials serves to confirm that the difference obtained in the experimental group is indeed due to transfer. This procedure has been tested successfully with 4-month-old babies (Milhet, 1989; Pineau and Streri, 1990; Streri and Spelke, 1988, 1989) and 2-month-old babies (Streri, unpublished manuscript). It can be applied equally well to both touch–vision and vision–touch intermodal transfer.

In this procedure, the subject makes two comparisons. The first is intermodal, between familiarization phase and test phase, and is the aim of the experiment. However, it is necessary to form a control group. The second is intramodal, at the test phase, when the subject compares the supposed familiar object with the supposed new object over the six trials. In this case, it is also possible to study the habituation curve obtained over the course of successive presentations of new and familiar objects. The data collected during this phase indicate whether transfer has occurred. Within this paradigm, as in that of 'paired comparison', preference for the new or familiar object is of only relative importance in the question of intermodal transfer.

What is essential is the difference obtained in the exploration times of familiar and new objects at the time of the test phase.

The empirical data

Unlike reaching behaviour, which is triggered or guided by vision, most experimental studies of intermodal transfer are based on the tactile modality, whether oral or manual.

Since the first experiment conducted by Bryant *et al.* (1972) research into the transfer of information from tactile modality to visual modality has principally been concerned with babies who are at least 6 months old. There are two reasons for this. First of all, most authors who are interested in the prehension–vision relationship have pointed to the poor quality of tactile manipulation in very young babies. Moreover, 6-month-old babies perform not only the grasping of the objects they see, but also their subsequent manipulation, with intense concentration.

Using a paired comparison technique, Gottfried, Rose and Bridger (1977, 1978), Ruff and Kohler (1978) and Rose, Gottfried and Bridger (1981*a*) have clearly demonstrated that babies from 6 months of age onwards are capable of memorizing a certain amount of haptic information during the familiarization phase, and then of visually recognizing the object they have previously handled.

This ability means that a central mechanism for processing information exists in babies of this age independently of the sensory modalities which apprehend the information. It could, however, be argued that infants detect correspondences between visual and haptic information through the newly acquired multimodal activity which they direct towards objects. If this hypothesis could be verified, it would constitute an argument in favour of Piaget's theory. The age of 6 months is probably an important stage in the way the baby perceives the space of places and objects. It would appear, however, that joint manual and visual exploration is not a necessary precondition for intermodal transfer.

Intermodal perception before the age of 6 months

Experiments by Meltzoff and Borton (1979) and Gibson and Walker (1984) have demonstrated that month-old neonates can visually recognize an object they have previously explored orally on the basis of information they have extracted concerning its properties of texture (smooth, rough) and substance (hard, soft).

In the tactile sensory sphere, however, the oral and manual modes, while exhibiting structural and physiological similarities, probably make use of different mechanisms in the apprehension of the space of objects: in addition to its perceptual function, the hand also possesses a carrying function which increases its field of action (Hatwell, 1986). Moreover, the existence of a coordination between oral and visual exploration may be of significance for the study of the neonate's intermodal perceptions, but it does not constitute a functional reality in the young infant. Thus, Rose, Gottfried and Bridger (1981*b*) failed to provide evidence of transfer from oral mode to visual mode at 6 months of age, although visual recognition of the shape of a felt object is possible at this age.

Furthermore, as the intramodal tactile discriminatory ability of 2-month-old babies indicates (Streri, 1987*a*), the manipulation of objects is far from being as poor as the literature suggests (Bower, 1974; Lockman and Ashmead, 1983). But beyond the ability to manipulate, we would also like to demonstrate:

1. that very young babies can perceptually relate information extracted through different sensory modalities;
2. that this capacity enables them to treat objects as equivalent or nonequivalent;
3. that there are constraints linked to the modal systems during the course of development. These constraints cannot be interpreted as divergences in the processing of information. On the one hand, during the first few months of life, the corresponding systems develop at different rates; on the other, new functions appear, particularly in the tactile system.

We have studied the intermodal transfer of object shapes at two very particular times in the baby's life: at 5 months, when voluntary prehension begins, and at 2 months when, under everyday conditions of observation, there is no apparent relation between vision and prehension – that is to say, when a visually presented object does not trigger reaching and, conversely, when an object held in the hand does not provoke the action of carrying it into view.

At the age of 5 months, babies show haptic recognition of the shape of objects which they have already seen, but it has not been possible to observe the reverse transfer (Streri and Pêcheux, 1986*b*). In order to make sure that the absence of a touch–vision transfer cannot be attributed to the new procedure, we have repeated the classic procedure. After a 90-second period of tactile familiarization, comparable to the duration obtained during the haptic habituation phase of the earlier experiment, the familiar and new objects were simultaneously presented in the baby's visual field for 20 seconds. This second experiment also failed to reveal any influence of the haptic familiarization phase on the durations of visual exploration of the objects. This result has also been confirmed, for the same age group, by an experiment conducted by Brown and Gottfried (1986), who used the classic matching of pairs method, with the variation that the visual presentation of objects was carried out either at the same time as or after tactile exploration. In neither of these conditions did they observe the manipulated object to have influenced the visual exploration times of the new or familiar objects.

There are a number of factors which may explain these results. First, the subjects of these experiments are a month younger than those observed in studies establishing an intermodal touch–vision transfer (Rose *et al.*, 1981*b*; Ruff and Kohler, 1978). Before the age of 6 months, it appears to be difficult to demonstrate visual recognition of a felt object. It is therefore necessary to explain why this visual recognition should exist on the basis of oral exploration at the age of just one month (Gibson and Walker, 1984; Meltzoff and Borton, 1979) and why this capacity should then disappear at the age of 5 months, when manual exploration is involved. Could it be that 5-month-old babies relate the two situations, tactile familiarization and visual recognition? Bahrick and Watson (1985) have shown that babies of 5 but not 3 months of age are able to detect invariants, and to establish intermodal relations between their own leg movements and those perceived visually on a video recording.

A second explanation would seem more plausible. At about 5 months of age, babies do not simply manipulate objects, they actively transport them, either by passing them from one hand to the other or by carrying them into view or to their mouths. This activity involves not only their hands but also their arms. This newly acquired function of transporting an object might disturb the perceptual function of the hand which, as we have seen, is present from the very first weeks of life. While babies attempt to look at an object through a screen, their attention to its shape would be insufficient for intermodal transfer but enough for intramodal recognition.

In 2-month-old babies, the function of transporting objects is barely present, if at all. In consequence, the hand's perceptual function should be predominant; as a result, it should be possible to find evidence of touch–vision transfer occurring at this age. We have been able to verify this hypothesis with a similar procedure to that already used with 5-month-old babies (Streri, 1987*a*). Two-month-old babies visually recognize objects which they have already felt. However, there is no haptic recognition of a visually familiarized object. In our opinion, a single test trial did not allow the 2-month-old babies sufficient time to perform a haptic comparison of the previously memorized visual information. We have therefore repeated the experiment using the same shapes, but employing the preferential choice procedure with different shapes (Streri, unpublished manuscript). Once again, vision–touch transfer could not be obtained, while touch–vision transfer was confirmed. Thus, the nonreversibility of transfer cannot be due to the procedure, or to the shapes used. A transfer of the shape of objects from touch to vision has also been obtained in 3-month-olds by Brown and Gottfried (1986), who observed transfer from the oral mode and from the hand to vision under conditions of successive presentation, but not under conditions of simultaneous presentation. They assumed, however, that the results were contradictory, and should therefore be disregarded. Babies look at the orally familiarized object for a longer time, but after manual familiarization they prefer to look at the object they have not already felt. The preference for the familiar or new stimulus is a great problem which has not yet been adequately explained by research into the visual discriminatory capacities of babies (see Lécuyer, 1988). Under these conditions, it is understandable that Brown and Gottfried (1986) concluded from their results that transfer had not occurred.

These results obtained from babies at 2 and 5 months old demonstrate that at times when vision–prehension coordination is active or, alternatively, does not exist, the information extracted via different sensory systems is related. Prehension–vision coordination is not a necessary condition for intermodal transfer. Before they even compare what they see with what they touch during multimodal exploration, babies are capable of comparing the information about their environment which they absorb via different modalities.

However, the nonreversibility of the obtained transfer is hardly compatible with the hypothesis of an amodal code existing early in life. Why is it that at 5 months of age no touch–vision transfer can be obtained, while at 2 months of age the reverse is observed? This absence of transfer cannot be attributed to a lack of discrimination, since at both ages babies differentiate between the shapes of objects perfectly during both visual and haptic exploration (Streri, 1987*a*; Streri and Pêcheux, 1986*a*). We shall explore the reasons for nonreversibility of transfer first at 5 and then at 2 months of age.

We have already noted that at the age of 5 months, the motor function could have a disruptive effect on the perceptual function of the hand (see Chapter 3). At this age, babies cannot simultaneously pay attention both to their own activity with the object and to the properties of the object (Streri and Pineau, 1988). If the baby's motor activity were channelled towards exploratory rather than transporting ends, might we perhaps obtain a touch–vision transfer? This is what seems to happen. In a series of experiments into the haptic exploration of the unity and boundaries of objects, Streri and Spelke (1988) demonstrated that 4-month-old babies actively explore objects (rings) connected by either a rigid or a flexible link (see Figure 3.3, p. 107 above) with both hands and without visual control. The rigidly connected objects require the baby to move both arms at once, while the objects with a flexible connection do not necessitate any joint activity of these limbs. This exploration is enough to allow the babies to perform an intramodal discrimination between the two displays (see Chapter 3). It is also sufficient for visual recognition. In order to test intermodal transfer, we adopted the preferential choice technique. After the tactile exploration stage, the familiar and new displays are visually presented in alternation in six trials. The nonmanipulated elements (rod or elastic) are visible. The objects are suspended in front of the infants and jiggled. Those connected by the bar move rigidly together, while those connected by elastic move independently of each other. These configurations thus present the same movement characteristics as those observed during haptic exploration. The results show that the babies look for longer at the display they have not manipulated than at the familiar one. Thus at 4 months of age, babies visually identify the movements which they performed during manipulation. In these experiments, however, it is above all the movement of the arms, and therefore the motor and proprioceptive afferences, which form the basis for transfer. In effect, since the rings held in both hands are identical, handling the edges of the assembly plays a very minor role.

A second experiment was undertaken to demonstrate the role of manipulation of the boundaries of the object in the perception of object unity. After haptic familiarization to one or other of the assemblies, these are then presented visually, fixed to a small white support. The support is made to swing to attract the baby's attention to the entire assembly. Transfer is also observed under these conditions. Thus, on the basis of holding only the edges of the assembly (the connection not having been touched), the infants visually recognize it as a whole.

This recognition is similarly realized in the visual perception of a partially occluded object (Kellman and Spelke, 1983). This situation involves a process of visual habituation to a rod whose centre is concealed by a wooden block placed in front of it. Only the ends of the rod are visible, and it is moved left and right alternately behind the block, which remains fixed. In the test phase, the rod is presented in alternation with two smaller rods corresponding to the visible ends of the rod used in the habituation phase (see Figure 4.1). The babies look at the whole rod for less time than the fragmented rod. Thus, in the test phase, they recognize the whole rod as being the same as the rod which was partially occluded by the wooden block during the familiarization phase. The unity of the object is therefore reconstructed, even though only its ends are visible.

As for the bimanual tactual exploration of objects, a plausible hypothesis would be to consider that the visual recognition of objects is facilitated by the fact that the ends of the object held in the babies' hands are identical. This would appear to confirm the Gestalt principles of good continuation and good form. Similar mechanisms are manifested in the haptic exploration of an assembly which is irregular in shape, texture and weight (Streri and Spelke, 1989; see Figure 3.4, p. 108 above). Unity is perceived with both an asymmetrical and a symmetrical assembly. The same phenomenon is

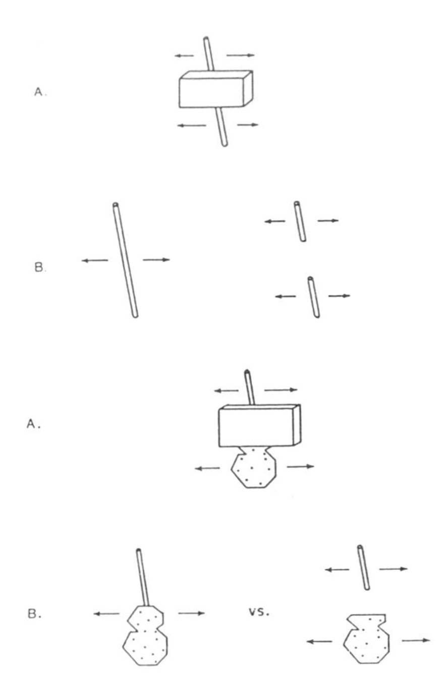

Figure 4.1 Symmetrical and asymetrical assemblies used in Kellman and Spelke's experiment (1983). (a) Objects for habituation. (b) Test objects.

observed in the visual modality in Kellman and Spelke's experiment (1983) in which the two visible ends of the object moving behind the block are different in shape, size and colour (see Figure 4.1).

These experiments show not only that babies are able to extract perceptual invariants using a process which is similar in both modalities – indeed, this has been demonstrated in the work of Streri and Pêcheux (1986*a*) and Streri (1987*a*) – but also that at 4 months of age babies haptically perceive an object as a whole unit when they are able to manipulate only part of it. This process is similar to the way in which they confer visual unity on an object on the sole basis of its visible extremities. Recently, other experiments (Streri, Spelke and Rameix, 1993, in press) have investigated the problem of object cohesion in the tactile modality using methods similar to those of von

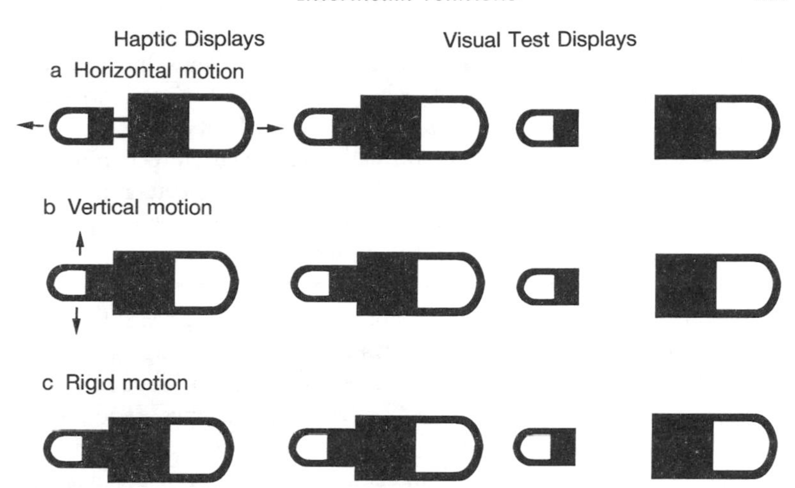

Figure 4.2 Tactual and visual displays.
(*Source*: Streri, Spelke and Rameix, 1993)

Hofsten and Spelke (1985) in the visual domain. Let us recall that these experiments involve two surfaces which are either adjacent or separate, and are either stationary or move together or independently. Adaptation of the material and experimental conditions is necessary for an investigation of the tactile modality. Four-month-old babies are given a display to manipulate. This consists of a large surface and a small surface which can be held in each hand by a handle (see Figure 4.2). These surfaces are either connected or can be moved relative to each other in either a horizontal or a vertical movement (active conditions). In two additional conditions it is the experimenter who moves the two surfaces (passive conditions). When the babies move the connected display, they perceive the object as a unit. When they move the small surface relative to the larger one, either horizontally or vertically, they perceive the object as two units. Under the passive conditions, the babies' responses are ambiguous. This research demonstrates once again that there are similar mechanisms for organizing information about the environment operating in both modalities. It also shows that active exploration on the part of the babies themselves is necessary if they are to organize haptically perceived information. This second point also indicates the specificity of the tactile modality in relation to the visual modality. In the visual mode, it is the experimenter who moves the objects, whereas haptically it is necessary for the baby to move them.

Other experiments provide confirmation of the visual recognition of the properties of felt objects in 5-month-olds. Pineau and Streri (1990) have attempted to discover whether the baby can haptically locate a strange object placed either between or outside two identical objects, then recognize this spatial information in the visual mode. The habituation procedure and the preferential testing were the same as those employed in previous experiments (Streri and Spelke, 1988, 1989). The stimulus consisted of a diamond shape positioned either between or at the left or right end of two ring shapes. The whole stimulus was no longer than 45 millimetres and could easily be held in the baby's hand. The results demonstrate that babies of this age not only detect the differences in the position of the odd object out (the diamond) in the tactile modality (intramodal transfer), but also visually recognize the spatial positioning of the three objects in the assembly they have manipulated. It therefore appears that the activity of locating one object amongst others in the hand is simpler for the baby than that of perceiving shape. Simple hand pressure is sufficient for the locating activity, but not for processing the shapes of the objects. Milhet and I (Streri and Milhet, in preparation) tested 4-month-old babies' ability to discriminate haptically between an assembly comprising two objects of the same weight (13 g) and another with two differently weighted objects (13 g and 47 g). The difference between the two assemblies is haptically perceived by the young baby. Using a visual display which represented a balance, we also observed that the haptically gained information about the difference in weight between the two assemblies was transferred to the visual modality (see Figure 4.3). In effect, the babies who were habituated to the same-weight haptic assembly looked for longer at the unequal balance than at the equal balance, and vice versa. It is certain that what we observed was a transfer not of the weight of the objects but of whether or not a weight difference existed within the assemblies. Experiments are now being undertaken to try to discover the information on which this recognition is based (proprioceptive or information concerning the idea of difference). This experiment was replicated with 2-month-old babies, who still have a low degree of global motor ability. The results are similar to those obtained with the

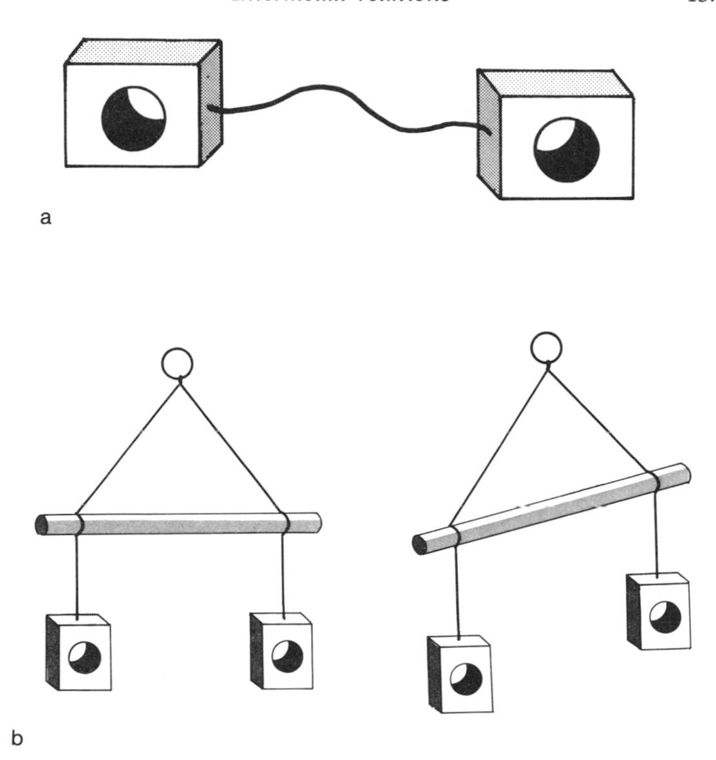

Figure 4.3 Haptic assembly and visual displays in Milhet and Streri's experiment. (a) Haptic assembly. The objects are either identically or differently weighted. (b) Visual displays. Showing either an equivalence or a difference in weight.
(*Source*: Streri and Milhet (in preparation))

4-month-olds. They indicate that the simple pressure of the weight of objects in the babies' hands is sufficient for them to be able to detect an equality or difference in weight, and for this information to be transferred to vision. Therefore, the 'unsupported holding' of the objects which adults perform under similar conditions (Lederman and Klatsky, 1987) seems unnecessary in infancy.

Why is it that we do not observe a reversible transfer in the case of the 2-month-old babies? We have not been able to demonstrate the existence of a vision–touch transfer in babies who do not attempt to reach for a visual object, or to carry a held object into view. Are we to conclude from this that at this age a correspondence of information is assured on the basis of touch? The transfer situation demands that information is memorized in one modality, then recognized in another. Let us recall that in order to demonstrate a mechanism which is common to both modalities at this age, we used an intermodal matching procedure which we judged to be simpler for the 2-month-old babies (Streri and Milhet, 1988). The results certainly revealed an intermodal matching response in the face of redundant information, and it was plausible to conclude that a central mechanism for information processing common to both vision and touch exists at an early age. However, these results demonstrated very clearly that this matching was obtained mainly on the basis of touch, and less so on the basis of vision. Thus, using two different experimental methods, we have obtained the same asymmetry at the level of the touch–vision relationship that we had already noted during the experiment concerning intermodal transfer in 2-month-old babies (Streri, 1987*a*).

These results suggest that we should reinterpret the disappearance of prehension–vision coordination which is characteristic of babies of this age. The hypothesis that this disappearance is due to a reorganization of the motor activity of the upper limbs as a result of growing maturity can no longer be regarded as adequate. Visual perceptual behaviour also undergoes a change. An initial argument emerges from the work of von Hofsten (1984). Analysis of the different development curves he obtains for reaching behaviour in babies of 1–19 weeks of age both in the presence of an object and in its absence (control condition) shows that at 7 weeks of age the number of reaches in the presence of an object decreases, while motor activity with no object present is at its maximum. From the age of 10 weeks, in contrast, this process is reversed. Babies try to catch the objects they see, and their motor activity decreases when no object is present. Thus although it is evident from their degree of motor activity when no object is present that 7-week-old babies are quite capable of raising their arms to the height of an object, it is difficult for them to do this when the activity has an underlying plan: that of reaching the object. The decline in motor activity in the presence of a visual target does not stem simply from a motor problem, but from the lack of ability to plan a goal-directed action. This inability, however, may modify the object's status for the baby, and herein lies our second argument.

The baby's visual perceptive capacities change considerably at about 2–3 months of age (Banks and Salapatek, 1983; Vurpillot, 1972). The tactual behaviour of babies of this age develops much more slowly, while they continue to show a large degree of reflex activity (Twitchell, 1965). It is possible that the information gained through the visual system is becoming more precise, while that gained through the tactile system is still rather blurred. Thus the status of the visual object is temporarily modified. It has become essentially an object for looking at, not for taking hold of, and it is not recognized by the tactile system. This is demonstrated by the ocular fixation times in habituation sequences, and by the baby's difficulty in turning away from the situation (Lécuyer, 1987).

In transfer situations, the nonconcordance between visual and tactile information-processing levels may explain why the transfer cannot be reversed. This means that the quality of information extracted haptically is imprecise, and the tactile percept is less sophisticated than the visual percept. It would be easier to recognize imprecise tactual information within the visual richness of an object than the reverse. When an object is seen in all its detail, it is no longer recognized in its cruder tactile form. In order to test this hypothesis, we conducted an intermodal transfer experiment (Streri and Molina, 1993*a*, in press) using the preferential choice technique with objects and very simplified illustrations (sketches) of these objects. This idea is not new. In their experiments with chimpanzees, Davenport and Rogers (1971) obtained visual recognition of manipulated objects when the visual test made use of life-size photographs and even simple sketches of the objects instead of the objects themselves. Similar results have also been obtained with the rhesus monkey (Malone, Tolan and Rogers, 1980; Tolan, Rogers and Malone, 1981).

In our experiments with 2-month-old babies, the objects consisted of a cross and a cotton reel, and the drawings were created by tracing the contours of the objects and then painting the trace-lines red. The first experiment tested touch–vision transfer. After haptic exploration of the object, the babies were visually presented with a sketch of the manipulated object, and with another sketch. The second experiment tested the reverse transfer. After visual exploration of a sketch, the babies were tactually presented with the object the sketch represented, and with another object. The results revealed the existence of a reversible transfer, but raise the problem of why a vision–touch transfer should be obtained when the visual presentation consists of a sketch but not when the actual object is presented. It will therefore be necessary to take great care in determining exactly what information really is processed by the two modalities, and is likely to be transferred.

What conclusions can be drawn about the unity of intermodal perceptions? We have collated all the experimental data which are so far available to us in the form of a table (see Table 4.1) showing the nature of the information, the perceptual systems involved, the direction of transfer, and the results obtained.

To sum up: from the age of at least 1 month, a transfer from the oral modality to vision is obtained for information about texture (Meltzoff and Borton, 1979) and substance (Gibson and Walker, 1984). In the latter experiment, only 60 seconds' oral exploration is needed for transfer to occur.

At 2 months of age, a transfer of the shape of objects from manual touching to vision is observed after about 140 seconds of manipulation (Streri, 1987*a*). However, pair matching of the seen object and the manipulated object is obtained after only 50 seconds (Streri and Milhet, 1988). None of the many studies above has been confirmed in the research of Brown and Gottfried (1986). It must, however, be emphasized that in this experiment the shapes of the objects used were very complex for such young babies. Moreover, the method (fixed 90 seconds' familiarization time, visual recognition in 20 seconds) could have limited the baby's exploration of the objects. Finally, it is not known whether the lack of transfer is due to a lack of intramodal discrimination in the visual modality or the tactile modality or, indeed, in both, since no study of this element was included in the research.

Numerous studies have tested 4-month-old babies' ability to carry out bimanual object-directed activity. The information which is transferred to vision concerns weight (Milhet, 1989), movement patterns (Streri and Spelke, 1988, experiment 2), the unity and boundaries of objects (Streri and Spelke, 1988, experiments 2 and 3),

Table 4.1 Research into intermodal transfer in babies under 6 months old

1st mode of information pick-up	Authors	Exploration times	Recognition (success or failure)	Nature of information	Age of babies
Oral			*Visual*		
	Meltzoff and Borton (1979)	90s	success	texture	1 month
	Gibson and Walker (1984)	60s	success	substance	1 month
	Brown and Gottfried (1986)	90s	failure	shape and texture	1 month
		90s	failure	shape	3 months
		90s	failure	shape	5 months
Manual			*Visual*		
	Brown and Gottfried (1986)	90s	failure	shape and texture	1 month
	Streri (1987*a*)	139s	success	shape	2 months
	Streri and Milhet (1988)	50s	success	shape	2 months
	Streri and Milhet (in prep.)	138s	success	weight	2 months
	Streri and Molina (1993)	170s	success	2D/3D	2 months
	Brown and Gottfried (1986)	90s	failure	shape	3 months
	Streri and	200s	success	movement	4 months
	Spelke (1988)	175s	success	object unity	4 months
	Streri and	121s	success	symmetry	4 months
	Spelke (1989)	130s	success	asymmetry	4 months
	Streri and Milhet (in prep.)	131s	success	weight	4 months
	Streri, Spelke and Rameix (1993)	117s (VM) 116s (HM) 130s (RM)	success success success	active movement condition	4 months
		160s (VM) 160s (HM)	failure failure	passive movement condition	4 months
	Streri and Pêcheux (1986*b*)	88s	failure	shape	5 months
	Pineau and Streri (1990)	137s	success	object arrangement	5 months
	Brown and Gottfried (1986)	90s	failure	shape	5 months
Visual			*Manual*		
	Streri (1987*a*)	111s	failure	shape	2 months
	Streri and Milhet (1988)	50s	failure	shape	2 months
	Streri and Molina (1993)	170s	success	2D/3D	2 months
	Streri and Pêcheux (1986*b*)	33s	success	shape	5 months

The table does not mention the factor of *procedure*

VM = vertical motion; HM = horizontal motion; RM =rigid motion their cohesion when they are connected (rigid motion) or moved horizontally or vertically relative to each other (Streri, Spelke and Rameix, 1993, submitted), and the symmetry or asymmetry of objects (Streri and Spelke, 1989, experiments 2 and 3). In all these studies the ability to explore objects bimanually was tested. Furthermore, the information gathered is both tactilokinaesthetic and proprioceptive in the exploratory behaviour involving the baby's upper limbs.

At 5 months of age the touch–vision transfer of the shape of objects disappears (Streri and Pêcheux, 1986*b*) or is no longer manifested (Brown and Gottfried, 1986), while a vision–touch transfer is observed for the first time at this age (Streri and Pêcheux, 1986*b*). However, the tactile locating of an object placed between two others is realized, and the transfer of this information to the visual modality is obtained at this same age (Pineau and Streri, 1990).

Most of these studies have shown that both a tactile and a visual intramodal tactile memory exist, indicating that the two modalities function in a similar way.

Therefore, there is unity, but nevertheless, also specificity of the sensory modalities . . . .

Originally, the researchers' primary concern was to reveal the existence of amodal perceptual invariants in babies at earlier and earlier ages. The studies we have discussed show that touch and vision are coordinated at a very early age. The demonstration of intermodal transfer in the first few months of the baby's life clearly indicates that the coordination of action schemes is not a prerequisite for a relationship between perceptions.

Nevertheless, we still know very little about the mechanisms which govern this behaviour. The theory of a nondifferentiation of the sensory systems (Bower, 1974, 1979) does not take the nonreversibility of transfer and behaviour into consideration. There would be no contradiction in thinking that, correlative to the existence of intersensory coordination, modal specificity might also exist very early in the infant's life. Rochat (1987) has observed that differences between oral and manual tactile exploration occur within the first few days. These differences must also exist *a fortiori* in the intramodal functioning of the visual, auditory, and other modalities.

For example, Lécuyer and Streri (1986) have demonstrated that at 5 months of age there was no correlation between the speeds at which the same baby became used to the same objects in visual and in tactile exploration. Thus a baby who habituates quickly in the visual modality may be slow to habituate haptically, and vice versa.

The modal specificities have been revealed through the very procedures which were designed to demonstrate intermodal transfer. The transfer situation requires the information to be encoded in one modality and decoded in another. When equivalent shapes are presented to both modalities, nonreversibility of transfer is due to a lack of complete agreement between the perception formed in one modality and the perception constructed in another (Streri, 1987*a*; Streri and Pêcheux, 1986*b*). We know very little about the quantity and nature of the information abstracted by the different sensory modalities.

In most of our experiments, transfer of information is based on properties which vary in given dimensions: rectilinear/curvilinear, shape with/without a hole, difference in weight, different arrangements of elements within an object. It seems unlikely that when these objects are treated as equivalent it is because the baby has identified all their dimensions. When babies are presented with objects which are too complicated and thus difficult to compare, as in Brown and Gottfried's experiment (1986), recognition is not obtained. Intermodal equivalence relies on the detection of differences or resemblances between the properties of objects (Pick, 1986). What we are observing, therefore, is a recognition which is relational in nature and is based on the extraction of invariants, rather than of absolute information. This interpretation seems to be the most plausible one for explaining mechanisms which we – perhaps wrongly – judge to be too complex to exist in the infant.

The development of intermodal transfer after the age of 6 months

There is a historical dimension to research into intermodal perception in babies aged 6 months to a year. It was the first research to reveal the existence of a relationship between vision and touch through a transfer mechanism in subjects who possess no language. In so doing, it has called into question a number of hypotheses involving the notion of a mediatory mechanism. Since the initial research conducted by Bryant *et al.* (1972), whose complex experimental procedure renders their results rather debatable, studies have multiplied and employed more simple techniques. Researchers looked first at 1-year-olds (Gottfried *et al.* 1977; Rose *et al.*, 1978) and then at 6-month-olds (Rose *et al.*, 1981*b*; Ruff and Kohler, 1978).

Table 4.2 provides a summary of the research bearing on transfer between touch and vision after monomodal exploration only. We shall examine the research relating to bimodal exploration later. The majority of the research explores the transfer of information from the tactile modality to the visual modality. The reverse transfer is studied in the work of Rose *et al.* (1981*a*) and Rose and Orlian (1991).

These studies specify the mechanisms involved in intermodal transfer in young babies under 6 months old. While most of the research is concerned with the shapes of objects, Gibson and Walker's (1984) looks at the transfer of information regarding substance at 1 year of age, while Rose, Gottfried and Bridger's (1983) deals with the two- or three-dimensional character of the information.

We noted above that visual recognition of the shape of a manipulated object was possible from the age of 2 months after about 140 seconds of manipulation (Streri, 1987*a*), while we failed to obtain a similar result in 5-month-old babies after tactile familiarization times of 88 seconds (experiment 1) and 90 seconds (experiment 2). After the age of 6 months, the exploration times allowed to the babies is considerably shorter. Rose *et al.* (1981*b*) obtained a positive result after a manual exploration time of just 60 seconds, though they failed to find evidence of a transfer after 30 seconds of tactile presentation only, even when there was no interval between tactile and visual presentations of the object. Paradoxically, Ruff and Kohler (1978) observe a touch–vision transfer at the same age after only 30 seconds of haptic presentation. However, the shapes used in this study were much simpler (a sphere and a cube) than those used by Rose *et al.* (1981*b*). The familiarity of the objects available to babies within their environments would seem to play a role from the age of 6 months onwards. Using an intermodal matching situation, Bushnell (1986) obtained a more effective transfer when the objects for comparison were familiar (a brush and a ball) than when they were not (a block and a pretzel).

At 1 year of age, 30 seconds (Gottfried *et al.*, 1977; Rose *et al.*, 1978) but not 15 seconds (Rose and Orlian, 1991) is sufficient for touch–vision transfer to be obtained, but on condition that the population studied is composed of full-term infants of middle-class

Table 4.2 Research into intermodal transfer after the age of 6 months

1st mode of information pick-up	Authors	Exploration times	Recognition (success or failure)	Nature of Information	Age of babies
Oral			*Visual*		
	Rose *et al.* (1981*a*)	30s	failure	shape	6 months
		60s	failure	shape	6 months
	Gottfried *et al.* (1977)	30s	success	shape	1 year
Manual			*Visual*		
	Ruff and Kohler (1978)	30s	success	shape	6 months
	Rose *et al.* (1981*a*)	30s	success	shape	6 months
		60s	success	shape	6 months
	Bushnell (1986)	30s	success	familiarity	6 months
	Walker-Andrews and Gibson (1986)	20s	failure	substance	6 months
	Bushnell (1982)	20s	failure	shape	8 months
		20s	success	shape	9.5 months
	Bryant *et al.* (1972)	time not specified	success	shape	about 9 months
	Bushnell (1982)	20s	success	shape	11 months
	Bushnell and Weinburg (1987)	30s	success	texture +shape	11 months
		30s	failure	texture/ shape	11 months
	Gottfried *et al.* (1977)	30s	success	shape	1 year
	Gibson and Walker (1984)	60s	success	substance	1 year
	Walker-Andrews and Gibson (1986)	20s	success	substance	1 year
	Rose *et al.* (1983)	30s	failure	2D/3D	1 year
		45s	success	2D/3D	
	Rose and Orlian (1991)	15s	failure	shape	1 year
		30s	success	shape	1 year
		60s	success	shape	1 year
Visual			*Manual*		
	Rose *et al.* (1981*b*)	30s	failure	shape	1 year
		60s	success	shape	1 year
	Rose and Orlian (1991)	15s	failure	shape	1 year
		30s	failure	shape	1 year
		60s	failure	shape	1 year

Other factors (procedure, socio-economic background, prematurity) are not mentioned in the table.

sociocultural backgrounds. If the infants are premature or from poor sociocultural backgrounds, transfer appears to be difficult under identical conditions of presentation.

Tactual recognition of a seen object has been obtained from 5-month-olds after a visual familiarization time of about 33 seconds (Streri and Pêcheux, 1986*b*). Rose *et al.* (1981*a*), on the other hand, failed to obtain a transfer in this direction with year-old babies after a 30-second visual familiarization time, though transfer was obtained after 60 seconds of familiarization. This latter result was not confirmed in Rose and Orlian's research (1991). It would appear, therefore, that vision–touch transfer is not a stable phenomenon at 1 year of age. This result contrasts with that of an experiment conducted with rhesus monkeys (DiMattia, Posley and Fuster, 1990) which analyzed the transfer of information regarding shape, size and texture in both vision–touch and touch–vision directions. Much better results were obtained for vision–touch than for touch–vision. Should we then conclude that in the baby there is no development in the speed at which information is extracted and transferred? The differences between the procedures and shapes employed in the research of Streri and Pêcheux (1986*b*) and that of Rose *et al.* (1981*a*, 1991) makes it difficult to compare the data. Nevertheless, the disappearance of vision–touch transfer at the age of a year, although it is obtained at 5 months of age, may be explained by the differing exploratory possibilities at the two ages. At 5 months, prehension–vision coordination is just beginning, and experiments concerned with intermodality are justified by the fact that objects are seen or touched at different moments. At a year, in contrast, the exploration of objects is multimodal, and vision is dominant. Perhaps the vision–touch intermodal transfer situation disturbs 1-year-old babies and impairs the tactile recognition of objects that have already been seen. Another interpretation would be that babies identify the objects visually, but cannot do so haptically. In the tactile modality, babies would abstract information about the properties of objects but would not necessarily identify them.

In the tactile modality, oral and manual modes have been studied concurrently. Thus in working with the 6-month age group, Rose *et al.* (1981*b*) failed to obtain visual recognition of an object explored orally, no matter how long the presentation time, although a transfer in this direction was obtained from the manual mode to vision after just 60 seconds of manipulation. The manipulation of an object would thus appear to be more effective than oral exploration. In contrast, with 1-year-olds, Gottfried *et al.* (1977) observed transfer of the shape of objects from oral to visual mode after 30 seconds of exploration. The oral–visual transfer obtained in 1-month-old babies by Meltzoff and Borton (1979) and Gibson and Walker (1984) after exploration times of 90 seconds and 60 seconds respectively has therefore disappeared by the age of 6 months. Rose and Ruff (1987) conclude simply that the relation between oral and visual exploration is weaker at 6 months of age than it is in older subjects.

Another interpretation would be that at this age the two systems are in competition. At 6 months of age, babies very frequently put objects into their mouths. The exploratory function of this activity is no longer exercised, since it has become redundant in relation to manual exploration. It is possible that at this age, the exploratory function of the oral modality has passed to the manual modality and been replaced by a more playful function. However, this temporary loss of the oral exploratory function is contradicted by the fact that the buccal cavity represents a goal, no doubt for exploration purposes, to which the hand carrying the object will most frequently be directed. This is what is revealed by Peters's observations (1983) on the establishment of manual laterality between the ages of 6 and 12 months. At 6 months, the grasped object is carried to the mouth, and these two activities are performed with either hand until the age of 12 months, when this behaviour alters. Oral exploration no longer has the same degree of importance, and the right hand is preferentially activated.

As for the coordination of tactual and visual information, let us return to the work of Bushnell (1982) in which she places babies of 8, 9·5 and 11 months of age into a situation of perceptual conflict. She observes an integration of tactile and visual space from the age of 9 months onwards. This result does not invalidate the possibility that a unity of the sensory information exists before this age, but it raises the problem of its establishment in situations of perceptual conflict. Do they require the same mechanisms as the transfer situation in order for a unity of one or more dimensions to be conferred on an object?

In another study, Bushnell and Weinberg (1987) used the intermodal matching technique with 11-month-old infants. The infants were sensitive to the difference between a smooth egg-shaped object and a fur-covered cube, and between a smooth cross and a fur-covered cube (shape + texture). In contrast, they did not react to the presentation of a smooth cube and a smooth cross (shape), although they did differentiate the smooth cube from the smooth egg. Thus, within the rectilinear dimension, objects with a similar texture are not easily differentiated, although the rectilinear is differentiated from the curvilinear. These results suggest that intermodal matching is easier when the objects differ in more than one dimension. The fact that 11-month-old infants fail to discriminate between the cube and the cross makes it reasonable to think that they are still insensitive to various interruptions in the linearity of the shapes, thus confirming Bryant *et al.*'s results (1972) with objects differing in this same characteristic. Moreover, 11-month-old infants fail to discriminate between objects which have the same shape but differ in texture, the smooth and fur-covered cubes, only under the condition in which the fur-covered cube is felt with the hands and the smooth cube is looked at. Under the reverse condition (fur-covered cube looked at, smooth cube felt with the hands) they are able to detect a difference. The role of visual information is therefore predominant in seeking differences between objects.

The relative difficulty experienced by several researchers in demonstrating touch–vision intermodal transfer could lie in the fact that the infants experienced difficulties in the tactual retention of information relating to the shape of objects, and then in visually recognizing and differentiating this from other information about object shapes. Gottfried and Rose (1980), Rose and Orlian (1991) and Soroka *et al.* (1979) demonstrate the existence of the tactile memory of complex shapes. Under conditions in which the objects are presented in darkness, infants manipulate new objects for longer than familiar objects during the test phase.

Nevertheless, there is still much to be researched if we are to understand the intermodal transfer mechanism at under 6 months of age as well as over 6 months. In all probability, the exploration time, the nature of the information, the complexity of the stimuli and the modalities concerned all play a part in this mechanism, as the descriptive model proposed by Wagner and Sakovits (1986) suggests. No study has deployed all these dimensions at once. It appears, however, that tactile exploration requires more time than visual exploration for transfer to be possible. The time required corresponds to the different way in which the two systems perceive objects. The speed of visual perception, even if it requires ocular scanning, contrasts with the slower, sequential perception of the tactile modality. In none of the cases observed do these differences in functioning contradict the idea of similar mechanisms for the apprehension of information existing in the two systems. Discrimination is possible in both systems.

Multimodal relations

Multimodal exploration and the reaction to novelty as evidence of intermodal coordination

From the time when joint visual and manual inspection of an object is assured, we might wonder how the amodal or specific properties of objects are integrated in multimodal exploration. Multimodal exploration is fully exercised from the time when prehension–vision coordination is realized: at about 5 to 6 months of age. At this age babies are able to compare identical information received simultaneously via different modalities. At the same time they are able to coordinate different information extracted from the same object. It was in order to examine these new possibilities that researchers conducted two-stage experiments with infants, similar in principle to the paired comparison procedure.

These experiments sought to demonstrate the effect of the functioning of one modality on that of another. Does the functioning of the first modality help or hinder the second modality in constructing a broader, multimodal knowledge about the object? Two procedures are possible: after bimodal visual and tactile (V + T) exploration, the effect of novelty

1. on the infant's visual behaviour (V) and
2. on the infant's tactile behaviour (T)

is tested.

The procedure is as follows: infants are allowed to explore an object bimodally. They look at it and manipulate it for a fixed period.

In the second stage, the familiar object is placed next to a new object, and the experiment continues as follows:

in condition (1), the researchers record the fixation times for the two objects, which are placed beyond the infant's reach. During the familiarization phase, a control group has received only visual information about the object (V condition). Thus in the test phase, fixation times for the two objects of both experimental and control group are compared, and the role of the tactile modality in gaining knowledge about the object is analyzed. With babies 6 to 12 months of age, depending on the experiment, Schaffer and Parry (1970), P.L. Harris (1972) and Gottfried, Rose and Bridger (1978) tested the hypothesis according to which manipulation of an object augments the visual knowledge extracted by the infant;

in condition (2), after the bimodal familiarization phase, either a new object (Schaffer and Parry, 1969) or the familiar object and a new object side by side (Bushnell, Shaw and Strauss, 1985; Ruff, 1976; Willatts, 1983) are placed within the infant's reach. Thus familiarization phase and test phase are conducted under the same conditions of bimodal exploration. When just one object is presented, as in Schaffer and Parry's research (1969), the behavioural indicators which are analyzed are the durations of visual fixation, of initial ocular fixation, and of the manipulations and the response latency in the prehensile activity directed towards the object. When two objects are presented, the initial behaviour of visual and prehensile choice and the durations of manipulation and looking at the held object are noted.

This last procedure is of particular interest in that it makes it possible to test the comparison not only of the amodal properties assimilated by the two systems (shape, texture) but also of the specific properties, such as colour in the case of vision, or temperature (Bushnell, 1985) or weight (Ruff, 1986) in the case of touch. This procedure may also make it possible to demonstrate that visual and tactual explorations are not independent of one another, even when the properties examined are specific to the different sensory modalities.

A variant of the above procedure has been employed by Gottfried and Rose (1980). At a year old, babies placed in the dark are able to recognize haptically the shape of objects which they have previously explored bimodally in the light.

Multimodal exploration

The visually controlled manipulation of objects has two important consequences. When infants look at the objects they handle, they see an object which is moving and therefore offers different perspectives but, above all, they are the authors of these changes in perspective through their active manipulation.

There are number of problems, which we shall attempt to solve in the light of research into babies' multimodal exploration. What are the characteristics of visually controlled object manipulation? Are there actions which are specific to particular object properties? Does visually controlled manipulation allow better knowledge of the object's properties to be gained or does it, on the contrary, interfere with visual gathering of information? Are the properties of objects belonging to one sensory system nevertheless taken into consideration by the other system?

The characteristics of multimodal exploration

Before the young baby's exploratory activity becomes visually controlled, at about 4 or 5 months of age, it is none the less quite considerable, even in the dark (Rochat, 1989). Karniol (1989) has analyzed the development of this activity in babies from birth until the age of 10 months. She defines ten ordered stages in the manipulation of objects which reveal how babies' potential to improve their understanding of their environment and extend their knowledge about the physical properties of objects develops. In the initial stages, during the first four months, babies are able to perform movements which rotate, displace or shake an object. Towards the age of 4 months they appear to discover that they can hold an object in one hand and do something else with their other hand. They can also hold an object with both hands. At about 4 or 5 months of age they succeed in passing an object from one hand to the other under visual control, but do not manage to do this without visual control (Streri and Pêcheux, 1986*a*). At about 5 or 6 months of age the hands begin to coordinate first of all in handling a single object, then about a month later in handling two objects at once. At the age of about 7 or 8 months, babies discover that objects can change in shape, produce a sound when squeezed, and so on – that is to say, their own actions on objects can make things happen. This discovery gives their actions an instrumental and sequential use so that, for example, at 10 months of age they can open a box with one hand and take an object out of it with the other.

Ruff's earlier research (1984) is nevertheless remarkable in its detailed understanding of the characteristics of multimodal exploration. In her initial experiment, Ruff analyzes babies' general behaviour during their multimodal exploration of objects. She analyzes the development of this behaviour during the course of several successive trials and its genesis at 6, 9 and 12 months of age. Then, in a second experiment, she attempts to discover whether babies' behaviour is more frequently directed towards one dimension than another.

She presents each subject with a series of six objects. Each series is presented over six trials with a 30-second familiarization period. A comparison of the effect of learning during the course of the trials is conducted between the first three and the latter three trials for each series of objects. The following elements of behaviour are analyzed: (1) total duration of visual exploration; (2) total duration of manual exploration; (3) oral exploration time; (4) the frequency with which buccal and visual explorations alternate; (5) rotations of the object using one hand, and using both hands; (6) fine manipulation of the object using the fingers; (7) passing the object from one hand to the other; and (8) banging the object on the table.

We should point out that several of these forms of behaviour were observed during our research into manual exploration without visual control in babies of 2 and 4 months of age. They are therefore used functionally at a very early age, with a quantitative and qualitative development in the frequency of occurrence between these two ages. Passing an object from hand to hand, carrying it to the mouth for oral exploration and even fine manipulation of the object are all behaviours which are not necessarily performed under visual control. They are not, therefore, specific to multimodal exploration.

The results of Ruff's first study indicate that some activities are modified with age. Oral exploration declines considerably between the ages of 9 and 12 months; so does the frequency of alternating oral and visual explorations. In contrast, the dexterity of fine manipulation with the fingers increases, above all between the ages of 6 and 9 months; rotating the object under visual control also increases, but this time between the ages of 9 and 12 months. These activities decrease significantly between the first three and the last three trials. This result was also obtained by Willatts (1983) under similar conditions of object presentation. Bimodal habituation is therefore possible in accordance with the same principle as visual or tactile unimodal habituation.

Is there any exploratory behaviour which is observed more frequently in connection with a given property of an object, since it is more effective than other behaviours in providing information about this property? Rotation of the object, for example, is more useful for perceiving it in its entirety than for assessing its weight. This is the second objective of Ruff's research with babies aged 9 and 12 months. During the familiarization phase she presents the infants with an object for three consecutive trials; then in a fourth trial, the test phase, she presents a new object which differs from the original by only one property – its shape, its texture or its weight. The results indicate a behavioural difference between the two phases as a function of the property studied. The babies react to changes in the characteristics of objects, and their responses are such that they maximize their likelihood of gaining information about these particular changes. A change in the object's weight leads to a greater decline in visual exploration than changes of texture or shape. Texture is a property which stimulates visual exploration and fine finger manipulation. Shape also gives rise to visual exploration and fine manipulation, but above all it stimulates the behaviour of rotating the objects, passing them from hand to hand and throwing them. In contrast, there is no particular behaviour pertaining to weight, which is a property specific to the tactilokinaesthetic modality. Therefore, infants do adjust or adapt their manipulations to the properties of objects in order to extract the most relevant information for the situation. This behaviour is compatible with the theory of affordances (J.J. Gibson, 1979) to the extent to which it is performed in a way which is adapted as a function of the particular properties of each object.

Are the sensory modalities complementary or in competition?

Schaffer and Parry's work (1969, 1970) provides evidence of hesitation behaviour in 9-month-old babies on coming into contact with a new object (the 'wariness' effect). The authors concluded from this reaction that there is a separation between the visual knowledge gained about an object and action. This research has since been the subject of much discussion and controversy (Hatwell, 1986; Rubenstein, 1976; Ruff, 1976) and similar results have not been obtained again (Willatts, 1983). We shall not reopen the debate here, but situate our analyses essentially at the level of the intersensory integration of the properties of objects.

In fact, the multimodal exploration of objects has another important consequence. Infants must judge certain information apprehended through both the visual and the tactile systems as being equivalent. In this case, are we observing a competition or an interference between the sensory modalities or, on the contrary, does the simultaneous apprehension of information in the two modalities allow better knowledge of the object to be gained? Moreover, does object-directed action have a positive effect on knowledge of object properties in the way that Piaget (1936, trans. 1936, 1953; 1937, trans. 1937, 1955) suggests?

These hypotheses have been put to the test in an experiment undertaken by Gottfried *et al.* (1978) with infants at 6, 9 and 12 months of age. The aim was to discover whether a multimodal exploration of the objects would allow better visual discrimination to be obtained than unimodal visual exploration. Three familiarization conditions were employed: one in which the object was presented solely visually; one bimodal presentation in which the babies could explore the object both manually and visually; and another condition of visual and manual presentation in which the object was inside a transparent box so that the babies could manipulate the box without having any direct access to tactile information about the object inside. The duration of familiarization in all three conditions was 20 seconds. In the test phase, the familiar object was presented with a new object, and the time spent visually exploring the two objects was recorded. The results revealed that better visual discrimination was achieved at the ages of 6 and 9 months after the solely visual familiarization condition than after the other two conditions. Only at 12 months of age did tactile exploration allow better visual recognition. From this experiment the authors conclude that until the age of 12 months the tactile modality interferes with the visual modality in the simultaneous exploration of objects, and that direct activity with the objects does not allow an efficient apprehension of information. The information would appear to be dispersed between the modalities. This interpretation is hardly compatible with the results obtained from combined exploration of objects, or with the hypothesis of an interference between perception and action. A second study undertaken with full-term and premature babies at 6 and 12 months of age gave comparable results (Rose, Gottfried and Bridger, 1978). Moreover, at the age of 12 months the manipulation of premature babies appears deficient compared to that of full-term babies, since at that age it still does not allow a high level of discrimination between objects.

These experiments are subject to criticism on two counts. First, the familiarization times are short, and identical in all three conditions (20 seconds). While this is suitable for the speed of vision, it is insufficient for an effective manipulation of objects. Secondly, the context in which the test phase is undertaken is uniform in the intramodal visual condition but differs in the other two conditions because the infants are not allowed to manipulate the objects. This difference in context between familiarization phase and test phase could itself be one of the causes of the absence of visual discrimination.

The hypothesis that the context of object presentation has an effect on the test phase has been examined in two studies (Rolfe and Day, 1981; Ruff, 1981). The first study, conducted with 6-month-old babies, employs an identical procedure to that used by Gottfried *et al.* (1978) for the familiarization phases. However, the test phases are identical to the familiarization phases in all three conditions. The results showed a high level of discrimination between familiar and new objects in each of the conditions apart from the one in which the object is enclosed within a transparent box. Thus the manipulation of objects does contribute to the gathering of better information about the object when it is associated with visual exploration, contrary to the findings of Gottfried *et al.* (1978) and Rose *et al.* (1979). The context of the test phase therefore plays a major role.

Ruff's second study (1981) focuses more precisely on the exact nature of the information which makes improved object recognition possible. The objects used in the familiarization phase and the test phase differ in colour while retaining the same surface structure, or conversely, they differ in shape but keep the same colour pattern. Colour is a property which is specific to the visual modality, whilst shape can be perceived through either modality. The familiarization time consisted of six trials of 30 seconds each, and was therefore longer than in the work of Gottfried *et al.* (1978). The results of Ruff's studies are the complete opposite of those obtained by Gottfried *et al.* (1978). In the visual intramodal condition, no discrimination is obtained in the test phase. In contrast, a preference for the new object is observed in the bimodal exploration condition. This preference appears to be realized more rapidly during exploration, when it relates to the shape rather than the colour of the new object. This latter result is important, since it indicates that visual information and tactile information concerning a specific property of objects supplement one another.

A greater efficiency in the gathering of information when this is jointly realized by two modalities has been the object of a second systematic research by Ruff (1982), who compares the bimodal gathering of information relating to different properties of objects. She draws a distinction between properties with structural characteristics, such as shape and texture, and properties without such characteristics, such as colour. The aim of her study is to discover whether manipulation augments visual attention in the case of structural properties and is less effective in the case of nonstructural properties. If so, then objects would be better discriminated by their shape or structure than by their colour. The results clearly show that the visually controlled manipulation of an object allows a high level of discrimination of its shape and texture – that is to say, its structural properties – but not of its colour. In the same way, better performances are obtained when the structural characteristics are shared by the two modalities than when they are not. This result confirms that of an earlier study by Steele and Pederson (1977).

The lack of discrimination between objects which differ only by virtue of their colouring poses a serious problem. It is unlikely that infants do not distinguish between the colours of objects (see Bornstein, 1978, 1981) and a result similar to Ruff's (1982) has also been obtained in more recent work by Bushnell, Shaw and Strauss (1985). This study had a different aim: to discover how 6-month-old babies reconstruct the information gathered during multimodal exploration of objects, given that these objects possess characteristics specific to the visual modality (colour) and the tactile modality (temperature). The infants spend longer touching objects than they do looking at them. It seemed to the authors that they were in some way haptically 'captured' by the objects, and that temperature is a salient dimension for this modality. When the temperature of the object is altered, the duration of tactile and visual exploration in the test phase is also modified. In contrast, the results concerning colour are not very clear. The babies do not visually or tactually explore an object whose colour is different in the test phase from that of the object in the familiarization phase. Thus the change in the colour of the object does not necessarily mean that it is a new object for the infant. It is therefore the structural properties of shape and texture which characterize an object, not its colour. Here, the tactile modality plays a fundamental role in multimodal exploration. In feeling objects, the hand produces visual and tactile sensory changes which allow the simultaneous extraction of perceptual invariants. However, manipulation is not simply a motor activity which is controlled by and at the service of vision. It rcmains a fundamental perceptual act.

To sum up: from the time when prehension–vision coordination becomes functional, the multimodal exploration of objects does not challenge the unity of the sensory modalities. On the contrary, analysis of infant behaviour reveals that the systems cooperate with each other in obtaining information about the properties of objects. This coordination is compatible with the development, after the age of 6 months, of touch–vision intermodal transfer, which is observed under even the shortest presentation conditions. Nevertheless, we still need to understand the processes through which babies organize, unite and coordinate their perceptions, and how this relation fits into the more general framework of the baby's representative activity. This question will be the subject of the next chapter.

Chapter 5

Perception and knowledge

Recent discoveries about infants' ability to know their environment have raised the question of what level of perceptual organization we should attribute to neonates if we are to understand their various forms of motor and perceptual behaviour. Do babies possess an organized conception of their environment, or a perception of it which is confused with all the activity in the sensory receptors? The newborn, long described as a collection of reflexes, had all the appearance of a badly adjusted robot rather than a person. With perceptual systems which were thought to be too immature, the neonate developed in a disorganized world which was in perfect symbiosis with it. Evidence of the ability to process information at a central level would mean that babies do organize reality and that they possess cognitive, representative systems allowing them, through their own perceptions and actions, to conceive of a reality which is independent of them.

The field of neurophysiology has opened a promising avenue of research with its description of neuronal cell reactions and, more specifically, with the notion of 'bar detectors', now known as 'feature detectors', which was originally established by Hubel and Wiesel (1963, 1968). However, none of the research since then has made it possible to understand the functioning of the visual cortex. The research describes a certain way of representing the elements perceived in the environment, but as Marr (1982) has pointed out, 'trying to understand perception by studying only neurons is like trying to understand bird flight by studying only feathers' (p. 27). The organism's biological development is a precondition for psychological development, but does not suffice to explain it. Psychology also ascribes significance to behaviour. It is the very notion of the meaning of babies' behaviour which is at the heart of the debate.

Like perception, cognition cannot be directly observed. The study of it must rely on behavioural indications from which its character and properties can be inferred. However, as Lautrey (1987) suggests, the difficulty lies in distinguishing, through such indirect indications, those properties which can be imputed to representation from those which characterize the behaviour. Bearing in mind the narrow range of neonatal responses which researchers have available to them, the problem becomes thornier still. We have very little data with which to evaluate such inferences. The discussion is therefore theoretical, and the problem is posed differently depending on whether we are looking at the relation between responses which are controlled by babies in accordance with their perceptions – that is to say, in cases where motor and perceptual responses are thought to be heterogeneous – or studying the organizational abilities of the perceptual systems.

Meaning and intentionality

Intentional behaviour is interpreted as revealing that subjects attribute a meaning to the events they perceive. It assumes that subjects regard themselves as different from their environment, and that in their behaviour they distinguish between the means and the end of an action. The concepts of intention, meaning and subject are closely connected. They are incompatible with the idea of the existence of an adualistic relationship between neonates and their environment, which has been proposed in certain theories of development such as those of Piaget and Wallon and, more recently, Mounoud and Bullinger. Here we shall be only tangentially concerned with the relation between babies and their environment. This has, however, been the object of a thorough analysis by Lécuyer (1988, 1989) which takes account of the different theoretical contexts in which this question is raised.

At an earlier stage of research, Bruner (1973) had placed great stress on the baby's intentionality in effecting particular movements in reaction to stimuli. According to Bruner, the infant's motor activity is controlled by a mentally represented intention which directs the infant towards a goal. It is, one might say, the 'motivation' which underlies the sensorimotor action. For example, before infants can systematically reach for and touch an object – at about 4 months of age – their poorly controlled movements are interpreted as attempts to reach for it. These action patterns which are evoked or triggered by the sight of an object or an event form an innate, pre-adapted repertoire of behaviours for achieving a goal. With practice, these action patterns gain in speed and precision. Bruner (1966) attributes the young infant with representations based on actions ('enactive representations') which are themselves due to the intentions underlying them. Once mastered, the habitual pattern through which action is represented is 'serially organized, governed by some sort of scheme that holds its successive segments together, and is in some sense related to other acts that either facilitate it or interfere with it' (Bruner, 1966, p. 6). Piaget (1945) had earlier dismissed the idea of a similar representation of action, particularly during the sensorimotor period. He places the sensorimotor representation at the heart of the process of accommodation and assimilation. Grasping an object is an action which is likely to be produced again, and to be generalized in such a way that an object is perceived not only once it has been grasped but also as an object which can be grasped (assimilation). Conversely, depending on how far away the object to be grasped is situated, there are perceptions of depth and displacement correlative to the hand (accommodation). However, while the action schemes bestow a meaning on objects, representations are not formed until a later stage, 'when the current sensorimotor data are assimilated into elements which are simply evoked but are not perceptible at the time in question' (Piaget, 1945, p. 291).

Does the mental representation – to adopt Bruner's use of the term – have any reality in the analysis of behaviours other than prehension? For example, Meltzoff and Moore (1977, 1983, 1989) observe the intermodal behaviour of imitation in the neonate. Does this behaviour necessitate a representation of the baby's own body? Does it imply intention on the neonate's part? Imitation possesses a dual nature. On the one hand it can be thought of as a response to promptings from the environment, and is based on an entirely congeneric exchange. In this case it is defined as a mode of affective interaction, its socialization function is fundamental. On the other, it is a means of acquiring knowledge, and is based on a pre-formed knowledge of the imitator's physical and intellectual capacities. In this perspective its cognitive and representative function is fundamental.

It is around this second characteristic that the debate concerning the neonate's imitations has revolved. The problem is of knowing whether the imitative behaviour observed in 1945 by Zazzo in his 25-day-old baby (Zazzo, 1988), and later observed in neonates by Meltzoff and Moore (1977, 1983), really constitutes the active reproduction of a model with the intention of doing so. Imitations occurring early in life had already been mentioned at the beginning of this century, but dismissed as a form of instinct. The initial interpretation of these imitations at an early age – which have been fiercely disputed since the first observations reported by Zazzo (see Zazzo, 1988) – was that they were false imitations (Guillaume, 1927) as against the 'true' imitations, 'echopraxia' and 'echolalia', occurring at a later age (Wallon, 1942) or sporadic self-imitations which depend on a circular reaction, not on an external model (Piaget, 1936, trans. 1936, 1953; 1937, trans. 1937, 1955).

It is mainly in opposition to Piaget's theories on the role of imitation in representation that these early manifestations of this behaviour have been studied. In effect, Piaget (1945) has provided a strong theoretical framework for the genesis of representation in which it is difficult to integrate the existence of neonatal imitations.

According to Piagetian theory, representation is defined on two levels: in its broader meaning it is thought; in its narrower sense it is a kind of figurative memory in which reality is converted into images. In its broader meaning, representation is aimed at a knowledge of reality – that is to say, the attribution of meanings. This knowledge is assured by perceptual cues and the baby's activity in relation to its environment.

In its narrower sense, representation allows the reconstruction of past events or absent objects. It is assured by three instruments: the mental image, the symbol and the sign. Access to these instruments at about 18 months of age enables the infant to evoke absent realities. The signifiers – that is to say, the instruments – serve to re-create the signified which, for Piaget, may be the action scheme, the event or object, or the concept. Representation is the union between signifier and signified: 'This specific connection between the "signifiers" and the "signified" forms the basis of a new function which goes beyond sensorimotor activity and to which we can give the general name of "symbolic function" ' (Piaget, 1945, p. 292).

The beginning of representation is marked by the observation of delayed imitation. This is the principal sign of the existence of an internal image. It was therefore in the genesis of imitation that Piaget sought to find the origin of representation. He thought that imitation should involve first the visible parts of the body, then the invisible parts. For him, babies would have to rely on representations of their own bodies in order to imitate facial gestures. This description of development therefore prevents imitation of, for example, tongue protrusion before imitation of pointing the index finger. According to Piagetian theory, the organizational and necessary role of imitation is essential in the process of constructing representations.

It is with regard to this role in particular that Piaget's theory has been subject to some profound re-examination. More recent observations of neonatal imitative behaviour (Meltzoff and Moore, 1977; Vinter, 1985; Zazzo, 1957) in babies ranging from 1 month to 6 months of age (Field, Woodson, Greenberg and Cohen, 1982; Fontaine, 1984*b*; Maratos, 1973; Vinter, 1985) using a longitudinal and transverse procedure have made it impossible to doubt any longer that this behaviour exists from the first few days of life.

Meltzoff (1990) and Meltzoff, Kuhl and Moore (1991) interpret the reproduction of facial and head movements as indicating a neonatal capacity for actively realizing intermodal matching between the model (visual modality) and the neonate's own actions (proprioceptive modality). This process of 'Active Intermodal Mapping' (AIM) does not depend on mechanisms which are reflex or innate (IRM for Innate Releasing Mechanism), or on learning. Rather, it is a case of a 'psychological primitive' – that is to say, a system of cognitive representation which is not comparable to that postulated in the older infant by Piaget.

Vinter (1985) supports this point of view, and has conducted a number of studies of imitation while emphasizing the necessity to take particular care with the methodologies employed in this field. She obtains results similar to those of other authors. Within this framework, imitation becomes an indication of and no longer a precursor to representation, as Piaget suggested. Vinter also interprets this behaviour as indicating the presence of representation in the very young infant. Nevertheless, she differs from Meltzoff and Moore over the nature of this representation.

Mounoud (1979; Mounoud and Vinter, 1985) believes that the notion of representation is closely linked to the notions of code and memory. In the baby, representations are rudimentary, partial and imperfect. They 'organize or structure the contents of reality in a way which is internal to the subject and are therefore involved as much in the processes of identifying and recognizing objects as they are in evocation' (Mounoud and Vinter, 1985, p. 256). The subject's perceptions and actions are interfaced both by a system for translating reality by a process of coding and by an internal organization in the form of traces of these transcriptions. Mounoud links this notion of representation to that of action programmes. Action programmes govern the modes of exchange between babies and their surroundings. The degree of accuracy with which a movement is calibrated would indicate how well space and objects are represented. The nature of the code for structuring the organization of contents is modified as a function of the subject's abilities. The neonate's sensorimotor behaviour is managed by a sensory code, and the representations which mediate this management cannot be referred to any external world.

Whether it is a case of an active matching process (Meltzoff, 1990) or of a sensory representation (Mounoud and Vinter, 1985), these authors are agreed in their view of imitation as involving the formation of a memory trace and a representation of the neonate's own body.

However, the existence of mediators in the baby has not led Vinter and Mounoud to believe that babies live in a dualistic relationship with their environment. Infants are not conscious of their actions, their imitations or their matchings. The sensory but not perceptual types of coding (the latter occur at a later stage) belong to a trace system similar to that described in the field of neurophysiology: an engram for each new piece of learning.

Nevertheless, it is not entirely accurate to consider that babies live in total fusion with their surroundings. The existence of compensatory reactions by babies in experiments in which the environment is unstable is not compatible with this form of relation (Butterworth and Hicks, 1977; Jouen, 1986, 1988; Jouen and Lepecq, 1989; Lee and Aronson, 1974).

The principle behind the experiments reported by these authors is to create a conflict between visual information which specifies an instability of the environment and vestibular information which specifies a stable posture for the baby. The entire structure (walls and ceiling) into which the baby is placed can be moved forwards or backwards in such a way that the visual flow pattern corresponds with the pattern that would normally accompany swaying of the infant's body. Even before babies are able to propel themselves autonomously, they compensate for this nonexistent loss of balance. They sway, stagger or fall in the direction opposite to the movement defined by the misleading visual information. Babies are thus highly dependent on 'visual proprioception' in order to maintain a stable posture. These experimental data clearly indicate that babies perceive their surroundings as something which is separate from their own bodies, and that 'the organism appears to distinguish between the movement of its own body and the movement of the environment since the internal structure of the optic array cannot specify either of these two events' (Butterworth and Pope, 1983, p. 126). According to Butterworth, this does not mean that the specification relation, in the Gibsonian sense, is 'objectively known'. Only when babies have a high degree of command over their posture are they able to take account of what is really happening in their environment. It seems plausible, therefore, to think that during their early imitations babies perceive their models as separate from themselves.

However, the observation of early imitation, like that of other neonatal behaviour, raises a second problem. Is it a case of reflex behaviour triggered by a stimulus, or should we regard it as demonstrating an intention to reproduce the model? How should we interpret the meaning of this behaviour in relation to that which appears in a more systematic way in older infants? There is certainly an identity of structure, but can we also postulate an identity of function? If we accept Piaget's definition, the 18-month-old infant has a plan to imitate, but can it be said that the newborn and the very young baby have the same plan? They may react to the situation without saying to themselves, 'I am trying to do the same thing as someone else'. In other words, the behaviour may not be programmed before its execution, in which case there would be no intention to imitate.

Intentionality in the baby is a concept which has only just begun to be studied. The aim is to discover whether early behaviour involves programming of action. It is in the observation of sensorimotor behaviour that intention on the part of neonate and baby can be best discerned. For Bower, Broughton and Moore (1970*b*), this intention governs the baby's reaching behaviour. The reaching gesture does not occur by chance, since it happens more frequently when neonates fixate on the object than when they are looking elsewhere (von Hofsten, 1982). Anticipation of the point of arrival at a moving object, which is revealed by the precise positioning of arm and hand at the contact point, presupposes an underlying intentionality, but this has been observed only from the age of 4 months (von Hofsten and Lindhagen, 1979).

Depending on the research, several operational definitions have made it possible to conclude that intentional behaviour does exist in the neonate. For example, the frequency of directed behaviour in relation to 'noise level' – that is to say, the totality of the baby's spontaneous movements – serves to indicate the presence of intention for some authors. Thus, Butterworth (1986*a*, *b*) filmed the arm movements of 72-hour-old newborns, and analyzed the positions of their heads, hands and mouths. He observed that about 15 per cent of the neonate's arm and hand movements are directed towards the mouth. Butterworth believes that this activity cannot be due to reflexes alone. Furthermore, he considers that anticipatory opening of the mouth before the end of the trajectory of the arm movement reveals the presence of an intentional hand–mouth coordination.

As for early imitative behaviour, it is the differences in behaviour which reveal intent. For example, Fontaine (1984*c*) detects an intention to imitate on the baby's part in so far as the frequency of imitation of a movement corresponding to a model is greater than that of another movement belonging to the same movement field. The results of his research (Fontaine, 1982, 1984*b*) demonstrate a capacity for fine discrimination in the baby's reproduction of facial movements. Although these results are interesting, they do not enable us to understand why the ability to distinguish facial features is limited in babies. In fact, the mouth is not distinguished as a dimension of the face until the age of about 4 or 5 months (E.J. Gibson, 1976). At the level of representation, this is probably due to different mechanisms being involved in discrimination.

Nevertheless, does the fact that babies respond to stimuli mean that we should necessarily deduce from this that they organize their perceptions? They can perceive their environment as an entity independent of themselves, yet still respond only to blurred, partial information. They may perceive only surfaces or surface differences, but not necessarily an organized world made up of distinct objects bearing particular physical properties, and so on. For example, postulating the existence of an 'amodal' centre will tell us nothing about babies' ability to organize their perceptions, and does not imply that any cognitive mechanism exists in the baby.

Perception and cognition

The nonreversibility of behaviour and of intermodal transfer leads to the idea of a specificity of the modalities. In this respect, it is compatible with the conception of modular thought defended by Fodor (1983). Contrary to the notion of direct, immediate perception confined to the level of proximal stimulation, Fodor's propositions divide the perceptual act into two discrete elements: peripheral modules, responsible for perception; and central systems, which support thought. The distinction between perception and cognition is not new, but it requires a definition of each of them, and of their interrelationship. The peripheral modules are highly specialized, each in a precise domain. For example, there is a module for the perception of linguistic sounds, and another for the perception of musical sounds. These modules have an obligatory functioning (a perception cannot be avoided). They process information rapidly and are biologically determined by a fixed, specific, wired neuronal architecture. They are compartmentalized, and develop endogenously in a determined order. The perceptual modules serve as relays between the sensory transcoders (sensory systems) and thought. They receive the representations of the proximal stimulus from the transcoders, and perform transformations which reflect the properties of the objects. These levels of representation become increasingly abstract as the distance from the transcoders grows. The task of perception is to represent the world in a way which is accessible to thought. The central systems have the reverse properties to those of the peripheral systems. Central processes are slow. They are responsible for thought, and for the planning of action. They are not constraining (thought can be avoided). Although they have access only to the final product of the peripheral modules, they are able to correct our perceptions. They have no functional domain of their own, but clarify our perceptual knowledge.

Fodor's modular perspective is attractive and rigorously defined. The module concept has also been used elsewhere to describe the organization of the neocortex (Paillard, 1986). However, the notion of a peripheral modular perception contrasted with a central organization of thought is incompatible with the idea of an 'amodal' perception which integrates the sensory information, since in Fodor's theory this information is, in principle, processed in a compartmentalized way by the peripheral modules. The retention of the unity of an object and the integration of its physical properties when they are perceived visually and haptically are the task not of thought, but of a general perceptual system. Moreover, such a biological and psychological determinism of the peripheral systems suggests the presence of a transcription mediator, and this is incompatible with the early existence of amodal perception. Furthermore, Fodor does not state whether all the peripheral systems function in an analogous way. Differences of functioning between the perceptual modules would also be incompatible with the existence of a unity of modalities at birth, and with the findings which we have demonstrated in our research. While perception and cognition are two separable notions, they are closely linked in the perceptual act and are not based on instances of heterogeneous knowledge.

The boundaries between perception and cognition are rarely defined as clearly in studies of perception in babies. When they are the focus of theoretical reflection, either the two notions are fused into one and their boundaries are abolished, or they remain separate, and perception and cognition are deemed to act upon distinct elements of reality. The theory defended by Lécuyer (1989) illustrates the former viewpoint. The baby's intelligence is described in a general way as having the function of establishing relations. On this premiss, since perception is the first level of understanding relations, it is an intelligent activity. In view of the fact that motor activity plays a minor role and is very inefficient in the first few months of life, intelligence is initially perceptual. Intermodal matching is an illustration of this type of intelligent activity which is essentially perceptual in nature. However, since this perspective is limited to the perceptual mechanisms, it regards action as playing only a secondary role in the production of intelligible situations, and does not attribute a cognitive status to motor activity during the course of development of prehension–vision coordination.

The second perspective is expressed in Spelke's theory (1988). Perceptual activity is defined within the Gibsonian perspective. But since she is interested in the baby's physical conception of objects, Spelke separates perception and cognition. The perception of objects does not depend solely on a perceptual mechanism but also on a broader cognitive mechanism which allows the baby to possess an abstract conception of the physical world. To say that babies have a concept of objects implies that they have cognitive capacities which enable them to organize stimuli into units on the basis of their perceptions. These stimuli specify the abstract properties of objects as defined by adults.

Spelke demonstrates that 4-month-old babies invest objects with four properties: cohesion, boundaries, consistency and spatio–temporal continuity. Each of these properties is abstract. They cannot be seen, touched or felt, but they impose limits on the way in which objects move. Cohesion limits the movements of an object by preserving its integrity (Kellman and Spelke, 1983; Kellman, Gleitmann and Spelke, 1987; Kellman, Spelke and Short, 1986). Boundaries limit the movements of an object by preserving its distinctiveness in relation to other objects. Consistency limits the movements of an object in that it cannot pass through other objects (Baillargeon, Spelke and Wasserman, 1985). Spatio–temporal continuity limits the movements of an object in continuous displacement: an object cannot move from one place to another without tracing a continuous path through space and time between the two points (Spelke and Kestenbaum, 1986).

This organization of the environment is initially based on the perceptual system. However, the perceptual system does not seek out the same invariants as the cognitive system. Specifically, the perceptual system searches for and detects invariants in the physical energies of the stimulus in such a way that it gains knowledge of those surfaces in the optic array that are continuous. It does not, however, organize the world into units. The discovery of units with the abstract characteristics which define them is the job of the cognitive system.

Research into the 4-month-old baby's perception of object unity when the object is partially occluded, and of the boundaries of objects

(Kellman and Spelke, 1983) demonstrates this perspective well. Let us recall that in this experiment, when babies are visually presented with a rod which is partially hidden behind a wooden block, they retain the rod's unity and integrity provided that the rod behind the block is moved. Thus, on the basis of only those surfaces which are visible, babies perceive not two separate elements, but one. The fact that this result has also been obtained in the tactile modality (Streri and Spelke, 1988) in an intermodal transfer situation reveals that there is a similar mechanism at work in both modalities. We already know that touch and vision function in an analogous way in the extraction of perceptual invariants from a stimulus, as the baby's intramodal discriminatory abilities in both tactile and visual modalities demonstrate. This experiment also confirms the existence of amodal mechanisms in touch and vision in the organization of objects into units.

Spelke's perspective makes it possible to understand how, from the age of 3 to 4 months, babies segment their perceptual field into three-dimensional objects according to the 'cohesion', 'boundedness', 'rigidity' and 'no action at a distance' principles (Spelke, 1990). All the above research suggests that perception of the object also depends on the way in which human beings reason about the physical world. Remaining on the perceptual level, however, how can we explain the lack of reversibility of transfer of essentially perceptual properties, such as shape, which do not imply any need to reason about things? In order for a reversible transfer to be obtained, evidence would need to be found not only that there are amodal mechanisms common to vision and touch – which has been achieved – but also that there is an 'amodal' knowledge – that is to say, knowledge which is common to both sensory systems. Evidently, the constraints which would need to be defined limit the possibility of such knowledge.

Marr's computational theory (1982), which is compatible with that of Fodor (1983) on this point, would make it possible to explain why intermodal matching is obtained from vision to touch in 2-month-old babies when the target is a sketch, but not when it is an object (Streri and Molina, 1993, submitted). The baby's difficulty in the second case lies at the level of tactile recognition. At 2 months of age, is the tactile percept the same in nature as the visual percept?

Let us recall that according to Marr's viewpoint (1982), the visual act is regarded as the faculty for extracting the relevant information from an image in order to execute a task. Only the information which is necessary for the action is retained. Perception is described as a hierarchy of 'sketches' which, in the visual modality, transform the optic array into a succession of representations, each one exhibiting increasingly complex properties of reality and enabling perception of an object's volume to be derived from a flat image of light intensities. Marr's thesis is not a theory of development, and the sequential representations are part of the visual act, not the development of perceptions. Moreover, the model is defined only for vision, not for the other modalities. Nevertheless, if we consider that vision and touch function in a similar way, we could postulate that there are also information-processing levels within the tactile modality. These levels would develop as a function of the degree of maturity and processing ability of the sensory receptors and of the meanings infants accord to objects and events in their environment. Intermodal transfer would be realized in both directions only when the levels of tactile and visual representation are equivalent. When touch and vision discern different stimuli they perform an initial level of processing which can, however, be insufficient for recognition by the other modality. Our knowledge about the nature and quantity of information extracted through the two modalities by babies of any given age is still imprecise. In transfer experiments where visual and tactile stimuli are identical, the possibilities of recognition are maximized. This is less evident when transfer is realized despite a difference in the objects presented in the two modalities, as in Meltzoff and Borton's experiment (1979).

On this point, this experiment is noteworthy in two ways. Not only does it demonstrate the ability of babies just 1 month old to recognize visually an object previously explored orally, but this recognition occurs when the objects presented to the oral and the visual modalities are made of different material. Gibson and Walker's experiment (1984) with the same age group but with identical objects also demonstrated the existence of a relation between the two modalities.

We should point out the differences between the experimental apparatus employed by Meltzoff and Borton (1979): the objects stimulating the buccal and visual receptors differ in a number of dimensions. The constraints imposed by the receptor systems (the still poor visual discriminatory abilities of babies and the physical capacity of the oral cavity) made a difference in size necessary. The objects were made of different materials: the dummies were rubber, while the visual spheres were wooden. The oral exploration of the dummies therefore led to a distortion of the object, while the visual spheres were presented immobile and undistorted. As well as their general material aspect, the function of the objects also differed. For example, the dummy, but not the visually presented ball, might have had a calming effect on the baby. Only two dimensions were held invariant, namely the presence or absence of bumps and, if present, their number. Both sets of objects were spherical in appearance, although the dummies were none the less liable to become misshapen during buccal exploration. Despite these differences, the experiment shows – remarkably – that the 1-month-old baby establishes an equivalence relationship between the two sets of stimuli. This relationship is evidently not based on the number of bumps, but on their presence or absence.

Relations of equivalence are established not at the level of the objects but at the level of a property common to these objects and to both modalities. This conclusion is compatible with Bower's theory (1979) according to which the internal representations resulting from perception are primarily abstract, and retain only the most general properties of reality.

Thus, the question which is now raised is of knowing to what dimension the intermodal relation refers, as well as the nature of the information extracted haptically and visually concerning the same object by babies of a given age. We have attempted to answer this question in a series of experiments comprising three conditions (Streri and Molina, 1991). In the first condition (intermodal) the baby explores an object tactually and is then visually presented with the familiar object and a two-dimensional silhouette picture of the same object. In the second condition (visual intramodal) the baby is visually habituated to an object and is then presented, in the visual test phase, with the seen object and a silhouette of the same object. A control group receives the same visual test without prior familiarization. A comparison of the responses from the visual test phase in these three conditions should reveal whether there is a difference in the babies' recognition of the object. The stimuli were the same as those employed in the earlier experiment by Streri and Molina (1993*a*, in press) – that is to say, a three-dimensional cross and a three-dimensional cotton reel versus their two-dimensional silhouette pictures. Conditions of presentation of the stimuli were identical.

After tactile habituation to the object, the results show that the order in which the visual stimuli are presented has an effect. When the object is presented first, it is looked at for significantly longer than the silhouette; when the silhouette is the first stimulus, it is looked at for significantly longer than the object. Such an effect of order is not apparent in the control group; neither does it appear under the visual familiarization condition. After visual habituation to the object, the baby always looks for longer at the two-dimensional picture. On the basis of this first experiment, therefore, we can conclude that after tactile exploration of an object the representation of it formed by the baby is ambiguous, since transfer is supported by both the object and the silhouette. On the other hand, after visual exploration of the object the results are unequivocal. The baby always prefers to look at the new stimulus – that is to say, the two-dimensional silhouette. This second result is not new, since transfer and discrimination between an object and its two-dimensional representation have been demonstrated in 6-month-old (Rose, 1977) and 5-month-old babies (Deloache, Strauss and Maynard, 1979). More recently, Slater, Morison and Rose (1984*b*) have shown that as soon as they are born, babies are able to detect similarities and differences between three-dimensional stimuli and their two-dimensional representations. In contrast, the results are very unclear after tactile habituation to the object. Since the information regarding contour and surface is similar in both stimuli, it is possible that the effect of order is due to the change of modality which renders both objects familiar, the first trial determining the preference for a stimulus. However, an important difference between the two stimuli concerns the volumetric aspect of the object and the flat aspect of the silhouette. At the time of transfer, does this information remain relevant for the babies, or do they simply ignore it?

In order to answer this question, we conducted a second series of experiments (Streri and Molina, 1991) in which the visual stimuli were homogeneous (two drawings) and only the contour was specified, so that we could represent the object either in perspective or flattened. We constructed two line drawings specifying the edges of a cube. In one of the drawings, all three dimensions were specified and the general organization of the cube was retained (Necker cube).

In the other, a flattened version of the object was drawn; this was thus devoid of the meaning of the represented object. In both drawings, the information about the number of edges and total surface area was kept constant. We tested visual recognition of these two drawings after tactile exploration of the cube (intermodal condition) and after visual exploration (intramodal condition) of the same object. A control group received the same visual test without prior familiarization. If, while exploring the cube, the babies construct a three-dimensional representation of it, then at the time of the visual test they should look at the representation of the cube in perspective differently from that of the flattened cube. If they take in only the contour information (edges) but not the object's structural organization, then at the level of the visual test they should look at one line drawing for as long as they look at the other. The clearest results were expected after visual habituation.

After tactile exploration of the cube, we again observed the effect of the order of presentation of the visual stimuli. When the drawing in perspective was presented first, it was looked at for longer than the flat drawing. When the flat drawing was presented first, it was looked at for longer than the perspective drawing. We did not observe an effect of order of presentation in the babies in the control group. After visual habituation to the cube, the results were much clearer: the babies always and unequivocally spent longer looking at the drawing specifying the three dimensions of the object.

Therefore, these two series of experiments show that at 2 months of age tactile perceptual organization is different from visual perceptual organization. Everything suggests that the volumetric aspect of the object is irrelevant at the level of intermodal transfer and contour is the only information which is transferred, since the babies recognize the object they have just manipulated in both the Necker cube and the flattened cube. This result appears to be specific to the intermodal transfer situation, since in the visual modality babies detect a difference in the thickness of objects of similar appearance which are presented in flattened or rounded form (Streri and Molina, 1993*a*, in press). It is quite probable that since 2-month-old babies' ability to manipulate objects is limited, the efficiency with which they can take in overall and structural information is reduced. Babies need full control of their grasping reflex in order to explore an object in more detail, and thus to gain a clearer representation of it. Such limitations do not appear to be observed in the visual modality (Streri, 1991; Streri and Molina, 1993*b*, in press).

At what age do we observe an equivalence between the visual and tactile perceptual representations formed for the same object? We replicated the cube experiment with 4-month-old babies. The experimental conditions and the visual and tactile stimuli presented were identical to those employed with the 2-month-old babies. The results indicate that after visual habituation to the cube the 4-month-old babies prefer to look at the flattened drawing of the object than at the one specifying the cube in three dimensions. This result is the opposite to the one we obtained in the experiment with the 2-month-old babies, who prefer the drawing of the Necker cube. Therefore, a development in the organization of visual perception is observed. After tactile habituation to the cube, the 4-month-olds prefer to look at the drawing in perspective than at the flattened drawing. No effect of order of presentation is observed. The control group show no preference for either of the stimuli. Therefore, tactile perceptual organization has changed, and appears to be clearer at the age of 4 months. As for intermodal transfer, the volumetric aspect seems to have become relevant. Nevertheless, there still appears to be a disparity between the two conditions, since the preference shown for one type of drawing is not the same under visual and tactile conditions. All the same, this experiment does not help us to decide whether the 4-month-old baby is able to organize the manipulated object as a whole entity. The baby may be sensitive to contour and volume, but may still not form a clear representation of the object.

These results need to be complemented by further experiments employing other objects. Nevertheless, they do specify the nature of the information extracted during exploration of the surface areas of the object, and determine in more detail those elements which are actually transferred. Thus, on the basis of the levels of representation obtained in these experiments, we are in a better position to understand the degree of meaning that babies attribute to stimuli.

Equivalence and identity

All the research into intermodal transfer reveals early abilities to relate information gathered manually to information gained visually.

The baby treats heterogeneous information as equivalent at the sensory level. On the basis of the experiments analyzed, however, it is not possible to distinguish, among the totality of the information gathered by the baby, which is treated as equivalent and which is not differentiated. We still do not know precisely on the basis of what specific property, or feature of this particular property, this equivalence is established. In effect, babies are given a multimodal object to handle, not simply one property of that object. Yet we infer that it is this property that gives rise to transfer. If the contour of a complex object – that is to say, one with little redundancy of shape – is a salient dimension when the object is manipulated, on what characteristic of this contour of the object will visual recognition be based? Curves? Angles? Straight lines? Surfaces? We still do not have sufficient information to be able to answer this question.

Another question arises in this connection. Intermodal transfer is based on an equivalence relationship between the properties of objects, but not necessarily between the objects themselves. If this is so, how do babies know that objects which exhibit common characteristics are nevertheless different? The identification of an object requires more complex mechanisms than those involved when a single property is considered. When a parent slips a soft toy in with the sleeping baby, who then cuddles it for the rest of the night, how does the baby know it is teddy, not panda or koala? In an experimental situation, if a wooden ring is placed into a baby's hands while a circlet of flowers or a ring doughnut or a dress ring is visually presented, how does the baby know that all these objects, which share the same topology, are not the same? As Spelke in particular has suggested (1984), the problem posed by intermodal transfer is that of how the identity of objects is recognized. According to Bower (1979), it is through repeated experience that objects are perceived with their specific properties. However, we do not know through what mechanisms the baby passes from an abstract level to a more specific level. This problem is also familiar within the perspective of affordance theory. In order for infants to recognize, in a visual object, the tactually familiar object rather than some other one, Gibson's theory postulates the existence of limitations on the class of invariants which they must detect if they are to act correctly. However, as Spelke comments, this credits infants with a much higher capacity than that of extracting invariants; it implies that they have perceptual mechanisms for selecting which one of the set of logically possible stimuli corresponds to the object in question. This viewpoint concurs with the highly empirical perspective developed by Harnad (1987) of the genesis of perceptual categorization skills. He explains the learning of perceptual categorization in terms of an inductive 'bottom–up' process involving two kinds of internal representation:

- iconic representations situated at modality level which are translations of the sensory input. At this level, discrimination between stimuli is possible. These representations are reinforced by repeated exposure to one class of stimuli.
- categorial representations which result from the filtering of iconic representations. This filtering eliminates specificities or gross features which are linked to the modality, and retains only elements which are invariant. These representations are multimodal and make possible the identification and categorization of objects.

If we accept that intermodal transfer relies on a process of categorization, the research we have conducted corresponds well to this model. However, it is necessary to extend the range of stimuli. As far as we know, no experiment has yet attempted to find evidence that such mechanisms for filtering and selecting information exist in the baby.

Nevertheless, an idea proposed by Rose and Ruff (1987) constitutes the beginnings of an answer. They suggest trying Kluver's method (1933) of using stimuli which are equivalent or nonequivalent. The objective of this method is to find the different conditions under which a response can be elicited. More precisely, it consists of determining the range of stimuli for which infants respond in the same way, and the range of stimuli for which they respond differently. The important element of this perspective is to define the two classes. To some extent, this is what we attempted to achieve with 2-month-old babies when we investigated whether a drawing of an object is sufficient to support the transfer of haptically gained information. This is what Rose *et al.* (1983) aimed to find in a more complex way with 12-month-old babies. After haptic familiarization to an object, the babies were presented with a photograph of it and a drawing which portrayed only its contours. It would certainly appear that the contour of an object is an early-detected invariant which is necessary for information transfer between touch and vision to occur, and is common to the object, the photo and the drawing.

This method is well suited for the understanding of the underlying mechanisms of intermodal transfer. It enables the class of invariants to which babies respond to be more clearly defined. However, it does not fully resolve the problem of the identity of the object. After tactile familiarization to a ring-shaped object, babies might respond to visual presentation of a ring doughnut or a dress ring, since these objects have a hole in common, and not respond to a flower or a sphere, since they have no hole. A class of invariants would then have been defined, but the mechanism through which the babies manage to identify the information specific to each object would not be determined. Although this method represents an attempt to understand the process of categorization in transfer, it does not succeed in resolving the question of thc objcct's identity.

A second way of attempting to solve this problem which would constitute a further development of the above-mentioned method would be to examine the way in which babies find a control object amongst all the objects belonging to the same category. We could then be certain that babies discriminate between objects of the same category. The procedure proposed by Rose and Ruff (1987) would constitute a necessary stage in attaining this goal. Fagan (1976, 1979) has provided ample evidence that 7-month-old babies differentiate visually between a number of pictures of men's faces, then treat them as equivalent when contrasted with a picture of a woman's face. Might we, perhaps, be able to obtain similar results in the process of information transfer? This, however, requires far more complex mechanisms than those which are employed to detect equivalence of information.

Conclusions

The necessity of comparing different approaches

Our approach to the study of vision and touch has fallen mainly within the perspective of the interaction between perception and action, and between the perceptual systems. Analysis of the multiple aspects of the relationship between the visual and tactile systems is necessary if we are to obtain a more complete understanding of the nature of the links which organize our behaviour from the time we are born. The observation of the manual behaviour of reaching for and grasping a visual target, the demonstration of intermodal transfer of information gained about the properties of objects, and the analysis of multimodal exploration of objects are all different ways of approaching the problem of the relationship between eye and hand.

These approaches complement one another, and it seemed appropriate to us to compare and contrast them (Streri, 1987*b*). They are attempts to understand how, from birth onwards, babies take account of, coordinate, unify or, on the contrary, contrast the information made available to them through heterogeneous systems.

It is necessary to establish a relationship between these different approaches because of the existence of a specificity of systems and the presence of motor and sensory constraints from birth onwards. It is on the basis of information gathered through vision that the behaviour of reaching for an object, and therefore the motor activity of arm and hand, has been examined. The analysis of this behaviour has proved insufficient to provide real evidence of the perceptual possibilities of the hand, and to demonstrate adequately the baby's manipulatory abilities. The majority of research in this field has approached the transfer of information on the basis of touch. This means that the intermodal relation has essentially been studied from the tactile modality to the visual modality. Such research has shown itself to be inadequate for an understanding of the reverse process. The information which is taken into account by the systems also diverges depending on whether interest is focused on prehensile behaviour or on intermodal transfer. It is tangibility, size, orientation or the direction of the target which come under particular analysis in studies of motor response, whereas it is more often shape, texture, substance, weight, and so on, which are the object of transfer. Therefore the information tested would certainly seem to be a function of the approach, and it becomes necessary to establish an overall view of the way in which babies apprehend their environment. Thus the space of both places and objects comes under consideration.

The study of multimodal exploration of objects can account for the level of integration of the modalities in the simultaneous consideration of object properties. However, this is possible only when prehension–vision coordination is established systematically, at about 5 or 6 months of age; it cannot, therefore, provide evidence of how the functioning of the modalities begins.

These areas have thus been studied in such divergent ways that it has been difficult to find interactions between the various modes of investigating the touch–vision relationship. On the basis of our research analyzing the prehensile gesture in the first six months after birth and the multimodal exploration occurring from 5 to 6 months of age, we are able to define these interactions in five ways:

1. Vision–prehension coordination is not a prerequisite for intermodal transfer between vision and touch, since perceptual relations are obtained before the age of 5 or 6 months. In other words, joint exploration of the same object in more than one modality – that is, multimodal investigation – is not a necessary condition for the perceptual unity of an object to be realized.
2. There is an interval between the baby's ability to perform perceptual processing and the translation of this processing at the

motor level. An obvious example of this is the pre-positioning of the hand in prehensile movements as a function of the properties of the object to be grasped. Translation to the motor level becomes manifest several months after these properties are visually perceived by the baby.

3. When motor activity with objects, such as carrying them, becomes apparent, this disturbs the hand's perceptual function and temporarily prevents the transfer of information from touch to vision. The object is there to be taken, and no longer to be recognized visually.
4. Conversely, the asynchronies in the development of the visual and tactile receptors can contribute to the inhibition of the prehensile gesture. For 2-month-old babies, the object is no longer there to be grasped, since the hand will not recognize it haptically.
5. The joint realization of multimodal exploration of objects, once prehension–vision coordination is established, prolongs and reinforces the unity of perceptions which is evident from birth, and does not destabilize this unity.

Integration of the systems . . .

The volume of research into the prehension of objects during the first few months of life, which was the subject of the first half of this book, is much greater than that devoted to the relations between tactile and visual perceptions. There are a number of reasons for this disparity. The degree of interest in the baby's prehensile gesture is no doubt due to the fact that it represents the clearest behavioural demonstration of the instrumental function of the hand's motor and sensory system. Moreover, perceptual behaviour is never directly observable. It is inferred from motor or physiological indicators, and is therefore difficult to identify; while motor behaviour, on the other hand, is directly discernible even under 'free' observation conditions. Consequently, for a long time it was considered to be simpler for babies to gain control of their motor abilities than to organize their perceptions. The methods of studying the perceptions of the newborn have changed this view. These methods, applied to the study of vision in particular, have clearly demonstrated that neonates' sensory afferences are richer than their actions. A disparity is thus observed between the reality of perceptual organization, which has recently been demonstrated, and that of motor ability which, it had been thought, was well known. However, the necessity of employing sophisticated apparatus for studying fine behaviour such as the prepositioning of fingers and hand for an adapted grasp of an object has emerged only recently, and we are still far from having discovered all the fine motor skills of the baby. In these circumstances, many questions about the motor programming of the reaching action remain unanswered, or have received only ambiguous answers. Until recent years, however, the rigidity of the motor component of the baby's hand has been the main focus of research, at the expense of tactile sensoriality. The demonstration of a sensorial – indeed, perceptual – functioning of the hand has become indispensable to an in-depth study of intermodal transfer.

The question of integration of the systems is therefore posed differently depending on whether the elements involved in the relation are heterogeneous, as in the prehensile gesture, or homogeneous, as in intermodal transfer or multimodal exploration.

The interpretation of the neonate's approach of the hand towards a visual object remains, if not ambiguous, then at least limited. Joint orientation of eyes and hand towards the target is observed. Since the movement refers only to a defined point in space, the coordination is restricted to a vision-to-motor system which is directional in nature. There is no true vision–prehension coordination, since when reaching is successful the manipulatory component does not emerge. Moreover, proprioceptive reafferences seem to play a very small part, since no corrections are made to the action, and the movement is ballistic. The absence of readjustments of actions which have failed leads us to doubt whether a central command of control and comparison of the kind postulated by Bernstein (1967) and Adams (1971), exists in the newborn. The success of the neonate's action is largely dependent on posture and visual attention, as is clearly demonstrated by experiments employing the condition known as 'freed motor activity'. In these observations, the altered distribution of muscle tonicity has an organizing effect: the slow, saccadic action and the slight flexion of the fingers before the object is reached indicate that the system exists in a latent state. However, even under these conditions, which allow a particular level of vigilance, the reaching action of the neonate (without prehension, since the object is only stroked) is not the same as that which appears a few months later.

Control of prehension is established during the first four months: the neonatal approach movement becomes a reaching movement which ends in grasping the object. The neonate's sensori–motor relationship is transformed into a relationship between perception and action which will considerably increase the integration of visual information by the tactile motor system. And indeed, at 4 months of age the results are clearer, and vision–prehension coordination is evident. It is not so much the degree of success of the reaching action which is important for us as the way in which the visual sensory information is translated into the motor programming of the action while it is taking place. While vision plays a guiding role and is essential for success, it is nevertheless the organization of the movement which best testifies to the level of integration of the systems. Babies are able to anticipate the trajectory of a moving target, and the approach strategies from the very beginning of the programming of the action bear witness to the predictive nature of their movements. In the same way, the hand is prepared to receive visually gained information. This pre-positioning of the hand before grasping as a function of the properties of the object shows an improvement in the effectiveness of the behaviour. Therefore, when the elements of the relation are heterogeneous, integration of the systems is dependent on a motor organization which the subject gains control of gradually.

As for intermodal transfer, there is no evidence so far that it is present at birth. It is at the age of one month that a perceptual relation between the different sensory information gained from buccal tactile exploration and vision is first demonstrated. Our experiments have shown that at 2 months of age this relationship continues between manual exploration and vision.

However, a perceptual unity between vision and touch is possible only if, at the same age, a similar level of functioning is realized in both modalities in the apprehension and processing of information. The grasp and avoiding reflexes of the hand are predominant in the young baby, and prevent the fine exploration of objects. Nevertheless, our research reveals that the hand shows itself to be perfectly capable of taking in information about objects without the help of vision, despite the rigid and restrictive nature of the grasp reflex. The hand extracts and processes information about the properties of objects in situations of habituation which are similar to those employed in the study of visual perception. We have been able to establish that the perceptual function of the hand is present at the age of 2 months, since babies of this age are able to discriminate between the different shapes of the objects they hold as finely as they can in the visual modality. Thus at a time when babies' effections are still clumsy and do not fully reflect their abilities, the study of tactile sensoriality offers a clearer picture of what haptic information babies are capable of gathering about their environment. This unity of information is realized because vision and touch function in a similar manner in detecting the invariants in a stimulus. This is a necessary condition for transfer to occur. If the modalities were to apprehend and process information in different ways, we would have to postulate the existence of a translational or symbolic code at birth, which seems unlikely.

Nevertheless, not all the information gathered regarding objects is transferable from one modality to another. Only those items of information which are processed and represented in an analogous way by both modalities are recognized; the rest are neglected. Meltzoff and Borton's experiment (1979) illustrates this point of view. Although there are considerable differences between visual and tactile objects, transfer is obtained in month-old babies. This result can make sense only if we accept the idea that the perceptual relation concerns only the dimension of the presence or absence of bumps on the stimuli. Other information is not the focus of recognition. This interpretation considerably limits the range of perceptual relations. It concerns not the object as a whole, but a single abstract property of the object which is common to both visual and tactile objects. This type of experiment will need to be replicated and extended if we are to discover exactly which dimensions, among the whole range of the dimensions characterizing objects, are actually transferred.

Analyses of multimodal exploration of objects clearly indicate that subjects attribute unity to the object. They coordinate the information which is specific to one modality, and judge that which is common to two modalities to be equivalent. Moreover, the various activities performed on the object are a function of the properties themselves and are not, therefore, realized arbitrarily. Perception and action are thus closely connected in multimodal exploration. Furthermore, towards the age of 4 months, when babies prepare their hands to receive tactile information corresponding to the already processed visual information, organization of the prehensile gesture begins to emerge, and it is possible to see in this a preparation for goal-directed activities with objects.

Unity but not nondifferentiation . . .

Analysis of the baby's perceptual and motor behaviour, however, also reveals that tactile and visual systems are not undifferentiated in the newborn. The asymmetries of behaviour which exist at birth specify the constraints of each system. For example, while neonates are capable of lifting their arms to a visual target, holding an object does not elicit the behaviour of carrying it into view. This form of relation between eye and hand is therefore not reversible. This asymmetry should not be interpreted solely in terms of the dominance of vision over touch, but as revealing that the carrying function is absent in the neonate. The held object might be an object for looking at in the same way as the seen object is palpable, but it is still necessary for the baby who is holding an object to have the plan to carry it. Thus there is indeed an independence of the systems at birth which correlates to this unity. The point of view which holds that development starts with nondifferentiation of the systems and progresses towards greater independence does not take all the relations between eye and hand into consideration. The absence of the object-carrying function in the neonate, the apparent disappearance of the behaviour of reaching for an object at the age of 2 months and the nonreversibility of transfer at the ages of 2 and 5 months are all evidence of the relative independence of the systems from birth and during the first six months of life.

To consider that a central mechanism coordinates all the information while the perceptual systems still retain their specificity of functioning is not contradictory. However, how should the unity of the systems be defined? If we consider the nonreversibility of transfer within the intermodal relation, it is not compatible with the hypothesis of an amodal centre even though the functional conditions of equivalence in the reception and processing of information are fulfilled. To postulate the existence of a mechanism for translating from one modality to another would be too costly, too premature and too difficult to verify, since our experiments are focused on subjects whose perceptual systems develop very fast and in an asynchronous way.

Not confirming the existence of an amodal perceptual centre, however, demands an interpretation of the observed perceptual relations. Intermodal transfers are obtained because babies are able to relate their sensory experiences. In other words, transfers are not an intrinsic fact in the baby. They are realized as a result of perceptual and intelligent activity on the infant's part. Despite the nonreciprocity of the behaviour observed, a form of relation between systems is maintained during the course of development. In fact, if all the data obtained in the different approaches analyzed are taken into consideration, it can be seen that throughout the course of development a relationship, assured by one or other of the systems, is maintained between vision and touch. Neonates extend their arms towards a visual target. However, while they do not carry a held object into view, a transfer to vision from the oral mode of the tactile modality is established. The perceptual component of the tactile system is functional. When reaching disappears at the age of 2 months, a touch–vision transfer nonetheless exists. Finally, while we have failed to obtain a touch–vision transfer in 5-month-olds, the visually triggered and controlled prehensile gesture (again) becomes functional and intensive. The carrying of objects is also assured. The eye–hand relationship is thus always maintained during the first six months of development under conditions in which both modalities are employed.

In other words, during the first six months of life, before vision–prehension coordination is complete, there is no time at which the systems are totally separate. They are never completely unconnected. Therefore, development does not progress from a unity towards an autonomy of the perceptual systems. The systems are autonomous at birth, and babies' activity consists of connecting the information gathered visually and haptically as a function of their sensorial, perceptual and motor development.

Hence, a description of the evolution of the baby's behaviour in terms of discontinuous stages marked by profound reorganizations can account for only one aspect of the relation between tactile and visual systems – namely, the one demonstrated by the prehensile gesture. We observe that this relation is maintained throughout development despite the fact that its evolution is subject to extensive – mainly motor – reorganizations.

Perception, action and knowledge

Analyses of the organization of the baby's activity of reaching for a visual target in terms of a reflex which is triggered or controlled by environmental influences attribute very little importance to the baby's cognitive capacities. These interpretations concentrate exclusively on visual information, and largely ignore the necessity for the subject to have command of a motor programming plan in the organization of the movement. Consequently, they ignore the existence of a cognitive ability in the baby. There are organized and programmed sensorimotor reflexes in the baby, such as saccadic eye movements and the ocular fixation reflex. However, although the reflex occurs, the response does not necessarily have any meaning for the baby, and does not have to involve a programming plan. In contrast, fine, anticipatory motor organization of the hand is a manifestation of such control of movement as a function of the visual information analyzed. This, however, is not performed efficiently until the age of about 4 months. Nevertheless, neonatal intention to perform a movement is operationally defined by some researchers as hand–mouth coordination or imitation. This intention is less clear in the activity of reaching towards a visual object. However, the potential consequences of this behaviour (contact with the object and its eventual displacement, alteration of the environment) indicate that it cannot be regarded as an uncontrolled reflex on the baby's part. This behaviour is dependent to a large extent on the degree of muscular and articulatory development in the limbs, and on the maturity of the nervous system. Babies are largely unable to translate the information they register during visual exploration of their environment into motor activity.

In contrast, current technology allows us a better appreciation of the young infant's perceptual capacities. But what do these perceptions translate? And how are we to understand the level of knowledge which babies possess about their environment? While we are able to begin to form an evaluation on the basis of their motor behaviour (presence or absence of a movement, pre-positioning of the hand, success or failure of an action, and so on), what degree of coherence or meaning do babies attribute to the stimuli they receive? Experiments which investigate perceptual discrimination inform us about babies' discriminatory abilities but tell us little about their level of perceptual organization. The intermodal transfer situation allows us to gain a better understanding of the baby's perceptuo–cognitive development. It then becomes necessary to shift the focus of our analysis from the perceiving subject – that is to say, in terms of the proximal stimulus – to the perceived object. Intermodal relations bear on the abstract properties of objects, not on the objects themselves. These are relations of equivalence, not of identity.

The unity of information which is established on the basis of one or other of the sensory modalities and the analogous functioning of these modalities in the apprehension of information are the two principal facts which have been demonstrated in our studies of intermodal transfer. They overturn a number of ideas about the way in which tactile sensoriality and motor ability in object manipulation should be regarded. Moreover, babies' capacity to relate situations and information enables them to invest their environment with a degree of stability and unity. This perceptual coherence is neither progressively constructed in the Piagetian sense nor established through association during the first few months of life. It is realized through babies' very early-acquired ability to relate their sensory experiences. Even before they are able to perform activities relating to their environment in order to gain new information about it or to effect changes in it, babies consider that in certain dimensions the object they see and the object they touch are not necessarily different objects.

We have analyzed only the relationship between vision and touch. Similar analyses still need to be undertaken to examine the integration of other systems. It is not certain, however, that the problems posed will be of the same nature.

Bibliography

Abramov, I., Gordon, J., Hendrickson, A., Hainline, L., Dobson, V. and Laboissière, E. (1982), 'The retina of the newborn human infant', *Science*, **217**: 265–7.

Adams, J.A. (1971), 'A closed-loop theory of motor learning', *Journal of Motor Behavior*, **3**: 111–50.

Ajuriaguerra, de J. (1978), 'Ontogenèse de la motricité', in H. Hecaen and M. Jeannerod (eds), *Du contrôle moteur à l'organisation du geste*, Paris: Masson.

Alegria, J. and Noirot, E. (1978), 'Neonate orientation behaviour towards human voice', *International Journal of Behavioural Development*, **1**: 291–312.

Amiel-Tison, C. and Grenier A. (1980), *Evaluation neurologique du nouveau-né et du nourisson*, Paris/New York/Barcelona/Milan: Masson.

Amiel-Tison, C. and Grenier, A. (1985), *La surveillance neurologique au cours de la première année de la vie*, Paris: Masson.

André-Thomas and Saint-Anne Dargassies, S. (1952), *Etudes neurologiques sur le nouveau-né et le nourisson*, Paris: Masson.

Annet, M. (1970), 'A classification of hand preference by association analysis', *British Journal of Psychology*, **61**: 303–21.

Aslin, R.N. (1987), 'Motor aspects of visual development in infancy', in P. Salapatek and L. Cohen (eds), *Handbook of Infant Perception: From sensation to perception* (vol. 1), New York: Academic Press, pp. 43–113.

Atkinson, J. and Braddick, O. (1982), 'Sensory and perceptual capacities of the neonate', in P. Stratton (ed.), *Psychology of the Human Newborn*, New York: Wiley, pp. 192–219.

Bach-y-Rita, P. (1972), *Brain Mechanisms in Sensory Substitution*, New York: Academic Press.

Bahrick, L.E. and Watson, J.S. (1985), 'Detection of intermodal proprioceptive. Visual contingency as a potential basis of self-perception in infancy', *Developmental Psychology*, **21**: 963–73.

Baillargeon, R., Spelke, E.S. and Wasserman, S. (1985), 'Object permanence in five-month-old infants', *Cognition*, **20**: 191–208.

Banks, M.S. and Bennett, P.J. (1988), 'Optical and photoreceptor immaturities limit the spatial and chromatic vision of human neonates', *Journal of the Optical Society of America*, **5**: 2059–79.

Banks, M.S. and Dannemiller, J.L. (1987), 'Infant visual psychophysics', in P. Salapatek and L. Cohen (eds), *Handbook of Infant Perception: From sensation to perception* (vol. 1), New York: Academic Press, pp. 115–84.

Banks, M.S. and Salapatek, P. (1983), 'Infant visual perception', in M.M. Haith and J.J. Campos (eds), *Infancy and Development Psychobiology*; P. Mussen (gen. ed.), *Handbook of Child Psychology* (vol. 2), New York: Wiley.

Bauer, J.A. and Held, R. (1975), 'Comparison of visual guided reaching in normal and deprived infant monkeys', *Animal Behavior Processes*, **1**: 298–308.

Bayley, N. (1933), *The California First Year Mental Scale*, Berkeley: University of California Press.

Bechtoldt, H.P. and Hutz, C.S. (1979), 'Stereopsis in young infants and stereopsis in an infant with congenital esotropia', *Journal of Pediatric Ophthalmology and Strabismus*, **16**: 49–54.

Beek, P.J. (1986), 'Perception–action coupling in the young infant: an appraisal of von Hofsten's research programme', in M.G. Wade and H.T.A. Whiting (eds), *Motor Development in Children: Aspects of coordination and control*, Amsterdam: Martinus Nijhoff, pp. 167–85.

Berkeley, G. (1709/1944), 'Essai d'une théorie nouvelle de la vision', *Œuvres choisies*, vol. I, Paris: Aubier.

Bernstein, N.A. (1967), *The Coordination and Regulation of Movement*, Oxford: Pergamon.

Bertalanffy, L. von (1973) *Théorie générale des systèmes*, Paris: Dunod.

Bertenthal, B.I., Haith, M.M. and Campos, J.J. (1983), 'The partial-lag design: a method for controlling spontaneous regression in the infant-control habituation paradigm', *Infant Behavior and Development*, **6**: 331–8.

Biguer, B., Jeannerod, M. and Prablanc, C. (1982), 'The coordination of eye, head, and arm movements during reaching at a single visual target', *Experimental Brain Research*, **46**: 301–4.

Biguer, B., Prablanc, C. and Jeannerod, M. (1984), 'The contribution of coordinated eye and head movements in hand pointing accuracy', *Experimental Brain Research*, **55**: 462–9.

Blass, E.M., Fillion, T.J., Rochat, P., Hoffmeyer, L.B. and Metzger, M.A. (1989), 'Sensorimotor and motivational determinants of hand–mouth coordination in 1–3-day-old human infants', *Developmental Psychology*, **25**: 963–75.

Bornstein, M.H. (1978), 'Chromatic vision in infancy', in H.W. Reese and L.P. Lipsitt (eds), *Advances in Child Development and Behavior* (vol. 12), New York: Academic Press.

Bornstein, M.H. (1981), 'Psychological studies of color perception in human infants: habituation, discrimination and categorization, recognition and conceptualization', in L.P. Lipsitt (ed.), *Advances in Infancy Research* (vol. 1), Norwood, NJ: Ablex.

Bornstein, M.H. (1985), 'Habituation of attention as a measure of visual information processing in human infants', in G. Gottlieb and N.A. Krasnegor (eds), *Measurement of Audition and Vision in the First Year of Life: A methodological overview*, Norwood, NJ: Ablex.

Bouissou, M.F. (1968), 'Effet de l'ablation des bulbes olfactifs sur la reconnaissance du jeune par sa mère chez les ovins', *Revue du Comportement animal*, **3**: 77–83.

Bower, T.G.R. (1965), 'The determinants of perceptual unity in infancy', *Psychonomic Science*, **3**: 323–4.

Bower, T.G.R. (1966), 'The visual world in infants', *Scientific American*, **215**: 80–92.

Bower, T.G.R. (1971), 'The object in the world of the infant', *Scientific American*, **225**: 31–8.

Bower, T.G.R. (1972), 'Object perception in infants', *Perception*, **1**: 15–30.

Bower, T.G.R. (1974/1982), *Development in Infancy*, San Francisco: Freeman.

Bower, T.G.R. (1977), *Le développement psychologique de la première enfance*, Brussels: Mardaga.

Bower, T.G.R. (1979), *Human Development*, San Francisco: Freeman.

Bower, T.G.R., Broughton, J.M. and Moore, M.K. (1970*a*), 'The coordination of visual and tactual input in infants', *Perception and Psychophysics*, **8**: 51–3.

Bower, T.G.R., Broughton, J.M. and Moore, M.K. (1970*b*), 'Demonstration of intention in the reaching behavior of neonate humans', *Nature*, **228**: 679–81.

Bower, T.G.R. and Wishart, J.G. (1972), 'The effects of motor skill on object permanence', *Cognition*, **1**: 165–72.

Bremner, J.G. (1980), 'The infant's understanding of space', in M.V. Cox (ed.), *Are Young Children Egocentric?*, London: Batsford Academic.

Bresson, F. (1971), 'La genèse des propriétés des objets', *Journal de psychologie normale et pathologique*, **68** (2): 143–68.

Bresson, F. (1972), 'Aspects génétiques de la perception', in H. Hecaen (ed.), *Neuropsychologie de la perception visuelle*, Paris: Masson, pp. 168–84.

Bresson, F., Maury, L., Piéraut-Le Bonniec, G. and de Schonen, S. (1977), 'Organization and laterilization of reaching in infants: an instance of asymmetric function in hand collaboration', *Neuropsychologia*, **15**: 311–20.
Bresson, F. and de Schonen, S. (1976), 'A propos de la construction de l'espace et de l'objet: la prise d'un objet sur un support', *Bulletin de Psychologie*, Hommage à Jean Piaget, **XXX**: 150–58.
Brown, K.W. and Gottfried, A.W. (1986), 'Cross-modal transfer of shape in early infancy: is there reliable evidence?', in L.P. Lipsitt and C.K. Rovee-Collier (eds), *Advances in Infancy Research* (vol. 4), Norwood, NJ: Ablex, pp. 163–70.
Bruner, J.S. (1966), 'On cognitive growth', in J.S. Bruner, R.R. Olver and P.M. Greenfield (eds), *Studies in Cognitive Growth*, New York: Wiley.
Bruner, J.S. (1969), 'Eye, hand and mind', in D. Elkind and J.S. Flavell (eds), *Studies in Cognitive Development*, New York, London: Oxford University Press.
Bruner, J.S. (1970), 'The growth and structure of skill', in K. Connolly (ed.) *Mechanisms of Motor Skill Development*, New York: Academic Press.
Bruner, J.S. (1973), 'Organisation of early skilled action', *Child Development*, **44**: 1–11.
Bruner, J.S. and Koslowski, B. (1972), 'Visually preadapted constituents of manipulatory action', *Perception*, **1**: 3–14.
Brunet, O. and Lézine, I. (1951/1965), *Le développement psychologique de la première enfance*, Paris: Presses Universitaires de France.
Bryant, P.E. (1974), *Perception and Understanding in Young Children*, London: Methuen.
Bryant, P.E., Jones, P., Claxton, V. and Perkins, G.H. (1972), 'Recognition of shapes across modalities by infants', *Nature* (London), **240**: 303–4.
Buka, S.L. and Lipsitt, L.P. (1991), 'Newborn sucking behavior and its relation to grasping', *Infant Behavior and Development*, **14**: 59–67.
Bullinger, A. (1982), 'Cognitive elaboration of sensorimotor behavior', in G. Butterworth (ed.), *Infancy and Epistemology: An evaluation of Piaget's theory*, New York: Harvester.
Bullinger, A. and Rochat, P. (1985), 'L'activité orale du nourrisson comme indice du comportement', in P.-M. Beaudonnière (ed.), *Etudier l'enfant de la naissance à trois ans*, Paris: Centre National de la Recherche Scientifique, 55–68.
Bushnell, E.W. (1981), 'The ontogeny of intermodal relations: vision and touch in infancy', in R.D. Walk and H.L. Pick (eds), *Intersensory Perception and Sensory Integration*, New York: Plenum Press, pp. 5–37.
Bushnell, E.W. (1982), 'Visual–tactual knowledge in 8-, 9½-, and 11-month-old infants', *Infant Behavior and Development*, **5**: 63–75.

Bushnell, E.W. (1985), 'The decline of visually-guided reaching during infancy', *Infancy Behavior and Development*, **8**: 139–55.

Bushnell, E.W. (1986), 'The basis of infant visual–tactual functioning – amodal dimensions or multimodal compounds?' in L.P. Lipsitt and C.K. Rovee-Collier (eds), *Advances in Infancy Research* (vol. 4), Norwood, NJ: Ablex, pp. 182–94.

Bushnell, E.W., Shaw, L. and Strauss, D. (1985), 'Relationship between visual and tactual exploration in 6-month-olds', *Developmental Psychology*, **21**: 591–600.

Bushnell, E.W. and Weinberg, N. (1987), 'Infants' detection of visual–tactual discrepancies: asymmetries that indicate a directive role of visual information', *Journal of Experimental Psychology: Human Perception and Performance*, **13**: 601–8.

Butterworth, G. (ed.) (1982), *Infancy and Epistemology*, Brighton: Harvester.

Butterworth, G. (1983), 'Structure of the mind in human infancy', in L.P. Lipsitt (ed.), *Advances in Infancy Research* (vol. 2), Norwood, NJ: Ablex.

Butterworth, G. (1986*a*), *The structure of Spontaneous Movement in Newborn Human Infants: Evidence for innate intentionality?*, paper presented at the 2nd European Conference on Developmental Psychology, Rome, September 1986.

Butterworth, G. (1986*b*), 'Some problems in explaining the origins of movement control', in M.G. Wade and H.T.A. Whiting (eds), *Motor Development in Children: Aspects of coordination and control*, Amsterdam: Martinus Nijhoff, pp. 23–32.

Butterworth, G. and Castillo, M. (1976), 'Coordination of auditory and visual space in newborn infants', *Perception*, **5**: 155–60.

Butterworth, G. and Hicks, L. (1977), 'Visual proprioception and postural stability in infancy: a developmental study', *Perception*, **6**: 255–62.

Butterworth, G.E., Jarret, N. and Hicks, L. (1982), 'Spatio–temporal identity in infancy: perceptual competence or conceptual deficit?', *Developmental Psychology*, **18** (3): 435–49.

Butterworth, G. and Pope, M.J. (1983), 'Origine et fonctions de la proprioception visuelle chez l'enfant', in S. de Schonen (ed.), *Le développement dans la première année*, Paris: Presses Universitaires de France.

Campos, J., Langer, A. and Krowitz, A. (1970), 'Cardiac responses on the visual cliff in premotor human infants', *Science*, **170**: 195–6.

Caplan, P. and Kinsbourne, M. (1976), 'Baby drops the rattle: asymmetry of duration of grasp by infants', *Child Development*, **47**: 532–4.

Carnahan, H. and Marteniuk, R.G. (1991), 'The temporal organization of hand, eye, and head movements during reaching and pointing', *Journal of Motor Behavior*, **23**: 109–19.

Clark, J.E. (1986), 'The perception–action perspective: a commentary on von Hofsten', in M.G. Wade and H.T.A. Whiting (eds), *Motor Development in Children: Aspects of coordination and control*, Amsterdam: Martinus Nijhoff, pp. 197–206.

Cohen, L.B. (1973), 'A two process model of infant visual attention,' *Merrill-Palmer Quarterly*, **19**: 157–80.

Connolly, K. (ed.) (1970), *Mechanisms of Motor Skill Development*, New York: Academic Press.

Connolly, K. and Elliott, J. (1972), 'The evolution and ontogeny of hand function', in N.B. Jones (ed.), *Ethological Studies of Child Behavior*, London: Eastern Press.

Corballis, M.C. (1989), 'Laterality and human evolution', *Psychological Review*, **96**: 492–505.

Cornwell, K.S., Harris, L.J. and Fitzgerald, H.E. (1991), 'Task effects in the development of hand preference in 9-, 13-, and 20-month-old infant girls', *Developmental Neuropsychology*, **7**: 19–34.

Coryell, J.F. and Michel, F. (1978), 'How supine postural preferences of infants can contribute toward the development of handedness', *Infant Behavior and Development*, **1**: 245–57.

Costall, A. (1982), 'On how much information controls so much behavior: James Gibson's theory of direct perception', in G. Butterworth (ed.), *Infancy and Epistemology: An evaluation of Piaget's theory*, New York: St Martin's Press.

Cowey, A. and Weikrantz, L. (1975), 'Demonstration of cross-modal matching in Rhesus monkeys (Macaca mulatta)', *Neuropsychologia*, **13**: 117–21.

Crook, C.K. (1977), 'Taste stimulation and the temporal organization of neonatal sucking', in J. Weiffenbach (ed.), *Taste and Development: The ontogeny of sweet preference*, Washington, DC: US Government Printing Office, pp. 146–58.

Cruikshank, R.M. (1941), 'The development of visual size constancy in early infancy', *Journal of Genetic Psychology*, **58**: 327–51.

Davenport, R.K. and Rogers, C.M. (1970), 'Intermodal equivalence of stimuli in apes', *Science*, **168**: 279–80.

Davenport, R.K. and Rogers, C.M. (1971), 'Perception of photographs by apes', *Behavior*, XXXIX, 318–20.

Davenport, R.K., Rogers, C.M. and Russel, I.S. (1973), 'Cross-modal perception in apes', *Neuropsychologia*, **11**: 21–8.

Davenport, R.K., Rogers, C.M. and Russel, I.S. (1975), 'Cross-modal perception in apes: altered visual cues and delay', *Neuropsychologia*, **13**: 229–36.

Deloache, J., Strauss, M.S. and Maynard, J. (1979), 'Picture perception in infancy', *Infant Behavior and Development*, **2**: 77–89.

Diamond, A. (1987), 'Differences between adult and infant cognition: is the crucial variable presence or absence of language?', Communication présentée au Symposium de la Fondation Fyssen, *Thought without Language*, 3–7 April 1987.

Diamond, A. and Gilbert, J. (1989), 'Development as progressive inhibitory control of action: retrieval of a contiguous object', *Cognitive Development*, **4**: 223–49.

DiFranco, D., Muir, D.W. and Dodwell, D. (1978), 'Reaching in very young infants', *Perception*, **7**: 385–92.

DiMattia, B.V., Posley, K.A. and Fuster, J.M. (1990), 'Cross-modal short-term memory of haptic and visual information', *Neuropsychobiologia*, **28**: 17–33.

Dodwell, P.C., Muir, D.W. and DiFranco, D. (1976), 'Responses of infants to visually presented objects', *Science*, **203**: 1138–9.

Ettlinger, G. (1967), 'Analysis of cross-modal effects and their relationship to language', in F.L. Dailey and C.H. Millikan (eds), *Brain Mechanisms Underlying Speech and Language*, New York: Grune and Stratton, pp. 53–60.

Fagan, J.F. (1976), 'Infant's recognition of invariant features of faces', *Child Development*, **47**: 627–38.

Fagan, J.F. (1979), 'The origins of facial pattern recognition', in M. Bornstein and W. Kessen (eds), *Psychological Development from Infancy*, Hillsdale, NJ: Erlbaum.

Fantz, R.L. (1961), 'The origin of form perception', *Scientific American*, **204**: 66–72.

Fantz, R.L. (1963), 'Pattern vision in newborn infants', *Science*, **140**: 296–7.

Fantz, R.L. (1965), 'Visual perception from birth as shown by pattern selectivity', *Annals of the New York Academy of Science*, **118**: 793–814.

Fantz, R.L., Fagan, J.F. and Miranda, S. (1975), 'Early vision selection', in L.B. Cohen and P. Salapatek (eds), *Infant Perception: From sensation to cognition* (vol. 1), New York: Academic Press, pp. 249–345.

Fantz, R.L. and Nevis, S. (1967), 'Pattern preference and perceptual–cognitive development in early infancy', *Merrill-Palmer Quarterly*, **13**: 77–108.

Field, J. (1976), 'Relation of young infant's reaching to stimulus distance and solidity', *Developmental Psychology*, **12**: 444–8.

Field, J. (1977), 'Coordination of vision and prehension in young infants', *Child Development*, **48**: 97–103.

Field, T.M., Dempsey, J., Hatch, J., Ting, G and Clifton, R. (1979), 'Cardiac and behavioural responses to repeated tactile and auditory stimulation by preterm and term neonates', *Developmental Psychology*, **15**: 406–16.

Field, T.M., Woodson, R., Greenburg, D. and Cohen, D. (1982), 'Discrimination and imitation of facial expression by neonates', *Science*, **218**: 179–81.

Fodor, J.A. (1983), *The Modularity of Mind: An essay on faculty psychology*, Cambridge, MA: MIT.

Fodor, J.A. and Pylyshyn, Z.W. (1981), 'How direct is visual perception? Some reflections on Gibson's "ecological approach" ', *Cognition*, **9**: 139–96.

Fogel, A. and Thelen, E. (1987), 'Development of early expressive and communicative action: reinterpreting the evidence from a dynamic systems perspective', *Developmental Psychology*, **23**: 747–61.

Fontaine, R. (1982), *Conditions d'évocation des conduites imitatives chez l'enfant de 0 à 6 mois*, Paris: L'Ecole des Hautes Etudes en Sciences Sociales.

Fontaine, R. (1984*a*), 'Fixation manuelle de la nuque et organisation du geste d'atteinte chez le nouveau-né', in J. Paillard (ed.), *La lecture sensorimotrice et cognitive de l'expérience spatiale*, Paris: Centre National de la Recherche Scientifique.

Fontaine, R. (1984*b*), 'Imitative skill between birth and six months', *Infant Behavior and Development*, **7**: 323–33.

Fontaine, R. (1984*c*), 'Les imitations précoces: problèmes méthodologiques et théoriques', *Cahiers de Psychologie cognitive*, **4** (3): 517–35.

Fontaine, R. and Piéraut-Le Bonniec, G. (1988), 'Postural evolution and integration of the phehension gesture in children aged 4 to 10 months', *British Journal of Developmental Psychology*, **6**: 223–33.

Frost, D.O. (1990), 'Sensory processing by novel, experimentally induced cross-modal circuits', in A. Diamond (ed.), *The Development and Neural Bases of Higher Cognitive Functions*. Annals of the New York Academy of Sciences, pp. 92–109.

Gesell, A. and Ames, L. (1947), 'The development of handedness', *Journal of Genetic Psychology*, **70**: 155–75.

Gesell, A. and Halverson, H. (1942), 'The daily maturation of infant behavior: a cinema study of postures, movements, and laterality', *Journal of Genetic Psychology*, **61**: 3–32.

Gesell, A. and Ilg, L. (1943), *Le jeune enfant dans la civilisation moderne*, Paris: Presses Universitaires de France.

Gibson, E.J. (1969), *Principles of Perceptual Learning and Development*, New York: Appleton-Century-Crofts.

Gibson, E.J. (1982), 'The concept of affordances in development: the renascence of functionalism', in W.A. Collins (ed.), *The Concept of Development: The Minnesota symposium on child psychology* (vol. 15), Hillsdale, NJ: Erlbaum.

Gibson, E.J. (1984), 'Perceptual development from the ecological approach', in A. Brown, M. Lamb and B. Rogoff (eds), *Advances in Developmental Psychology*, (vol. 30), Hillsdale, NJ: Erlbaum.

Gibson, E.J. and Spelke, E.S. (1983), 'The development of perception', in J.H. Flavell and E.M. Markman (eds), *Handbook of Child Psychology*, vol. 3, *Cognitive Development*, New York: Wiley.

Gibson, E.J. and Walk, R.D. (1960), 'The "visual cliff" ', *Scientific American*, **202**: 64–71.

Gibson, E.J. and Walker, A. (1984), 'Development of knowledge of visual–tactual affordances of substance', *Child Development*, **55**: 453–60.

Gibson, J.J. (1950), *The Perception of the Visual World*, Boston, MA: Houghton Mifflin.

Gibson, J.J. (1962), 'Observation on active touch', *Psychological Review*, **69**: 477–91.

Gibson, J.J. (1966), *The Senses Considered as Perceptual Systems*, Boston, MA: Houghton Mifflin.

Gibson, J.J. (1979), *The Ecological Approach to Visual Perception*, Boston, MA: Houghton Mifflin.

Gibson, K.R. (1982), 'Comparative neuro-ontogeny: its implications for the development of human intelligence', in G. Butterworth (ed.), *Infancy and Epistemology*, Brighton: Harvester.

Gielen, C.C.A.M., Van den Heuvel, P.J.M. and Van Gisbergen, J.A.M. (1984), 'Coordination of fast eye and arm movements in a tracking task', *Experimental Brain Research*, **56**: 154–61.

Gordon, F.R. and Yonas, A. (1976), 'Sensitivity to binocular depth information in infants', *Journal of Experimental Child Psychology*, **22**: 413–22.

Gottfried, A.W. and Rose, S.A. (1980), 'Tactile recognition memory in infants', *Child Development*, **51**: 69–74.

Gottfried, A.W., Rose, S.A. and Bridger, W.H. (1977), 'Crossmodal transfer in human infants', *Child Development*, **48**: 118–23.

Gottfried, A.W., Rose, S.A. and Bridger, W.H. (1978), 'Effects of visual, haptic and manipulatory experiences on infants' visual recognition memory of objects', *Developmental Psychology*, **14**: 305–12.

Gottlieb, G. (1983), 'The psychobiological approach to developmental issues', in M.M. Haith and J.J. Campos (eds), *Infancy and Developmental Psychobiology: Handbook of Child Psychology* vol. 2, New York: Wiley.

Gottlieb, G. and Krasnegor, N.A. (1985), *Measurement of Audition and Vision in the First Year of Postnatal Life: A methodological overview*, Norwood, NJ: Ablex.

Granrud, C.E. (1987), *Size Constancy in Newborn Human Infants*, paper presented at the meetings of the Association for Research in Vision and Ophthamology, Sarasota, FL, 6–10 May 1987.

Granrud, C.E. (1988), *Visual Size Constancy in Newborn Infants*, paper presented at the Congress of ICIS, Washington, DC, 21–24 April 1988.

Grenier, A. (1980), 'Révélation d'une expression motrice différente par fixation manuelle de la nuque', in A. Grenier and C. Amiel-Tison (eds), *Evaluation neurologique du nouveau-né et du nourrisson*, Paris: Masson.

Grenier, A. (1981), 'La "motricité libérée" par fixation manuelle de la nuque au cours des premières années de la vie', *Archives françaises de Pédiatrie*, **38**: 557–61.

Guillaume, P. (1927), *L'imitation chez l'enfant*, Paris: Presses Universitaires de France.

Guillaume, P. (1937), *La psychologie de la forme*, Paris: Flammarion.

Haeckel, E. (1891), *Anthropogenie oder Entwicklung geschichte des Menschen*, Leipzig: Wilhelm Engelmann.

Halverson, H.M. (1931), 'An experimental study of prehension in infants by means of systematic cinema records', *Genetic Psychology Monographs*, **10**: 110–286.

Halverson, H.M. (1937), 'Studies of the grasping response of early infancy', *Journal of Genetic Psychology*, **51**: 371–449.

Harnad, S. (1987), 'Category induction and representation', in S. Harnard (ed.), *Categorial perception: The groundwork of cognition*, Cambridge: Cambridge University Press, pp. 535–65.

Harris, L.J. (1983), 'Laterality of function in the infant: historical and contemporary trends in theory and research', in G. Young, S.J. Segalowitz, C.M. Corter and S.E. Trehub (eds), *Manual Specialization and the Developing Brain*, **10**, New York: Academic Press, pp. 117–239.

Harris, L.J. and Fitzgerald, H.E. (1983), 'Postural orientation in human infants: changes from birth to three months', in G. Young, S.J. Segalowitz, C.M. Corter and S.E. Trehub (eds), *Manual Specialization and the Developing Brain*, **14**, New York: Academic Press, pp. 285–304.

Harris, P.L. (1972), 'Infants' visual and tactual inspection of objects', *Perception*, **62**(1): 141–6.

Harris, P.L. (1974), 'Perseverative search at a visibly empty place by young infants', *Journal of Experimental Child Psychology*, **18**: 535–42.

Harris, P.L. (1983), 'Infant cognition', in P.H. Mussen (ed.), *Handbook of Child Psychology*, vol. 2, *Infancy and Developmental Psychobiology*, New York: Wiley.

Harris, P.L. (1987), 'The devlopment of search', in P. Salapatek and L. Cohen (eds), *Handbook of Infant Perception: From perception to cognition* (vol. 2), New York: Academic Press, pp. 155–207.

Hatwell, Y. (1981), *La fonction perceptive de la main: perception tactile de l'espace et intégration de la vision et du toucher*, thesis submitted to the Faculty of Letters and Human Sciences, Université René Descartes, Paris.

Hatwell, Y. (1986), *Toucher l'espace*, Lille: Presses Universitaires de Lille.

Hatwell, Y. (1987), 'Motor and cognitive functions of the hand in infancy and childhood', *International Journal of Behavioral Development*, **10**: 509–26.

Hawn, P.R. and Harris, L.J. (1983), 'Hand differences in grasp duration and reaching in two- and five-month-old infants', in G. Young, S.J. Segalowitz, C.M. Corter and S.E. Trehub (eds), *Manual Specialization and the Developing Brain*, **17**, New York: Academic Press, pp. 331–48.

Hay, L. (1985), 'La transition des comportements réflexes aux comportements volontaires: l'exemple de l'atteinte manuelle', *Année psychologique*, **85**: 407–28.

Hein, A. and Held, R. (1967), 'Dissociation of the visual placing response into elicited and guided components', *Science*, **158**: 390–92.

Held, R. (1968*a*), 'Plasticity in sensori–motor coordination', in S.J. Freedman (ed.), *The Neuropsychology of Spatially Oriented Behavior*, Homewood, IL: Dorsey.

Held, R. (1968*b*), 'Dissociation of visual functions by deprivation and rearrangement', *Psychologische Forschung*, **31**: 338–48.

Held, R. and Bauer, J.A. (1967), 'Visually guided reaching in infant monkeys after restricted rearing', *Science*, **155**: 718–20.

Held, R. and Hein, A. (1963), 'Movement produced stimulation in the development of visually guided behavior', *Journal of Comparative and Physiological Psychology*, **56**: 872–6.

Helmhotz, H. von (1885/1962), *Treatise on Physiological Optics*, ed., J.P.C. Southall, vol. 3, New York: Dover.

Hickey, T.L. and Peduzzi, J.D. (1987), 'Structure and development of the visual system', in P. Salapatek and L. Cohen (eds), *Handbook of Infant Perception: From sensation to perception* (vol. 1), New York: Academic Press.

Hofsten, C. von (1979), 'Development of visual directed reaching: the approach phase', *Journal of Human Movement Studies*, **30**: 369–82.

Hofsten, C. von (1980), 'Predictive reaching for moving objects by human infants', *Journal of Experimental Child Psychology*, **30**: 369–82.

Hofsten, C. von (1982), 'Eye–hand coordination in the newborn', *Developmental Psychology*, **18**: 450–61.

Hofsten, C. von (1983*a*), 'Foundations for perceptual development', in L.P. Lipsitt (ed.), *Advances in Infancy Research* (vol. 2), Norwood, NJ: Ablex, pp. 241–64.

Hofsten, C. von (1983*b*), 'Catching skills in infancy', *Journal of Experimental Psychology: Human Perception and Performance*, **9**: 75–85.

Hofsten, C. von (1984), 'Developmental changes in the organization of prereaching movements', *Developmental Psychology*, **20**: 378–88.

Hofsten, C. von (1986), 'The emergence of manual skills', in M.G. Wade and H.T.A, Whiting (eds), *Motor Development in Children: Aspects of coordination and control*, Amsterdam: Martinus Nijhoff, pp. 197–206.

Hofsten, C. von (1989), 'Motor development as the development of systems: comments on the special section', *Developmental Psychology*, **25**: 950–53.

Hofsten, C. von and Fazel-Zandy, S. (1984), 'Development of visually guided hand orientation in reaching', *Journal of Experimental Child Psychology*, **38**: 208–19.

Hofsten, C. von and Lindhagen, K. (1979), 'Observations on the development of reaching for moving objects', *Journal of Experimental Child Psychology*, **28**: 158–73.

Hofsten, C. von and Rönnqvist L. (1988), *Preparation for Grasping an Object: A developmental study*, paper presented at the Congress of ICIS, Washington, DC, 21–24 April 1988.

Hofsten, C. von and Spelke, E.S. (1985), Object perception and object-directed reaching in infancy', *Journal of Experimental Psychology: General*, **114**: 198–211.

Holst, E. von and Mittelstädt, H. (1950), 'Das Reafferenzprinzip. Wechselwirkungen zwischen Zentralnervensystem und Peripherie, *Naturwissenschaft*, **37**: 464–76.

Hooker, D. (1938), 'The origin of the grasping movement in man', *Proceedings of the American Philosophical Society*, **79**: 597–606.

Hooker, D. (1952), *The Prenatal Origin of Behavior*, Lawrence: University of Kansas Press.

Hornbostel, E.M. von (1925), 'Die Einheit der Sinne', *Melos, Zeitschrift für Musik*, **4**, 290–7. Translated as 'The unity of senses', *Psyche*, 1927, **7**, 83–9.

Horowitz, F.D., Paden, L., Bhana, K. and Self, P. (1972), 'An infant-controlled procedure for studying infant visual fixations', *Developmental Psychology*, **7**: 90.

Hubel, D.H. and Wiesel, T.N. (1959), 'Receptive fields of single neuron in the cat's striate cortex', *Journal of Physiology*, **148**: 574–91.

Hubel, D.H. and Wiesel, T.N. (1963), 'Receptive fields in striate cortex of very young visually inexperienced kittens', *Journal of Neurophysiology*, **26**: 944–1002.

Hubel, D.H. and Wiesel, T.N. (1968), 'Receptive fields binocular interaction and functional architecture of monkey striate cortex', *Journal of Physiology*, **195**: 215–43.

Humphrey, T. (1964), 'Some correlations between the appearance of human fetal reflexes and the development of the nervous system', *Progress in Brain Research*, **4**: 93–135.

Humphrey, T. (1970), 'The development of human fetal activity and its relation to postnatal behavior', in H. Reese and L. Lipsitt (eds), *Advances in Child Development and Behavior* (vol. 5), New York: Academic Press.

Insel, F. (1987), *La prise au contact palmaire dans la première semaine de vie: le positionnement des doigts de la main, d'après la réalisation d'empreintes, lors de la saisie*, Paris: Centre d'Etude des Processus cognitifs et du Langage, l'Ecole des Hautes Etudes en Sciences Sociales.

Jarrett, N. (1981), *The Development of Detour Reaching in Human Infancy*, unpublished study, University of Southampton.

Jeannerod, M. (1981), 'Intersegmental coordination during reaching at natural visual objects', in J. Long and A. Baddelely (eds), *Attention and Performance* (vol. 9), Hillsdale, NJ: Erlbaum.

Jeannerod, M. (1984), 'The timing of natural prehension movements', *Journal of Motor Behavior*, **16**: 235–54.

Jeannerod, M. (1986), 'The formation of the finger grip during prehension: a cortically-mediated visuo–motor pattern', in H.T.A. Whiting and W.G. Wade (eds), *Themes in Motor Development*, Amsterdam: Martinus Nijhoff.

Jeannerod, M. and Biguer, B. (1982), 'Visuo–motor mechanisms in reaching within extrapersonal space', in D.J. Ingle, R.J.W. Mansfield and M.A. Goodale (eds), *Advances in the Analysis of Visual Behavior*, Cambridge, MA: MIT Press.

Jeannerod, M. and Prablanc, C. (1978), 'Organisation et plasticité de la coordination œil–main,' in H. Hecaen and M. Jeannerod (eds), *Du contrôle moteur à l'organisation du geste*, Paris: Masson.

Jouen, F. (1986), 'La contribution des récepteurs visuels et labyrinthiques à la détection des déplacements du corps propre chez le nourrisson', *L'Année psychologique*, **86**: 169–92.

Jouen, F. (1988), 'Visual proprioceptive control of posture in newborn infants', in B. Amblard, A. Berthoz and F. Clarac (eds), *Posture and Gait: Development adaptation and modulation*, Amsterdam: Elsevier.

Jouen, F. and Lepecq, J.C. (1989), 'La sensibilité au flux optique chez le nourrisson', *Psychologie française*, **34**: 13–18.

Karniol, R. (1989), 'The role of manual manipulative stages in the infant's acquisition of perceived control over objects', *Developmental Review*, **9**: 205–33.

Kellman, P.J., Gleitman, H. and Spelke, E.S. (1987), 'Object and observer motion in the perception of objects by infants', *Journal of Experimental Psychology: Human Perception and Performance*, **13**: 586–93.

Kellman, P.J. and Spelke, E.S. (1983), 'Perception of partly occluded objects in infancy', *Cognitive Psychology*, **15**: 483–524.

Kellman, P.J., Spelke, E.S. and Short, K. (1986), 'Infant perception of object unity from translatory motion in depth and vertical translation', *Child Development*, **57**: 72–86.

Kessen, W. (1967), 'Sucking and looking: two organized congenital patterns of behavior in the newborn', in H.W. Stevenson, E.H. Hess and H.L. Rheingold (eds), *Early Behavior: Comparative and developmental approaches*, New York: Wiley, pp. 147–79.

Kessen, W., Salapatek, P. and Haith, M.M. (1965), *The Ocular Orientation of Newborn Human Infants to Visual Contours*, Communication to the Psychonomic Society, Chicago.

Kluver, H. (1933), *Behavior Mechanisms in Monkeys*, Chicago: University of Chicago Press.

Koffka, K. (1959), *The Growth of the Mind*, Paterson, NJ: Littlefield, Adams.

Köhler, W. (1964), *Psychologie de la forme*, Paris: Gallimard.

Kugler, P.N., Kelso, J.A.S. and Turvey, M.T. (1982), 'On the control and coordination of naturally developing systems', in J.A.S. Kelso and J.E. Clark (eds), *The Development of Movement Control and Coordination*, New York: Wiley, pp. 5–78.

Kuypers, H.G.J.M. (1973), 'The anatomical organization of the descending pathways and their contribution to motor control especially in primates', in J.E. Desmet (ed.), *New Developments in Electromyography and Clinical Neurophysiology* (vol. 3), New York: S. Karger, 38–68.

Lamb, M.E. and Campos, J.J. (1982), *Development in Infancy*, New York: Random House.

Lasky, R.E. (1977), 'The effect of visual feedback of the hand on the reaching and retrieval behavior of young infants', *Child Development*, **48**: 112–17.

Lautrey, J. (1987), *Structure et fonctionnement dans le développement cognitif*, thesis submitted to the Faculty of Letters and Human Sciences, Université René Descartes, Paris.

Lecanuet, J.-P., Granier-Deferre, C. and Busnel, M.-C. (1989), 'La sensorialité fœtale: ontogenèse des systèmes sensoriels, conséquences de leur fonctionnement fœtal', in J.P. Relier, B. Salle and R. Laugier (eds), *Fœtus et nouveau-né. Pathologie, Biologie*, Paris: Flammarion.

Lécuyer, R. (1987), 'Habituation, réaction à la nouveauté et intelligence', *Bulletin de Psychologie*, **381**: 815–31.

Lécuyer, R. (1988), *L'intelligence des bébés*, thesis submitted to the Faculty of Letters and Human Sciences, Université René Descartes, Paris.

Lécuyer, R. (1989), *Bébé astronome, bébé psychologue. L'intelligence de la première année*, Brussels: Mardaga.

Lécuyer, R. and Streri, A. (1986), 'Information intake during habituation in infants: links between visual and tactual habituation', *Cahier de Psychologie cognitive*, **6**: 565–74.

Lederman, S.J. and Klatzky, R.L. (1987), 'Hand movements: a window into haptic object recognition', *Cognitive Psychology*, **19**: 342–68.

Lederman, S.J. and Klatzky, R.L. (1990), 'Haptic classification of common objects: knowledge-driven exploration', *Cognitive Psychology*, **22**: 421–59.

Lee, D.N. and Aronson, E. (1974), 'Visual proprioceptive control of standing in human infants', *Perception and Psychophysics*, **15**: 529–32.

Liederman, J. (1983), 'Is there a stage of left-sided precocity during early manual specialization?' in G. Young, S.J. Segalowitz, C.M. Corter and S.E. Trehub (eds), *Manual Specialization and the Developing Brain*, **16**, New York: Academic Press, pp. 321–30.

Lipsitt, L.P. (1979), 'The pleasures and annoyances of infants: approach and avoidance behavior', in E.B. Thoman (ed.) *Origins of the Infant's Social Responsiveness*, Hillsdale, NJ: Erlbaum, pp. 125–53.

Lockman, J.L. and Ashmead, D.H. (1983), 'Asynchronies in the development of manual behavior', in L.P. Lipsitt and C.R. Rovee-Collier (eds), *Advances in Infancy Research* (vol. II), Norwood, NJ: Ablex, pp. 113–35.

Lockman, J.J., Ashmead, D.H. and Bushnell, E.W. (1984), 'The development of anticipatory hand orientation during infancy', *Journal of Experimental Child Psychology*, **37**: 176–86.

Malone, D.R., Tolan, J.C. and Rogers, C.M. (1980), 'Crossmodal matching and photographs in the monkey', *Neuropsychologia*, **18**: 693–7.

Maratos, O. (1973), *Les origines et le développement de l'imitation dans les six premiers mois de la vie*, thesis, University of Geneva.

Marks, L.E. (1978*a*), 'Multimodal perception', in E.C. Carterette and M.P. Friedman (eds), *Perceptual Coding*, **9**, New York: Academic Press.

Marks, L.E. (1978*b*), *The Unity of Senses*, New York: Academic Press.

Marr, D. (1982), *Vision: A computational investigation into the human representation and processing of visual information*, San Francisco: Freeman.

Martinius, J. and Papousek, H. (1970), 'Responses to optic and exteroceptive stimuli in relation to state in the human newborn: habituation', *Neuropaediatrie*, **1**: 452–60.

Maury, L. and Streri, A. (1981), 'Recherche de l'objet: modifications des références spatials chez le bébé de 8 à 14 mois', *L'Année psychologique*, **81**: 51–67.

McCormick, C.M. and Maurer, D.M. (1988), 'Unimanual hand preferences in 6-month-olds: consistency and relation to familial-handedness', *Infant Behavior and Development*, **11**: 21–9.

McDonnell, P.M. (1975), 'The development of visually-guided reaching', *Perception and Psychophysics*, **18**: 181–5.

McDonnell, P.M. (1979), 'Patterns of eye–hand coordination in the first year of life', *Canadian Journal of Psychology*, **33**: 253–65.

McDonnell, P.M. and Abraham, W.C. (1979), 'Adapting to displacing prisms in human infants', *Perception*, **8**: 175–85.

McDonnell, P.M., Anderson, B.E.S. and Abraham, W.C. (1983), 'Assymmetry and orientation of arm movements in three- to eight-week-old infants', *Infant Behavior and Development*, **6**: 287–98.

McGuire, I. and Turkewitz, G. (1979), 'Approach–withdrawal theory and the study of infant development', in M. Bortner (ed.), *Cognitive Growth and Development: Essays in memory of Herbert Birch*, New York: Bruner/Mazel, pp. 57–84.

Mebert, C.J. (1983), 'Laterality in manipulatory and cognitive-related activity in four- to ten-month-olds', in G. Young, S.J. Segalowitz, C.M. Corter and S.E. Trehub (eds), *Manual Specialization and the Developing Brain*, **18**, New York: Academic Press, pp. 349–65.

Mehler, J. and Fox, R. (1985), *Neonate Cognition: Beyond the Blooming Buzzing Confusion*, Hillsdale, New Jersey: Erlbaum.

Meltzoff, A.N. (1982), 'Imitation, intermodal coordination and representation in early infancy', in G. Butterworth (ed.), *Infancy and Epistemology*, Brighton: Harvester.

Meltzoff, A.N. (1990), 'Towards a developmental cognitive science: the implications of cross-modal matching and imitation for the development of representation and memory in infancy', in A. Diamond (ed.), *The Development and Neural Bases of Higher Cognitive Functions*, Annals of the New York Academy of Sciences, pp. 1–37.

Meltzoff, A.N. and Borton, R.W. (1979), 'Intermodal matching by human neonates', *Nature*, **282**: 403–4.

Meltzoff, A.N., Kuhl, P.K. and Moore, M.K. (1991), 'Perception, representation, and the control of action in newborns and young infants: toward a new syntheses', in M.J.S. Weiss and P.R. Zelazo (eds), *Newborn Attention: Biological constraints and the influence of experience*, Norwood, NJ: Ablex, pp. 377–411.

Meltzoff, A.N. and Moore, M.K. (1977), 'Imitation of facial and manual gestures by human neonates', *Science*, **198**: 75–8.

Meltzoff, A.N. and Moore, M.K. (1983), 'The origins of imitation in infancy: paradigm, phenomena and theories', in L.P. Lipsitt (ed.), *Advances in Infancy Research* (vol. 1), Norwood, NJ: Ablex, pp. 265–301.

Meltzoff, A.N. and Moore, M.K. (1989), 'Imitation in newborn infants: exploring the range of gestures imitated and the underlying mechanism', *Developmental Psychology*, **25**: 954–62.

Michel, G.F. (1981), 'Right-handedness: a consequence of infant supine head-orientation preference?', *Science*, **212**: 685–7.

Michel, G.F. (1983), 'Development of hand-use preference during infancy', in G. Young, S.J. Segalowitz, C.M. Corter and S.E. Trehub (eds), *Manual Specialization and the Developing Brain*, **3**, New York: Academic Press, pp. 33–70.

Michel, G.F., Harkins, D.A. and Meserve, A.L. (1990), 'Sex differences in neonatal state and laterilized head orientation', *Infant Behavior and Development*, **13**: 461–7.

Michel, G.F., Ovrut, M.R. and Harkins, D.A. (1986), 'Hand-use preference for reaching and object manipulation in 6- through 13-month-old infants', *Genetic, Social, and General Psychology Monographs*, **111**: 409–27.

Michotte, A. (1905), *Les signes régionaux. Nouvelles recherches expérimentales sur la répartition de la sensibilité tactile dans les états d'attention et d'inattention*, Paris: Alcan.

Michotte, A. (1950), 'A propos de la permanence phénoménale. Faits et théories', *Acta Psychologica* **VII**: 298–322.

Milhet, S. (1989), *Cross-Modal Transfer of Weight in 4-month-old Infants*, paper presented at the 10th biennal meeting of ISSBD, Jyväskyla (Finland), July 1989.

Minkowski, M. (1938), 'L'élaboration du système nerveux', *Encyclopédie française*, **8**: 14; 5–16; **8**; 16, 1–15, Dépositaire Librairie Larousse.

Morrongiello, B.A. and Rocca, P.T. (1989), 'Visual feedback and anticipatory hand orientation during infants' reaching', *Perceptual and Motor Skills*, **69**: 787–802.

Mounoud, P. (1976), 'Les révolutions psychologiques de l'enfant', *Archives de Psychologie*, **171**: 103–14.

Mounoud, P. (1979), 'Développement cognitif: construction de structures nouvelles ou construction d'organisations internes', *Bulletin de Psychologie*, **343**: 107–18.

Mounoud, P. (1983), 'L'évolution des conduites de prehension comme illustration d'un modèle du développement', in S. de Schonen (ed.), *Le développement dans la première année*, Paris: Presses Universitaires de France.

Mounoud, P. (1986), 'L'utilisation du milieu et du corps propre par la bébé', in J. Piaget, P. Mounoud and J.-P. Bronckart (eds), *La Psychologie*, Encyclopédie La Pléiade, Paris: Gallimard.

Mounoud, P. and Vinter, A. (1982), 'Representation and sensori–motor development', in G. Butterworth (ed.), *Infancy and Epistemology*, Brighton: Harvester.

Mounoud, P. and Vinter, A. (1985), 'La notion de représentation en psychologie génétique', in S. Erhlich (ed.), *Les représentations, Psychologie française*, **30**, 253–8.

Mounoud, P., Vinter, A. and Hauert, C.-A. (1985), 'Activités manuelles et développement cognitif', *Comportements*, **3**: 101–23.

Newell, K.M., Skully, D.M., McDonald, P.V. and Baillargeon, R. (1989), 'Task constraints and infant grip configurations', *Developmental Psychobiology*, **22**: 817–32.

Noirot, E. (1983), 'Réflexions sur la stratégie de recherche dans le domaine du développement humain précoce', *Enfance*, **1–2**: 169–95.

Paillard, J. (1971), 'Les déterminants moteurs de l'organisation spatiale', *Cahiers de Psychologie*, **14**: 261–316.

Paillard, J. (1974), 'Le traitement des informations spatiales', in *De l'espace corporel à l'espace écologique*, Paris: Presses Universitaires de France.

Paillard, J. (1986), 'Development and acquisition of motor skills: a challenging prospect for neuroscience', in M.G. Wade and H.T.A. Whiting (eds), *Motor Development in Children: Aspects of coordination and control*, NATO, ASI Series, Amsterdam: Martinus Nijhoff.

Paillard, J. and Beaubaton, D. (1978), 'De la coordination visuo-motrice à l'organisation de la saisie manuelle', in H. Hecaen and M. Jeannerod (eds), *Du contrôle moteur à l'organisation du geste*, Paris: Masson.

Pêcheux, M.G. and Lécuyer, R. (1989), 'Les méthodes d'étude du nourrisson', in J.-P. Rossi (ed.), *Les méthodes en psychologie expérimentale*, Paris: Dunod.

Pêcheux, M.G., Lepecq, J.-C. and Salzarulo, P. (1988), 'Oral activity and exploration in 1–2 month-old infants', *British Journal of Developmental Psychology*, **6**: 245–56.

Pedersen, P. and Blass, E.M. (1982), 'Prenatal and postnatal determinants of the 1st sulking episode in albino rats', *Developmental Psychobiology*, **15**: 349–55.

Peters, M. (1983), 'Lateral bias in reaching and holding at six and twelve months', in G. Young, S.J. Segalowitz, C.M. Corter and S.E. Trehub (eds), *Manual Specialization and the Developing Brain*, **19**, New York: Academic Press, pp. 367–74.

Petrie, B.F. and Peters, M. (1980), 'Handedness: left/right differences in intensity of grasp response and duration of rattle holding of infants', *Infant Behavior and Development*, **3**: 215–21.

Piaget, J. (1936), *La naissance de l'intelligence chez l'enfant*, Neuchâtel: Delachaux & Niestlé; trans. *The Origins of Intelligence in the Child*, London: Routledge & Kegan Paul (1936, 1953).

Piaget, J. (1937), *La construction du réel chez l'enfant*, Neuchâtel: Delachaux & Niestlé; trans. *The Child's Construction of Reality*, London: Routledge & Kegan Paul (1937, 1955).

Piaget, J. (1945), *La formation du symbole chez l'enfant*, Neuchâtel: Delachaux & Niestlé.

Pick, H.L. (1970), 'Systems of perceptual and perceptual–motor development', in J.P. Hill (ed.), *Minnesota Symposia on Child Psychology* (vol. 4), Minneapolis: University of Minnesota Press, pp. 199–219.

Pick, H.L., Jr (1986), 'Reflections on the data and theory of cross-modal infancy reasearch', in L.P. Lipsitt and C. Rovee-Collier (eds), *Advances in Infancy Research* (vol. 4), Norwood, NJ: Ablex, pp. 230–39.

Piéraut-Le Bonniec, G. (1985), 'Hand–eye coordination and infant construction of convexity and concavity', *British Journal of Developmental Psychology*, **3**: 273–80.

Piéraut-Le Bonniec, G. (1986), 'Genèse de propriétés des objets chez le nourrisson: propriété physique de concavité et propriété fonctionnelle de contenant', *Psychologie française*, **31**: 73–8.

Piéraut-Le Bonniec, G., Fontaine, R., Hombessa, E. and Jacquet, A.Y. (1988), *Anticipation of Object Size: One aspect in the organization of grasping behavior*, Communication at the Congress of ICIS, Washington, DC, 21–24 April 1988.

Pineau, A. and Streri, A (1985), 'Etude de l'invariance d'une relation spatiale chez les bébés de 4 à 9 mois: être entre deux objets', *L'Année psychologique*, **85**: 489–502.

Pineau, A. and Streri, A. (1990), 'Intermodal transfer of spatial arrangement of the component parts of an object in 4/5-month-old infants', *Perception*, **19**, 795–804.

Prechtl, H.F.R. (1969), 'Problems of behavioral studies in newborn infants', in C. Lehrman and R. Hinde (eds), *Advances in the Study of Behavior*, New York: Academic Press.

Prechtl, H.F.R. and Beintema, D.J. (1964), *The Neurological Examination of the Full-Term Newborn Infant*, London: Heinemann.

Prechtl, H.F.R. and O'Brien, M.J. (1982), 'Behavioral states of the full-term newborn: the emergence of a concept', in P. Stratton (ed.), *Psychobiology of the Human Newborn*, New York: Wiley.

Previc, F.H. (1991), 'A general theory concerning the prenatal origins of cerebral lateralization in humans', *Psychological Review*, **98**: 299–334.

Provine, R.R. and Westerman, J.A. (1979), 'Crossing the midline: limits of early eye–hand behavior', *Child Development*, **50**: 437–41.

Rader, N. and Stern, J.D. (1982), 'Visually elicited reaching in neonates', *Child Development*, **53**: 1004–7.

Ramsay, D.S. (1983), 'Unimanual hand preference and duplicated syllable babbling in infants', in G. Young, S.J. Segalowitz, C.M. Corter and S.E. Trehub (eds), *Manual Specialization and the Developing Brain, 9*, New York: Academic Press, pp. 161–76.

Ramsay, D.S., Campos, J.J. and Fenson, L. (1979), 'Onset of bimanual handedness and speech in infants', *Infant Behavior and Development*, **3**: 67–77.

Reed, E.S. (1982), 'An outline of a theory of action systems', *Journal of Motor Behavior*, **14**: 98–134.

Reisman, J.E. (1987), 'Touch, motion and proprioception', in P. Salapatek and L. Cohen (eds), *Handbook of Infant Perception: From sensation to perception* (vol. 1), New York: Academic Press, pp. 265–303.

Revesz, G. (1933, 1950), *Psychology and Art of the Blind*, New York: Longmens, Green.

Rochat, P. (1983), 'Oral touch in young infants: response to variation of nipple characteristics in the first months of life', *International Journal of Behavioral Development*, **6**: 123–33.

Rochat, P. (1985), *Mouthing and Grasping in Newborns: Crossmodal responsiveness to soft and rigid objects*, paper presented to the 8th biennal meetings of the ISSBD, Tours.

Rochat, P. (1986), *Unity of the Senses and Early Development of Action*, paper presented at the Second European Conference on Developmental Psychology, Rome.

Rochat, P. (1987), 'Mouthing and grasping in neonates: evidence for the early detection of what hard and soft substances afford for action', *Infant Behavior and Development*, **10**: 435–49.

Rochat, P. (1989), 'Object manipulation and exploration in 2- to 5-month-old infants', *Developmental Psychology*, **25**: 871–84.

Rochat, P., Blass, E.M. and Hoffmeyer, L.B. (1988), 'Oropharyngeal control of hand–mouth coordination in newborn infants', *Developmental Psychology*, **24**: 459–63.

Rochat, P. and Reed, E.S. (1987), 'Le concept d'affordance et les connaissances du nourrisson', *Psychologie française*, **32**: 97–104.

Rock, I. and Victor, J. (1964), 'Vision and touch: an experimentally induced conflict between the two senses', *Science*, **143**: 594–6.

Rolfe, A. and Day, R.H. (1981), 'Effects of the similarity and dissimilarity between familiarisation and test objects on recognition memory in infants following unimodal and bimodal', *Child Development*, **52**: 1308–12.

Rose, S.A. (1977), 'Infants' transfer of response between two-dimensional and three-dimensional stimuli', *Child Development*, **48**: 1086–91.

Rose, S.A., Gottfried, A.W. and Bridger, W.H. (1978), 'Cross-modal transfer in infants: relationship to prematurity and socio-economic background', *Developmental Psychology*, **14**: 643–52.

Rose, S.A., Gottfried, A.W. and Bridger, W.H. (1979), 'Effects of haptic cues on visual recognition memory in full-term and preterm infants', *Infant Behavior and Development*, **2**: 55–67.

Rose, S.A., Gottfried, A.W. and Bridger, W.H. (1981*a*) 'Cross-modal transfer and information processing by the sense of touch in infancy', *Developmental Psychology*, **17**: 90–98.

Rose, S.A., Gottfried, A.W. and Bridger, W.H. (1981*b*) 'Cross-modal transfer in 6-month-old infants', *Developmental Psychology*, **17**: 661–9.

Rose, S.A., Gottfried, A.W. and Bridger, W.H. (1983), 'Infants' cross-modal transfer from solid objects to their graphic representations', *Child Development*, **54**: 686–94.

Rose, S.A. and Orlian, E.K. (1991), 'Asymmetries in infant cross-modal transfer', *Child Development*, **62**: 706–18.

Rose, S.A. and Ruff, H.A. (1987), 'Cross-modal abilities in human infants', in J.D. Osofsky (ed.), *Handbook of Infant Development*, 2nd edn, New York: Wiley.

Rose, S.A., Schmidt, K. and Bridger, W.H. (1976), 'Changes in tactile responsivity during sleep in the newborn infant', *Developmental Psychology*, **12**: 311–20.

Rose, S.A., Schmidt, K. and Bridger, W.H. (1978), 'Changes in tactile responsivity during sleep in the newborn infant', *Developmental Psychology*, **14**: 163–172.

Rose S.A., Schmidt, K., Riese, M. and Bridger, W.H. (1980), 'Effects of prematurity and early intervention on responsivity to tactual stimuli: a comparison of preterm and full-term infants', *Child Development*, **51**: 416–25.

Rubenstein, J. (1976), 'Concordance of visual stimuli and manipulative responsiveness to novel and familiar stimuli: a function of test procedures or prior experience?', *Child Development*, **47**: 1197–9.

Ruff, H.A. (1976), 'The coordination of manipulation and visual fixation: a response to Schaffer (1975)', *Child Development*, **47**: 868–71.

Ruff, H.A. (1981), 'Effect of context on infants' responses to novel objects', *Developmental Psychology*, **17**: 87–9.

Ruff, H.A. (1982), 'Role of manipulation in infants' response to invariant properties of objects', *Developmental Psychology*, **18**: 682–91.

Ruff, H.A. (1984), 'Infants' manipulative exploration of objects: effects of age and object characteristics', *Developmental Psychology*, **20**: 9–20.

Ruff, H.A. (1986), 'Components of attention during infants' manipulative exploration', *Child Development*, **57**: 105–14.

Ruff, H.A. and Halton, A. (1978), 'Is there directed reaching in the human neonate?', *Developmental Psychology*, **14**: 425–6.

Ruff, H.A. and Kohler, C.J. (1978), 'Tactual–visual transfer in six-month-old infants', *Infant Behavior and Development*, **1**: 259–64.

Salapatek, P. and Kessen, W. (1966), 'Visual scanning of triangles by the human newborn', *Journal of Experimental Child Psychology*, **3**: 155–67.

Schaffer, H.R. and Parry, M.H. (1969), 'Perceptual-motor behavior in infancy as a function of age and stimulus familiarity', *British Journal of Psychology*, **60**: 1–9.

Schaffer, H.R. and Parry, M.H. (1970), 'The effects of short term familiarisation on infants' perceptual motor coordination in a simultaneous discriminative task', *British Journal of Psychology*, **61**: 559–69.

Schmidt, R.A. (1975), 'A schema theory of discrete motor skill learning', *Psychological Review*, **82**: 225–60.

Schneirla, T.C. (1965), 'Aspects of stimulation and organization in approach withdrawal processes underlying vertebrate behavioral development', in D.S. Lehrman, R.A. Hinde and E. Straus (eds), *Advances in the Study of Behavior* (vol. 1), New York: Academic Press.

Schonen, S. de (1977), 'Functional asymmetries in the development of bimanual coordinations in human infants', *Journal of Human Movement Studies*, **3**: 144–56.

Schonen, S. de (1980), 'Développement de la coordination visuo–manuelle et de la latéralisation manuelle des conduites d'atteinte et de prise d'objet', *Travaux du Centre d'Etude des Processus cognitifs et du Langage*, Paris: L'Ecole des Hautes Etudes en Sciences Sociales.

Schonen, S. de (1981), 'Données sur le développement du geste et de la représentation de l'espace', in *Psychologie française, Hommage à Jean Piaget*, **26**: 274–81.

Schonen, S. de and Bresson, F. (1984), 'Développement de l'atteinte manuelle d'un objet chez l'enfant', in J. Paillard (ed.), *La lecture sensorimotrice et cognitive de l'expérience spatiale. Directions et distances*, Paris: Centre National de la Recherche Scientifique, pp. 99–114.

Seth, G. (1973), 'Eye–hand coordination and "handedness": a developmental study of visuomotor behavior in infancy', *British Journal of Educational Psychology*, **43**: 35–49.

Sivak, B. and MacKenzie, C.L. (1990), 'Integration of visual information and motor output in reaching and grasping: the contributions of peripheral and central vision', *Neuropsychologia*, **28**: 1095–116.

Slater, A., Morison, V. and Rose, D. (1984*a*), 'Habituation in the newborn', *Infant Behavior and Development*, **7**: 183–200.

Slater, A., Morison, V. and Rose, D. (1984*b*), 'Newborn infants' perception of similarities and differences between two- and three-dimensional stimuli', *British Journal of Developmental Psychology*, **2**: 287–94.

Soroka, S.M., Corter, C.M. and Abramovitch, R. (1979), 'Infants' tactual discrimination of novel and familiar tactual stimuli', *Child Development*, **50**: 1251–3.

Spear, N.E. and Molina, J.C. (1987), 'The role of sensory modality in the ontogeny of stimulus selection', in N.A. Krasnegor, E.M. Blass, M.A. Hofern and W.P. Smotherman (eds), *Perinatal Development: A psychobiological perspective*, New York: Academic Press, pp. 83–110.

Spelke, E.S. (1984), 'Constraints on intermodal perception', in L.S. Liben (ed.), *Piaget and the Foundations of Knowledge*, Hillsdale, NJ: Erlbaum.

Spelke, E.S. (1985), 'Preferential-looking methods as tools for the study of cognition in infancy', in G. Gottlieb and N.A. Krasnegor (eds), *Measure-*

ment of Audition and Vision in the First Year of Postnatal Life: a methodological overview, Norwood, NJ, Ablex, 323–63.

Spelke, E.S. (1987), 'The development of intermodal perception', in P. Salapatek and L. Cohen (eds), *Handbook of Infant Perception: From perception to cognition* (vol. 2), New York: Academic Press.

Spelke, E.S. (1988), 'Where perceiving ends and thinking begins: the apprehension of objects in infancy', in A. Yonas (ed.), *Perceptual Development in Infancy: The Minnesota Symposia on Child Psychology* (vol. 20), Hillsdale, NJ, Erlbaum.

Spelke, E.S. (1990), 'Principles of object perception', *Cognitive Science*, **14**: 29–56.

Spelke, E.S., Hofsten, C. von and Kestenbaum, R. (1989), 'Object perception in infancy: interaction of spatial and kinetic information for boundaries', *Developmental Psychology*, **25**: 185–96.

Spelke, E.S. and Kestenbaum, R. (1986), 'Les origines du concept d'objet', *Psychologie française*, **31**: 67–72.

Steele, D. and Pederson, D.R. (1977), 'Stimulus variables which affect the concordance of visual and manipulative exploration in the six-month-old', *Child Development*, **8**: 104–11.

Stein, B.E. and Meredith, M.A. (1990), 'Multisensory integration: neural and behavioral solutions for dealing with stimuli from different sensory modalities', in A. Diamond (ed.), *The Development and Neural Bases of Higher Cognitive Functions*, Annals of the New York Academy of Sciences, pp. 51–65.

Strauss, E. (1982), 'Manual persistence in infancy', *Cortex*, **18**: 319–22.

Streri, A. (1987*a*), 'Tactile discrimination of shape and intermodal transfer in 2- to 3-month old infants', *British Journal of Developmental Psychology*, **5**: 213–20.

Streri, A. (1987*b*), *Intermodal Transfer and Sensorimotor Coordination in Infancy*, paper presented to the IXth biennal meeting of ISSBD, Tokyo.

Streri, A. (1988*a*), 'Confirmation of intermodal transfer from touch to vision in 2–3-month-old infants' (unpublished manuscript).

Streri, A. (1988*b*), *The Motor Function of the Hand: Help or handicap the perceptual function?*, paper presented to the 3rd European Conference on Developmental Psychology, Budapest, 15–19 June 1988.

Streri, A. (1991), 'L'espace et les relations inter-modalités', *L'Année psychologique*, **91**: 87–102.

Streri, A. and Milhet, S. (1988), 'Equivalences intermodales de la forme des objets entre la vision et le toucher chez les bébés de 2 mois', *L'Année psychologique*, **88**: 329–41.

Streri, A. and Milhet, S. (1992), 'Haptic perception of weights and intermodal transfer in infancy' (in preparation).

Streri, A. and Molina, M. (1991), 'The development of tactual representation of objects shape in infancy: a comparison with vision', communication presented to the 11th meeting of ISSBD, Minneapolis.

Streri, A. and Molina, M. (1993*a*), 'Visual–tactual and tactual–visual transfer between objects and pictures in 2-month-old infants', *Perception*, in press.

Streri, A. and Molina, M. (1993*b*), 'Constraints on intermodal transfer between touch and vision in infancy', in D.J. Lewkowicz and R. Lickliter (eds), *The Development of Intersensory Perception: Comparative perspectives*, Hillsdale, NJ: Erlbaum.

Streri, A., Molina, M. and Millet, G. (1989), *Representation tactile chez le bébé de 2 mois*, lecture notes, Université René Descartes, Paris.

Streri, A. and Pêcheux, M.-G. (1986*a*), 'Tactual habituation and discrimination of form in infancy: a comparison with vision', *Child Development*, **57**: 100–104.

Streri, A. and Pêcheux, M.-G. (1986*b*), 'Cross-modal transfer of form in 5-month-old infants', *British Journal of Developmental Psychology*, **4**: 161–7.

Streri, A. and Pineau, A. (1988), *Cognitive and Motor Functions of the Hand*, paper presented at the 10th Congress of ICIS, Washington, DC, 20–24 April 1988.

Streri, A. and Spelke, E.S. (1988), 'Haptic perception of objects in infancy', *Cognitive Psychology*, **20**: 1–23.

Streri, A. and Spelke, E.S. (1989), 'Effects of motion and figural goodness on haptic object perception in infancy', *Child Development*, **60**: 1111–25.

Streri, A., Spelke, E.S. and Rameix, E. (1993), 'Specific and amodal mechanisms of object perception and exploration in infancy: the case of active touch', *Cognition*, in press.

Teicher, M.H. and Blass, E.M. (1977), 'First response of the newborn albino rat: the role of olfaction and amniotic fluid', *Science*, **198**: 635–6.

Thelen, E. (1985), 'Developmental origins of motor coordination: leg movements in human infants', *Developmental Psychobiology*, **18**: 1–18.

Tighe, T.J. and Leaton, R.N. (1976), *Habituation: Perspectives from child development, animal behavior and neurophysiology*, Hillsdale, NJ: Erlbaum.

Tolan, J.C., Rogers, C.M. and Malone, D.R. (1981), 'Cross-modal matching in monkeys: altered visual cues and delay', *Neuropsychologia*, **19**: 289–300.

Trehub, S.E., Corter, C.M. and Schosenberg, N. (1983), 'Neonatal reflexes: a search for lateral asymmetries', in G. Young, S.J. Segalowitz, C.M. Corter and S.E. Trehub (eds), *Manual Specialization and the Developing Brain*, New York: Academic Press, pp. 257–74.

Trevarthen, C. (1974), 'The psychobiology of speech development', *Neurosciences Research Programme Bulletin*, **12**: 570–85.

Turkewitz, G. (1980), 'Mechanisms of a neonatal rightward turning bias: a reply to Liederman and Kinsbourne', *Infant Behavior and Development*, **3**: 239–44.

Turkewitz, G., Gordon. E.W. and Birch, H.G. (1965), 'Head turning in the human neonate: spontaneous patterns', *Journal of Genetic Psychology*, **107**: 143–8.

Turkewitz, G. and Birch, H.G. (1971), 'Neurobehavioral organization of the human newborn', in J. Hellmuth (ed.), *Exceptional Infant* (vol. 2), New York: Bruner/Mazel.

Twitchell, T.E. (1965), 'The automatic grasping response of infants', *Neuropsychologia*, **3**: 247–59.

Twitchell, T.E. (1970), 'Reflex mechanisms and the development of prehension', in K. Connolly (ed.), *Mechanisms of Motor Skill Development*, New York: Academic Press.

Vince, M.A. and Billing A.E. (1986), 'Infancy in the sheep: the part played by sensory stimulation in bonding between the ewe and lamb', in L.P. Lipsitt and C. Rovee-Collier (eds), *Advances in Infancy Research* (vol. 4), Norwood, NJ: Ablex.

Vinter, A. (1985), *L'imitation chez le nouveau-né*, Neuchâtel/Paris: Delachaux & Niestlé.

Vurpillot, E. (1972), *Les perceptions du nourrisson*, Paris: Presses Universitaires de France.

Vurpillot, E. and Bullinger, A. (1983), 'Y-a-t-il des âges clés dans la première année de vie de l'enfant?', in S. de Schonen (ed.), *Le développement dans la première année*, Paris: Presses Universitaires de France.

Wagner, S.H. and Sakovits, L.J. (1986), 'Process analysis of infant visual and cross-modal recognition memory: implications for an amodal code', in L.P. Lipsitt and C. Rovee-Collier (eds), *Advances in Infancy Research* (vol. 4), Norwood, NJ: Ablex.

Walker-Andrews, A.S. and Gibson, E.J. (1986), 'What develops in bimodal perception?', in L.P. Lipsitt and C. Rovee-Collier (eds), *Advances in Infancy Research* (vol. 4), Norwood, NJ: Ablex, pp. 171–181.

Wallon, H. (1942), *De l'acte à la pensée*, Paris: Flammarion.

Werner, H. (1934), 'L'unité des sens', *Journal de Psychologie*, **XXXI**: 190–205.

Wertheimer, M. (1961), 'Psychomotor coordination of auditory and visual space at birth', *Science*, **134**: 16–92.

White, B.L. (1970), 'Experience and the development of motor mechanisms in infancy', in K. Connolly (ed.), *Mechanisms of Motor Skill Development*, New York: Academic Press.

White, B.L., Castle, P. and Held, R. (1964), 'Observations on the development of visually guided reaching', *Child Development*, **35**: 349–64.

White, B.W., Saunders, F.A., Scadden, L., Bach-y-Rita, P. and Collins, C.C. (1970), 'Seeing with the skin', *Perception and Psychophysics*, **7**: 23–7.

Willatts, P. (1983), 'Effects of object novelty on the visual and manual exploration of infants', *Infant Behavior and Development*, **6**: 145–9.

Yang, R. and Douthitt, T. (1974), 'Newborn responses to threshold tactile stimulation', *Child Development*, **45**: 237–42.

Yonas, A., Cleaves, W. and Pettersen, L. (1978), 'Development of sensitivity to pictorial depth', *Science*, **200**: 77–9.

Yonas, A. and Granrud, C.E. (1984), 'The development of sensitivity to kinetic, binocular, and pictorial depth information in human infants', in D. Ingle, D. Lee and M. Jeannerod (eds), *Brain Mechanisms and Spatial Vision*, Amsterdam: Martinus Nijhoff.

Yonas, A. and Granrud, C.E. (1985), 'Development of depth sensitivity in infants', in J. Mehler and R. Fox (eds), *Neonate Cognition: Beyond the Blooming, Buzzing Confusion*, Hillsdale, NJ: Erlbaum.

Yonas, A., Granrud, C.E. and Smith, I.M. (1982), *Infants Perceive Accretion/ Deletion Information for Depth*, paper presented at the meeting of the Association for Research in Vision and Ophthalmology, Sarasota, FL.

Yonas, A. and Owsley, C. (1987), 'Development of visual space perception', in P. Salapatek and L. Cohen (eds), *Handbook of Infant Perception: From perception to cognition* (vol. 2), New York: Academic Press, pp. 80–122.

Young, G., Bowman, J.G., Methot, C., Finlayson, M., Quintal, J. and Boissonneau, P. (1983), 'Hemispheric specialization development: what (inhibition) and how (parents)', in G. Young, S.J. Segalowitz, C.M. Corter and S.E. Trehub (eds), *Manual Specialization and the Developing Brain*, **7**, New York: Academic Press, pp. 119–40.

Young, G., Segalowitz, S.J., Corter, S.M. and Trehub, S.E. (1983), *Manual Specialization and the Developing Brain*, New York: Academic Press.

Young, G., Segalowitz, S.J., Misek, P., Ercan Alp, I. and Boulet, R. (1983), 'Is early reaching left-handed? Review of manual specialization research', in G. Young, S.J. Segalowitz, C.M. Corter and S.E. Trehub (eds), *Manual Specialization and the Developing Brain*, **2**, New York: Academic Press, pp. 13–32.

Zazzo, R. (1957), 'Le problème de l'imitation chez le nouveau-né', *Enfance*, **10**: 135–42.

Zazzo, R. (1988), 'Janvier 1945: découverte de l'imitation néonatale', in J. Nadel (ed.), 'L'imitation immédiate: bilan et perspective', *Psychologie française*, **33**.

Name Index

Subject Index